Elizabeth A. Lyons in front of her Haddonfield home.

ELIZABETH HADDON ESTAUGH
1680–1762

BUILDING THE QUAKER COMMUNITY OF
HADDONFIELD, NEW JERSEY,
1701–1762

~~~~~~~~~~~~~~~

Jeffery M. Dorwart
and
Elizabeth A. Lyons

𝔥𝔞𝔡𝔡𝔬𝔫𝔣𝔦𝔢𝔩𝔡. 𝔑.𝔍.:
Published by
THE HISTORICAL SOCIETY OF HADDONFIELD

2013

> This publication made possible by funding from:
> Joseph E. Murphy
> Bequest of Elizabeth Alice Lyons
> Historical Society of Haddonfield Book Fund

Historical Society of Haddonfield
343 King's Highway East
Haddonfield, New Jersey 08033
© 2013 by the Historical Society of Haddonfield

All rights reserved. No part of this publication
may be reproduced in any form or by any means,
including electronic formats, except by permission
of the publisher. Published in 2013
Printed in the United States of America

International Standard Book Number 978-09723949-1-8

∞ The paper used in this publication meets the minimum requirements of the American National Standard for Information Sciences—Permanence of Paper for Printed Library Materials, ANSI Z39.48-1984.

"[John Estaugh] bestowed much labor and time
For the good of the People of the Neighborhood
Where he dwelt: and especially on the Poor"

—*Elizabeth Haddon Estaugh, July 1743*

CONTENTS.

	PAGE
List of Illustrations	iii
Acknowledgements	v
Preface	vii

Chapter 1:
Legend of the "Youthful Emigrant," Elizabeth Haddon 1

Chapter 2:
Observe the Pious and Godly Example of Tender Parents ..27

Chapter 3:
"That There is Such a *Province* as *New-Jersey* is Certain"...47

Chapter 4:
"My New and Lawful Attorney for Me in My Name,"
1699–1701 69

Chapter 5:
A Faithful and Loving Wife, 1702 101

Chapter 6:
The Search for Unity, 1703–1713......127

Chapter 7
"Most Dear Children...We Cannot Come to You," 1713–1719...153

Chapter 8:
"Lett the Plantation to Make Yourselves Easy," 1720–1726...181

Chapter 9:
To See Good Order among Friends, 1727–1742 205

Chapter 10:
Maintaining Love and Unity, 1743–1762 235

Conclusions......261

Bibliography......269

Index......281

ILLUSTRATIONS.

	PAGE
Tablet in Friends Cemetery in Memory of Elizabeth Haddon	4
"The Proposal" Tableau from 1913 Pageant	9
Temperance Fountain Dedicated to Elizabeth Haddon	13
Seal of the Borough of Haddonfield	14
Elizabeth A. Lyons and Her Brother George Stuart Lyons	20
John Worlidge Map Identifying "Haddon Feild," c.1706	74
Thomas Sharp Map of Newton Township, NJ, 1700	89
Details of Sharp Map Showing John Haddon Properties	90-91
S.N. Rhoads Pointing to E. Haddon's First House Location	92
Wedding Signatures of John Estaugh and Elizabeth Haddon	97
Painting of New Haddonfield by John Evans Redman	156
Floor Plan of the First Floor of New Haddonfield	156
John and Elizabeth Haddon Estaugh's "Brew House"	162
1713 Letter from the Haddons to the Estaughs	165
Craig Receipt for Educating Ebenezer Hopkins	215
John Estaugh Document Regarding Control of Two Slaves	222
Quaker Burial Ground at Tortola	230
Minute Book of Haddonfield Friends Women's Meeting	232
Title Page of *A Call to the Unfaithful Professors of Truth*	236
Receipt from Benjamin Franklin for Printing, 1744	237

ACKNOWLEDGEMENTS.

This book was made possible by a nearly half-century crusade by local Haddonfield, New Jersey historian Elizabeth "Betty" Lyons to write a definitive biography of Elizabeth Haddon Estaugh, the reputed founder of her town. Over the years Betty, accompanied by her brother Stuart, traveled widely to discover long-lost records of the Haddon family. They accumulated boxes of notes and wrote several rough drafts in preparation for the publication of an Elizabeth Haddon Estaugh biography. Betty and Stuart passed away before they could complete their project, leaving all their research material to the Historical Society of Haddonfield, New Jersey. Here the Lyons Project notes joined the collections of documents about Elizabeth Haddon Estaugh's life gathered over the years by earlier generations of local society historians, most notably John Clement, Samuel Nicholson Rhoads, Rebecca Nicholson Taylor and Carrie Elizabeth Nicholson Hartel, among many other less accomplished researchers.

Betty Lyons had hoped to finish her biography for the 300th anniversary celebration of the Haddonfield community. Society members and authors of *Lost Haddonfield*, Katherine Mansfield Tassini and Douglas B. Rauschenberger had, for many years, encouraged and helped Betty with her project and refused to let the dream of an Elizabeth Haddon Estaugh biography die with her. The Lyons's research might have remained unpublished had it not been for the vision and generosity of former Historical Society of Haddonfield president Joseph Murphy to hire a professional historian to complete Betty's unfinished work. Tassini and Rauschenberger, joined later by noted South Jersey historian Paul W. Schopp, formed a committee to edit and oversee the publication of this book. The following biography of Elizabeth Estaugh was greatly strengthened by their comments, suggestions for revision and constant guidance in preparing the final manuscript.

I received encouragement in finishing this project from my former history colleagues at Rutgers University, Camden, Professor Howard Gillette and Dean Margaret Marsh, both Haddonfield residents. Archivist Patricia Chapin O'Donnell and curator Christopher Densmore of Friends Historical Library of Swarthmore College, John Anderies, Ann Upton and Diana Franzusoff Peterson of the Quaker and Special Collections of Haverford College and Maria Gonzalez, curator of the Stewart collection, Rowan University in Glassboro, New Jersey and the staff of the Historical Society of Pennsylvania provided archival assistance. My wife Nelly read the rough draft of the manuscript and made valuable suggestions to improve the work, as did my brother David A. Dorwart, who spent long hours copyediting, revising and correcting the final drafts of this work. Leona Pellot, secretarial assistant III of Rutgers University, Camden gave me the technical support to produce the manuscript. The following story of Elizabeth Haddon Estaugh and her part in building the town of Haddonfield, New Jersey would not have been possible without all their help.

      Jeffery M. Dorwart,
      Professor Emeritus of History
      Rutgers University, Camden, New Jersey

PREFACE.

For nearly 300 years, scores of writers, poets, collateral descendants and even a few professionally-trained historians told the tale of a courageous, romantic, unmarried Quaker woman named Elizabeth Haddon almost single-handedly founding the suburban town of Haddonfield, New Jersey. The Haddon legend begins with the teenager Elizabeth, the daughter of a London, England, Quaker blacksmith, John Haddon, sailing to America entirely on her own in 1701 to represent her father's real estate interests in the Province of West New Jersey. Here, according to most accounts, Elizabeth Haddon trudged through the wilderness forests among the Native Americans to settle her father's affairs. Then she met a handsome, charismatic Quaker minister John Estaugh, and proposed marriage. With her new husband by her side, the legend continues, Elizabeth founded the town of Haddonfield in 1713 and in 1721 the Haddonfield Monthly Meeting for the Religious Society of Friends in Newton Township, Old Gloucester County, Province of West New Jersey in America.

According to an enduring Haddon tale, Elizabeth was supposedly too frail and diminutive to bear children. So, she devoted her life to comforting the poor and sick children of other Quaker women and those of Native Americans in West New Jersey. Without having children to inherit her father's lands in West New Jersey, Elizabeth presumably adopted her sister's son Ebenezer Hopkins in London and brought him to the Delaware Valley to carry on the family line in America. In the process, Elizabeth built a prosperous house and plantation where she entertained some of the wealthiest and most influential Pennsylvania, New Jersey and English Quaker leaders in her magnificent "Haddon Hall" mansion.

Each account of Elizabeth Haddon's life increasingly embellished the truth. In the end, Haddonfield residents and local historians created a larger than life "founder" of their town of Haddonfield, New Jersey. They had little choice, argued Haddonfield historian John Clement, because no one could find real evidence of Elizabeth Haddon's most intimate personal activities or views about the world around her. "It is unfortunate that she did not, near the close of her life, prepare or dictate her autobiography," Clement wrote in 1877, "so that the incidents of her eventful career could have been preserved, as she would not then have left the most interesting and romantic parts of her life to vague and uncertain tradition."[1]

Finding few original sources with which to work, future biographers relied on oral traditions and undocumented sources that assumed much in the story of Elizabeth Haddon. Writers often placed Elizabeth within the larger nineteenth century literary image of Quaker women as the "noblest of creatures."[2] Accordingly, Quaker women such as Elizabeth Haddon embodied the highest spiritual and moral values in American culture and society. These pious women members of the Religious Society of Friends symbolized egalitarianism, pacifism, sobriety, individualism and benevolence. Reformist authors imagined that they stood at the forefront of the movements for women's rights, temperance and abolition of slavery. Stories of Elizabeth Haddon's almost single-handed development of a wilderness town in America reinforced the image of the legendary founder of Haddonfield. And so it remained for generation after generation who passed down those often-told tales and stories well into the twentieth century, when even the latest Internet web pages, including Wikipedia, repeated the centuries-old traditional accounts of this heroic Quaker woman who founded the town of Haddonfield.

Almost lost in the constant reiteration of the Elizabeth Haddon story was the crusade by two members of the Historical Society of Haddonfield to discover the truth about the actual historical rather than legendary figure. This search for the "real" Elizabeth Haddon behind the legend started in the late 1960s when Haddonfield residents Elizabeth "Betty" Lyons and her brother George Stuart Lyons decided to probe more deeply into the traditional undocumented view of Elizabeth Haddon as the founder of their town. The Lyons brother-sister research team began what became a more than forty-year mission to unearth the facts behind the familiar Elizabeth Haddon legend. They started out by asking some basic questions? Did she really found Haddonfield, New Jersey, and, if so, when and how did she accomplish this non-traditional task for a woman? Was Elizabeth Haddon a person of unusual courage, as portrayed by earlier biographers, who crossed the ocean and struggled nearly alone in the New World wilderness? Did she have only one sibling in her family back in England, as most writers claimed? Why did her father John Haddon, who was proprietor of the West Jersey land that became Haddonfield, never come to America? What part, if any, did her father have in the founding of Haddonfield? Did her mother have any influence on Elizabeth? How did Elizabeth's childhood in England and upbringing in the Religious Society of Friends impact on her future in America?

The Lyons inquired more deeply into the innermost secrets of Elizabeth Haddon's life. They wondered if the demure Elizabeth Haddon, as early stories and poems about this Quaker heroine revealed, really had a passionate love affair with the handsome Quaker minister John Estaugh, pursued him to America and while riding through the woods unabashedly proposed marriage. They asked: What role did John Estaugh play in the Haddonfield saga? Why did Elizabeth Haddon and John Estaugh never have children in a community that valued child bearing and motherhood above all other family functions? Why have so many Haddonfield residents, over time, claimed kinship to the childless Elizabeth Haddon? Did she comfort the sick, help the poor, preach to Native Americans and support the women in her community and, if so, how? Was Elizabeth Haddon a slave owner? What was her relationship with William Penn and other important founders of the Quaker communities in the Delaware Valley?

Betty and Stuart Lyons tried to answer these and many other questions about Elizabeth Haddon Estaugh through research trips to libraries, archives and historic sites in England, the West Indies, Pennsylvania and New Jersey. They employed their extensive collection of information to write several drafts for a biography of Elizabeth Haddon. In the midst of their writings, Stuart died suddenly in 2001. Betty Lyons became more dedicated than ever to writing a "definitive" biography of Haddonfield's reputed founder Elizabeth Haddon. She hoped to have the biography published by 2013 in time for Haddonfield's 300th Anniversary Celebration. With the editorial help of Haddonfield librarians Katherine Mansfield Tassini and Douglas B. Rauschenberger, co-authors of the Historical Society publication *Lost Haddonfield,* Betty Lyons revised an earlier manuscript draft that by 2008 was closer than ever before to becoming ready for publication. "This book is an attempt to reconstruct the true story of Elizabeth Haddon Estaugh," she announced. At this point, Betty decided to take a brief vacation to Norway, planning to put the final touches on the Elizabeth Haddon Estaugh biography when she returned.[3]

Tragically, Betty died while on vacation in Oslo, Norway. It appeared as though her lifetime mission would never be completed and that her boxes of notes and manuscript pages would join those of previous generations of Elizabeth Haddon biographers tucked away in the files of the Historical Society of Haddonfield. Then, the Society asked Rutgers Professor Emeritus of History Jeffery M. Dorwart to look at the last draft of the Lyons manuscript to see what could be done to publish it by 2013 for Haddonfield's 300th Anniversary Celebration. Dorwart reviewed the boxes of notes and several typed rough drafts of a proposed book for what the Society called the Lyons Project. He determined that the disorganized forty-year accumulation of research material could be used as the basis for the book that Betty and Stuart Lyons had long dreamed of publishing; a definitive biography of Elizabeth Haddon Estaugh. In response, the Historical Society of Haddonfield asked Dorwart to write this book.

The following work completes Betty and Stuart Lyons's "Search for Elizabeth" begun more than forty years ago. It adopts the basic concept and themes developed by the Lyons Project, explaining that Elizabeth Estaugh played a significant role during the first sixty years of the eighteenth century in developing the Quaker community of Haddonfield in Old Gloucester County, Province of West New Jersey. Though based in part on the "Lyons Project" collection of documents, notes and manuscript drafts on deposit in the Library of the Historical Society of Haddonfield, this book is rewritten as an original work with extensive new research. This study's interpretation of the documents and of Elizabeth Haddon Estaugh's life and relationship with those people closest to her, particularly with her father and husband, differs conceptually from what local historians Betty and Stuart Lyons depicted in their writings.

In the beginning, the Lyons had raised serious questions about the traditional view of Elizabeth Haddon as a heroic and romantic figure who single-handedly founded their adopted town. However as their work progressed, Betty and Stuart struggled in trying to answer all the questions that they had originally posed, largely because of the paucity of sources found that related directly to Elizabeth Haddon Estaugh's character, personality and view of the secular world around her. Therefore, after so many years dedicated to their search for the "real" Elizabeth Haddon Estaugh, Betty and Stuart Lyons gradually portrayed their subject in much the same light as her previous biographers. "Perhaps one marvels most," the longtime Haddonfield residents wrote, "when learning of her daring solo undertaking to the New World and her subsequent trips back to England under hazardous conditions, challenged by motives at which we can only guess." The Lyons began to "guess" about Elizabeth Haddon Estaugh's personal life, her feelings and how she interacted with others. Without the discovery of any personal letters, diaries or correspondence written directly by Elizabeth, these dedicated Historical Society of Haddonfield biographers, much like their nineteenth century predecessors, could only imagine the Quaker woman's most intimate feelings and views held by their subject.[4]

The following study steps back from the Elizabeth Haddon legend and examines Elizabeth's world through the religious and business relationships that she had with the men and women around her. This biography is concerned less with guessing about Elizabeth Haddon Estaugh's innermost motives and feelings than with discovering how her life (seen largely through the eyes of her contemporaries who left more documented evidence) helps us to understand the place that colonial Quaker women had in the entire process of building a community in the English mid-Atlantic colonies. Most previous studies of Quaker women in America focused on Philadelphia and Pennsylvania Friends; hence Elizabeth Estaugh's story offers one of the first studies of the experience of colonial Quaker women across the Delaware River in New Jersey.[5]

The legacy of Elizabeth Haddon Estaugh exists within the conceptual context of how her connections to a complex set of Quaker family, religious, social, business and economic organizations led to the late eighteenth and early nineteenth century settlement of West New Jersey. Moreover, the story of Elizabeth illuminates West New Jersey's inter-relationship with Quaker communities in Great Britain, the British West Indies, Philadelphia and the surrounding Pennsylvania countryside. Her life as a highly religious woman and as a manager of a great New Jersey plantation also offers a chance to apply for the first time to New Jersey, the eminent Quaker historian Frederick B. Tolles's paradigm of how Philadelphia Quakers merged their religious lives (Meeting House) and business affairs (Counting House) into building community. More importantly, Elizabeth Estaugh's life provides a model with which to test the assumptions presented in recent studies about how Quaker women influenced American history.[6]

Though this study of Elizabeth Haddon Estaugh's life holds a much larger meaning for the history of American women, business, colonization and the Religious Society of Friends, it is written primarily, as the late Betty Lyons had long envisioned, for those most interested in the history of Haddonfield, New Jersey. On the local level as one of the original settlers of Newton Township, Old Gloucester County, West New Jersey, Elizabeth Haddon Estaugh's biography provides a good method with which to examine the earliest history and founding of the community that eventually became Haddonfield. It demonstrates when, why and how the area was settled. It follows the actions of the people closest to Elizabeth in conducting her business and religious pursuits. As to her place in Haddonfield's history, I will leave it to the readers of this biography to find their own interpretation of the "real" Elizabeth Haddon Estaugh and to decide whether three-hundred-years ago, she became the first woman in American history to single-handedly found a town.

PREFACE NOTES.

[1] John Clement, *Sketches of the First Emigrant Settlers in Newton Township, Old Gloucester County, West New Jersey* (Camden, NJ: Sinnickson Chew, 1877), 124.

[2] See James Emmett Ryan, *Imaginary Friends: Representing Quakers in American Culture, 1650–1950* (Madison: University of Wisconsin Press, 2009), 22ff.

[3] Elizabeth and George Lyons, "The Search for Elizabeth," unpublished manuscript, and loose notes, in box 5, Lyons Project Papers, the Historical Society of Haddonfield Library, Haddonfield, NJ (hereafter, cited as HSHL). For the most accurate study of Haddonfield's history, to date, see Douglas B. Rauschenberger and Katherine Mansfield Tassini, *Lost Haddonfield* (Haddonfield, NJ: The Historical Society of Haddonfield, 1989).

[4] Lyons, "Search for Elizabeth," HSHL; Ryan, *Imaginary Friends*.

[5] See, Karin A. Wulf, *Not all Wives: Women of Colonial Philadelphia* (Ithaca, NY and London: Cornell University Press, 2000).

[6] See, Hugh Barbour and J. William Frost, *The Quakers* (Westport, CT: Greenwood Press, 1988); Frederick B. Tolles, *Meeting House and Counting House: The Quaker Merchants of Colonial Philadelphia, 1682–1763* (Chapel Hill: University of North Carolina Press, 1948); Carol and John Stoneburner, eds. *The Influence of Quaker Women on American History: Biographical Studies* (Lewiston, NY: Edwin Mellen Press, 1986); Rebecca Larson, *Daughters of Light: Quakers Women Preaching and Prophesying in the Colonies and Abroad, 1700–1775* (New York: Alfred A. Knopf, 1999); Cristine Levenduski, *Peculiar Power: A Quaker Woman Preacher in Eighteenth-Century America* (Washington and London: Smithsonian Institution Press, 1996); and Ryan, *Imaginary Friends*.

Eliz.ᵃ Estaugh

CHAPTER 1.
Legend of the "Youthful Emigrant," Elizabeth Haddon.

Doubt not, my child, that we shall be willing to give thee up to the Lord's disposings, however hard the trial may be. But when thou wert a very little girl, thy imagination was much excited concerning America; therefore, thou must be very careful that no desire for new adventures, founded in the will of the creature, mislead thee from the true light in this matter.
—Lydia Maria Child[1]

Long before the legend of the "Youthful Emigrant" emerged, Elizabeth Haddon, a young unmarried Quaker woman, landed at New Castle, Delaware in spring 1701. Based on her extensive earlier research, Betty Lyons concluded that Elizabeth arrived later, in fall 1701, on the merchant ship DOLMAHOY. Here on the banks of the Delaware River, Betty Lyons believed that Elizabeth Haddon encountered Pennsylvania Governor William Penn, his wife Hannah and daughter Letitia.

Betty based the date of Elizabeth's arrival and the Haddon-Penn meeting on a letter from Dr. Griffith Owen to William Penn which states that "John Estoe [Estaugh],they say is like to marry a young woman that came fr[o]m London, came in when we were at New Castle hath a plantation in Jersey. I thinke [*sic*] her name is Haddon."[2] Penn was in New Castle in late October 1701, preparing to return to England. However, Elizabeth Haddon arrived many months earlier in 1701 and already was living on her father's land in West Jersey. Dr. Owen, in his letter to Penn, is using the "royal we" when he states "when we were at New Castle". Owen is saying that **he alone**, not he and Penn, met Elizabeth at New Castle. The Haddon-Owen meeting must have taken place in the spring of 1701, rather than in fall 1701.

If there had been a Haddon-Penn interlude, it would have been a defining moment in Delaware Valley history. William Penn, founder of the Province of Pennsylvania and City of Philadelphia, was about to depart for Bristol, England, on the DOLMAHOY, in the specially outfitted captain's cabin. Penn sailed to England to defend his proprietary government and personal estate against attacks from his many enemies who sought to destroy his Quaker enterprise in Pennsylvania. William Penn would never return to America. At the same time, Elizabeth Haddon was beginning what would become a sixty-year journey to represent her father's real estate and business interests and in the process to establish a Quaker community across the river in the Province of West New Jersey in America. In some respects, the unity of her experiment would endure longer than that of the more well-known Quaker founder of Pennsylvania, William Penn.

Meanwhile, Elizabeth Haddon spent the rest of her life (as Elizabeth Estaugh) representing and then developing her father John Haddon's real estate across the Delaware River from Philadelphia in old Gloucester County, Province of West New Jersey in America. Here, the historic records show that Elizabeth Haddon Estaugh established a highly profitable plantation, constructed a beautiful house near Cooper's Creek in 1713 and helped to build a vibrant Quaker community in rural Haddonfield, New Jersey, named after her father John Haddon. Future generations, though, insisted that Elizabeth Haddon, not Estaugh, founded the town of Haddonfield and gave her name to the place in 1713, and moreover, in 1721 founded the Haddonfield Monthly Meeting of the Religious Society of Friends. Gradually a legendary rather than historical Elizabeth emerged in local lore. Twentieth century Haddonfield residents actually celebrated the 200th anniversary of the founding of their town based on the 1713 construction of Elizabeth and John Estaugh's plantation house near Cooper's Creek. They erected a plaque to celebrate Elizabeth Haddon's place as founder of their historic southern New Jersey town, locating it close to the where it is believed she was buried. (As was the custom of the Quakers in the eighteenth century, her grave was unmarked.) Fifty years later Haddonfield officials even created a Founder's Day in honor of Elizabeth Haddon.

Such adoration for a female town founder was understandable. Few women left their names on places in the early settlement of colonial America. Fewer still established towns. Those who did were of noble birth. Queen Christina of Sweden, an early seventeenth century proponent of New Sweden on the Delaware, was the namesake for Christiana, Delaware. Anne Arundel County, Maryland, derived its name from Lady Anne Arundel, wife of Cecil Calvert, the second Lord Baltimore, founder of the Maryland Colony. East New Jersey's first governor Philip Carteret named the colony's capital Elizabethtown in honor of Lady Elizabeth Carteret, wife of his brother

Sir George Carteret, proprietor of the colony. The colony of Virginia took its name from the Virgin Queen Elizabeth I of England, and not after the commoner Virginia Dare, the first English child born in America. No one, it seemed, named a place in colonial America after a woman not of noble birth, especially a member of what many considered a "peculiar" religious sect that gave women equal rights with men.[3]

Tablet erected in October 1913 in Haddonfield Friends Cemetery to honor Elizabeth Haddon Estaugh. It was part of the Two Hundredth Anniversary of the Settlement of Haddonfield Celebration program. *Rhoads Collection, Historical Society of Haddonfield*

Then, early residents of a tiny, southern New Jersey village lying just across the Delaware River from the vibrant port of Philadelphia claimed that the quiet, diminutive Quaker Elizabeth Haddon founded their town of Haddonfield. Eventually Haddon's name came to dominate not only the small village of Haddonfield but nearby Haddon Township, Haddon Heights, Haddon Avenue and even the Elizabeth Haddon Elementary School. Over time, Elizabeth Haddon became bigger than life, a heroic romantic and legendary figure. It helped that no portrait or description existed of what she actually looked like. Only an article of clothing displayed in the Historical Society of Haddonfield museum suggests that Elizabeth was of very small stature. Although many Haddon-Estaugh business records exist, only a few pieces of private personal correspondence from her family survive.[4]

Thus, recorders of her memory invented an Elizabeth Haddon based on legendary tales, partial truths and an oral tradition handed down from generation to generation. The traditional story began with the little girl, Elizabeth, sitting on William Penn's knee when the Pennsylvania proprietor visited her father John Haddon's house on the Thames Riverfront in London. The tale continued that while she rested on the lap of the great Quaker founder of Pennsylvania, Elizabeth Haddon held a corn doll of the virgin Indian princess Pocahontas and listened while Penn recounted stories of the noble savages in America. According to legend, Penn's testimony so moved Elizabeth that she resolved to one day visit America. She planned to follow in the steps of so many Religious Society of Friends female traveling preachers and spread the Word of God among what most Quakers saw as the "heathen" Delaware Indians. She was driven, the legend of Elizabeth acclaimed, by "her desire to carry Christianity to the Indians."[5]

When her father John Haddon purchased land near William Penn's Quaker community in Philadelphia on the Delaware River and asked her to represent family interests in West New Jersey, Elizabeth, so the legend went, crossed the Atlantic alone, while only nineteen years old, and settled in the untamed wilderness in order to preach to the Indians. The tale of Elizabeth Haddon continued that once in America she first lived among the Indians in the remote Mountwell farmhouse that stood isolated from the homes and Friends meetings of the few widely scattered Quaker settlers of Newton Township in Old Gloucester County. Many of these Quakers reportedly resided in cave-like dugouts along the banks of the many creeks that emptied into the Delaware River. Once in West New Jersey, the Haddon saga continued, Elizabeth met the handsome and charismatic Quaker traveling minister John Estaugh. John had arrived already in America where he spread the Word of the Lord among Friends meetings throughout Maryland, Virginia, North Carolina, Pennsylvania, New England and finally West New Jersey. According to the often repeated tale, Elizabeth proposed marriage to John while the two were riding through the West Jersey wilderness to attend meeting at the Salem Quarterly Meeting, the oldest such gathering of the Religious Society of Friends in New Jersey.[6]

Elizabeth Haddon's legendary stature increased even more after she built, what contemporaries recalled was a magnificent brick mansion house near Cooper's Creek in Old Gloucester County, New Jersey. Traditional accounts of Elizabeth's life, based on observations made years later by visitors to her house that "Haddonfield 1713" appeared in burned headers on the estate's chimney, claimed that on that date Elizabeth founded the Quaker community of Haddonfield. The date 1713 became etched indelibly in history and has been celebrated ever since by local residents as the year designated for the founding by Elizabeth Haddon of their historic town of Haddonfield, New Jersey.

Gradually, the legend of Elizabeth Haddon as the founder of Haddonfield became popular history through magazine stories written by nineteenth century Quaker abolitionist author Lydia Maria Child, a strong advocate of women's rights. Apparently Child had learned about the Haddon saga while she resided in New York City in the same boardinghouse as Quaker book seller and abolitionist propagandist Isaac T. Hopper. Hopper was born in Deptford, New Jersey, near Haddonfield, and spent his youth in Philadelphia, where undoubtedly the story of the Quaker woman who founded Haddonfield was widely known. Hopper shared all the Haddon anecdotes with Child. Eventually, Child published "The Youthful Emigrant" in *Columbian Lady's and Gentleman's Magazine*. This story of Elizabeth Haddon, though based on some actual occurrences and partial truths, was a largely fictional account.[7] Leading West New Jersey newspapers at the time immediately picked up and reprinted the story, led by the *New Jersey Mirror and Burlington County Advertiser*, published in Mount Holly.

The increasingly popular story became even more famous years later when New England poet Henry Wadsworth Longfellow perpetuated the Elizabeth

Haddon-John Estaugh love story in his 1873 edition of *Tales of a Wayside Inn*. Though Longfellow used some of Elizabeth's own words from her introduction to John Estaugh's *A Call to the Unfaithful Professors of Truth*, the New England poet based his "The Theologian's Tale: Elizabeth" largely upon the Haddon romance recounted in Child's "The Youthful Emigrant." Longfellow's poem presented the young dynamic preacher John Estaugh, traveling with a group of Quakers going to a Quarterly Meeting and stopping for refreshment at Elizabeth Haddon's West New Jersey doorstep. Here they "Tasted the currant wine, and the bread of rye, and the honey brought from the hives that stood by the sunny wall of the garden." Thus flushed with honey and wine, the two young Quakers joined the others and headed for meeting. They lingered behind in the deepest part of the Jersey woods, and according to Longfellow's rendition of the Lydia Child's tale, here they embraced and Elizabeth proposed marriage. "I have received from the Lord a charge to love thee, John Estaugh." Surprisingly, according to this version of the tryst, John Estaugh replied that he needed time to think about her proposal. He explained that before making his decision he was to leave on another great mission to preach across the seas. Longfellow concluded this idealized version of the Haddon-Estaugh encounter in America with the immortal line: "Ships that pass in the night, and speak each other in passing."[8]

Generations of Haddonfield residents connected through marriage to the original settlers of late-seventeenth century Newton Township in Old Gloucester County, West New Jersey, came to identify their community with the Child and Longfellow versions of their

"The Proposal" tableau of Elizabeth Haddon's proposal to John Estaugh, part of the 1913 Pageant celebrating the Two Hundredth Anniversary of the Settlement of Haddonfield. *Rhoads Collection, Historical Society of Haddonfield*

saintly "founder" Elizabeth Haddon's romantic life. Collateral descendants of the children of Elizabeth's sister Sarah Haddon Hopkins began the veneration of Elizabeth Haddon. In the process, they completely ignored the Estaugh name that Elizabeth used throughout her entire life in America. Elizabeth never bore children, but her father John Haddon and younger sister Sarah first sent her daughter Sarah and later her son Ebenezer Hopkins to live with Aunt Elizabeth and Uncle John Estaugh. Haddon's collateral descendants in America traced their genealogy back to the marriage of Ebenezer Hopkins and Sarah Lord, a prominent Woodbury, New Jersey, Friend.

Ebenezer and Sarah had seven children all born in New Jersey, who intermarried with other original Quaker families in the area and handed down the Elizabeth Haddon story from generation to generation. They wrote tracts, articles, prayers and even carefully documented books (based on the few original letters left in the family records) that made Elizabeth Haddon the single founder and namesake of their town of Haddonfield.[9]

Historian John Clement, who was related to the Estaugh, Hopkins, Mickle and almost every other early Quaker family of the area that became Haddonfield, authored the most important work. In 1877, Clement honored his father Samuel's appeal that he record the "correct" history of the first settlers of their "native place" of Newton Township. Clement followed the emerging late nineteenth century professionalization of history by using archival primary sources, wills, deeds, marriage certificates and court and government records to reconstruct the founding of his Haddonfield community. He published his findings in *Sketches of the First Emigrant Settlers in Newton Township*. Clement admitted that there might be gaps in his history of Newton Township that future researchers could fill and that he had written about Elizabeth Haddon, who he referred to by her married name Elizabeth Estaugh, mainly to evoke pride and "deserving reverence" in the Haddon roots of Haddonfield.[10]

Though still the most important introduction to the subject and despite extensive research, Clement's study of Elizabeth became yet another stage in the creation of the Haddon legend. Even his use of the Elizabeth Estaugh name "mysteriously disappeared" in the work of later historians.[11] Worse, Clement repeated many earlier factual errors and partial truths. The local New Jersey historian claimed that Elizabeth Haddon was one of only two children born to John and Elizabeth Clarke Haddon of London, when in fact she had seven brothers and sisters most of whom died early in life. Another distortion portrayed Elizabeth as a lonely teenager in 1701 when crossing the Atlantic to West Jersey unaccompanied by Friends. She actually turned twenty-one on the trip to America and traveled with a Quaker woman and family from her own Friends meeting back in England, who had sailed with Elizabeth to Philadelphia to join her husband.

Clement presented as historical fact many other questionable undocumented observations. He accepted the West Jersey tradition that had Elizabeth first living in America at the Mountwell estate of a Newton Township founder Francis Collins, "a companion of her father." The fact that Collins was the first permanent settler on the land that one day became part of present-day Haddonfield probably created this connection to the town's reputed founder Elizabeth Haddon. However, Collins had moved to Burlington, a large town over twenty miles up the Delaware River from his Mountwell farmhouse, many years before Elizabeth arrived in the Newton colony. The most enduring legend perpetuated by Clement claimed that Elizabeth Haddon invited American Indians to her wedding, one of whom signed her certificate of marriage. Though several hundred Algonquin-speaking Lenape Native American people lived in the Newton Township neighborhood when Elizabeth arrived in West New Jersey, and many marriage witnesses at her wedding had purchased land from the local Lenape clans, no records show that any Indians attended her marriage.

Much of John Clement's research actually offered an appearance of historical legitimacy to the emerging legend of Elizabeth Haddon as a "female example" of a heroic colonial British-American woman who in 1713 founded the town of Haddonfield, New Jersey. In the end, Clement praised her for being one of the women that: "Having shared every sacrifice and met every requirement, [her] position in the first endeavor to settle our State with English colonists should be made a prominent one and must command respect."[12]

Another collateral descendant, Samuel Nicholson Rhoads, continued John Clement's research into the life of Elizabeth Haddon. He discovered more original documents and letters in order to write the "Story of Elizabeth Haddon: The Maiden Pioneer." Rhoads used his findings for an address to Haddonfield residents in July 1907 at the unveiling of an Elizabeth Haddon Memorial Fountain that was situated at the corner of Mechanic Street and King's Highway.[13] The Haddonfield Woman's Christian Temperance Union erected this fountain to honor Elizabeth as the supposed founder of the long crusade to prohibit, forever, the sale and use of alcoholic beverages in her town. It did not matter that the historical record showed that Elizabeth and John Estaugh made hard apple cider, "grape" wine (some even sent to Elizabeth's father in England) and had two stills on their eighteenth century Haddonfield plantation. One letter from John Haddon indicates that he had shipped Elizabeth two-hundred bottles of a highly alcoholic concoction of macerated roots of herbs and spices known as "bitters," for medicinal purposes. According to legend, she also distributed these "medicinal bitters" to local Native

Fountain dedicated to Elizabeth which the Woman's Christian Temperance Union erected at the corner of King's Highway East and Mechanic Street. *Photo Collection, Historical Society of Haddonfield*

Americans in an effort to raise the spiritual awareness and inner light among "heathen" doubters.[14] A story Historical Society of Haddonfield member Edna L. Haydock often recounted attempted to demonstrate that the local Native Americans trusted Elizabeth, but then admitted she gave strong liquor to the Indians. There is, however, no historical basis for this story, which endures as folklore in many cultures.[15]

The Borough of Haddonfield's seal further codifies the legend of Elizabeth Haddon as someone who helped the Indians through gifts of food and medicine. The borough derived its seal from a medal that prominent local artist Emlen McConnell designed for presentation to First World War veterans returning to Haddonfield. The Borough Commissioners officially adopted the seal on July 14, 1919.[16]

Haddonfield artist Emlen McConnell originally created a medal featuring Elizabeth Haddon Estaugh ministering to Native Americans for World War I Veterans. It later became the Seal of the Borough of Haddonfield.

Meanwhile, Samuel N. Rhoads began to research his own biography of Elizabeth Haddon Estaugh after his 1907 dedication of the Temperance fountain. He traveled to England in 1909 in search of facts about Elizabeth's early life. Rhoads asked everyone interested in Elizabeth's life to send documents to share with him. Few found any new evidence. But six years later, Rhoads organized a 200th anniversary celebration of Elizabeth's construction of her house in 1713 to commemorate the beginning of the town of Haddonfield. He hoped that new evidence about Elizabeth Haddon Estaugh would accompany this historical pageant. Instead, during this celebration of the town's founding the legends surrounding Elizabeth Haddon's life became institutionalized in poems, speeches and published works. The celebration committee concluded its morning ceremonies with the unveiling of a brass tablet in the old Friends Cemetery (near the present-day Haddonfield fire station). The memorial plaque called "Elizabeth Haddon," born in 1680, the "Founder and Proprietor of Haddonfield, NJ." As part of the same program, John Estaugh Hopkins's great-great-granddaughter Rebecca Nicholson Taylor read her poem "Elizabeth Haddon" (with no mention of the Estaugh name) at the Friends Meeting House in Haddonfield for the 200th anniversary of the settlement of Haddonfield. Taylor praised Elizabeth not only as the first temperance advocate in Haddonfield, but as the first suffragette. "And she would build a house of prayer, For worship, silent, pure and free," Taylor wrote, "with men and women equal there to speak the word or bend the knee."[17]

At the same time, Harriet Redman Willits read her "Incidents in the Life of Elizabeth Haddon" for the Haddonfield 200th Anniversary celebration. Willits' talk was filled with the same oral tradition, undocumented stories, legends and partial truths presented by earlier keepers of Elizabeth Haddon's memory. As part of her presentation Willits announced that they had little choice but to invent the legendary female founder of their town. "Elizabeth Haddon left no diary," Willits wrote, "so we too are obliged to be pioneers and to blaze again the forest trails, this time through the pages of books, a few old letters, note books and Meeting records from which we piece together a story, full of youth and romance and religious zeal."[18]

In 1925 another collateral descendant, Rebecca Nicholson Taylor, inherited a collection of original Haddon, Estaugh and Hopkins family documents and letters from her aunts Sarah and Rebecca Nicholson, who had been custodians of the Elizabeth Haddon and John Estaugh papers for many years. These documents revealed that much of the popular Elizabeth Haddon legend stemmed from romanticized partial truths and downright falsehoods. The correspondence in 1880 between English Quaker historian Hannah J. Sturge, and New York City Quaker Mary Sutton Wood, author of the then out-of-print *Social Hours with Friends,* proves particularly enlightening. Wood's book contains a chapter on Elizabeth Haddon that repeated Lydia Child's folklore story verbatim. Sturge asked, as she prepared to write a memorial to John and Elizabeth Haddon Estaugh, for a copy of Wood's book. Wood agreed, although warning "Friend Sturge" that the account of Haddon "was written by Lydia Maria Child from traditions of the family obtained from descendants of her nephew [Ebenezer Hopkins], but her story was considerably embellished, and some of our young women are quite indignant about the account of her offering herself to John Estaugh." One of those young women reported that many original letters were in the possession of her husband's family and none of them mentioned the romantic stories invented by the Quaker journalist Child.[19]

With these intriguing letters in her possession Rebecca Nicholson Taylor began to revise the Haddon story. Elizabeth Estaugh's distant collateral descendant crafted several articles about John and Elizabeth Haddon Estaugh's business dealings that she published in 1930 in the *Bulletin of Friends' Historical Society of Philadelphia*. These articles revealed new information about the Estaughs' real estate developments and the part they played in building the Quaker community of Haddonfield, New Jersey. However, as the latest keeper of the Elizabeth Haddon Estaugh papers and cherished memories of the Haddon-Hopkins lineage, Taylor actually enhanced and perpetuated the traditional view of Elizabeth "Haddon" as the heroic founder of Haddonfield.[20]

The legend of Elizabeth Haddon continued through the Great Depression Era (1929–1941) when unemployed historians, working for the New Jersey Writers' Project of the New Deal's Work Projects Administration (WPA), assembled a lesson plan for Haddonfield school children that repeated the accounts of past historians based largely on oral tradition. "It was her plan to make a home in the wilderness," the New Deal writers taught, "where Quaker missionaries could rest from their travels and to be a nurse and teacher to the Indians." The WPA story tellers insisted that the heroic Elizabeth Haddon became "the only woman who ever settled alone on (and managed) an American colonial plantation." The New Jersey Writers'

Project curriculum taught Haddonfield students that in 1713 Elizabeth Haddon had founded their historic little town. The New Deal historians went much further, however, claiming that Elizabeth should be memorialized as the "most famous woman in New Jersey history."[21]

The Elizabeth Haddon legend continued to expand with each passing year. In 1950, New Jersey Governor Alfred E. Driscoll, a Haddonfield resident, connected Elizabeth to the incorporation in 1875 of Haddonfield, formerly part of Haddon Township, as a borough. "From its beginning, when Elizabeth Haddon settled on her father's land," Driscoll announced at the 75th Anniversary celebration of the incorporation of his town as a borough, "Haddonfield has been an important part of the life of the colony, state and nation."[22] The Haddon legend became official Borough of Haddonfield policy in 1963, with the establishment of a Founder's Day celebration honoring Elizabeth Haddon. "We," the Haddonfield Borough Commissioners announced, "do hereby proclaim the year 1963 to be the 250th Anniversary Year of the founding of Haddonfield, and call upon all citizens to join in the observance thereof."[23] At this moment of devotion, surprisingly, at least one Historical Society of Haddonfield member voiced some doubt about all the legendary accounts. Camden County Historical Society Trustee Elmer Garfield Van Name, while agreeing with most assumptions about Elizabeth Haddon's place in history, called for more research into her life. Van Name even suggested making archaeological digs along the south side of Cooper's Creek at Coles Landing along present-day Coles Mill Road in order to discover what he and earlier, Samuel Nicholson Rhoads, believed was the long-lost site of Elizabeth's first house in America.[24]

After the 1963 Founder's Day celebration of the 250th anniversary of the first permanent settlement of Haddonfield by Elizabeth Haddon, no one really started any new research into her life and times. Then two Haddonfield Borough residents and ardent patrons of the Historical Society of Haddonfield, Elizabeth A. Lyons, a New Jersey Department of Health official with a degree in English from the University of Pennsylvania, and her brother George Stuart Lyons, a Drexel graduate and engineer with RCA Victor in Camden, began their lifelong "Search for Elizabeth." The Lyons's interest in Elizabeth Haddon arose in 1969 after the sudden death of their mother with whom they lived. That same year, Stuart lost his job at the Radio Corporation of America headquarter in nearby Camden, New Jersey. According to Betty Lyons the two siblings needed something to take their minds off of these losses and they started to devote their lives to researching the history of Haddonfield and its time-honored founder Elizabeth Haddon. The Lyons team discovered that nearly every published work repeated the same stories about Elizabeth. Betty and her brother struggled to locate original documents in local archives beyond the handful collected by Rhoads and other descendants and in possession of the Historical Society of Haddonfield. Eventually, they visited Elizabeth Haddon's birthplace in the Bermondsey neighborhood of Southwark, a London city borough located on the south banks of the Thames River. They hoped to discover historical evidence that might reveal once and for all the facts surrounding Elizabeth Haddon's role in the founding of their beloved town of Haddonfield.[25]

Betty and Stuart Lyons uncovered a treasure trove of original documents about Haddon family history while in London. These findings led to the location of documents

Elizabeth A. Lyons and her brother George Stuart Lyons who researched and wrote about Elizabeth Estaugh for over forty years. *Lyons Collection, Historical Society of Haddonfield*

in the Quaker archives at Swarthmore and Haverford colleges back in the Philadelphia area. The Quaker Collection at the Haverford College Library held the largest known accumulation of Haddon, Estaugh and Hopkins family documents. With such discoveries, the Lyons began in the late 1960s to write a book about Elizabeth Haddon. They spent the next forty years pouring through local historical society archives in Philadelphia, Pennsylvania, Gloucester and Camden counties in New Jersey and the New Jersey State Archives in Trenton always searching for the "real" Elizabeth Haddon history. Betty and Stuart returned to England and revisited Elizabeth Haddon's Southwark birthplace where they searched the records of the Haddon family's Horsleydown Monthly Meeting (and the surrounding Bermondsey and Rotherhithe neighborhoods) and for the Haddon family burial plots. They also discovered previously unknown information about Elizabeth's father John Haddon in the Mining Museum archives at Newcastle-on-Tyne. Next the Lyons brother and sister team visited Tortola in the British Virgin Islands, where Elizabeth Haddon Estaugh's husband John had died in 1742 while on a mission to Friends on the island. The Lyons team hoped to find his grave and those of the famous Quaker missionary and wealthy merchant ship owner Thomas Chalkley of Philadelphia and other Delaware Valley Quaker traveling ministers buried on Tortola. They discovered that the ancient cemetery was so overgrown with thorny thickets that they were unable to find the actual grave markers.

As her research intensified Betty started to question earlier accounts of the reputed founder of Haddonfield, particularly when she discovered that after Elizabeth

Haddon's marriage in 1702 to John Estaugh, Elizabeth always called herself and signed all documents as "Elizabeth Estaugh," never as "Elizabeth Haddon." Her contemporaries—family, friends, religious and business associates—always referred to her as Elizabeth Estaugh. So, if she never used the Haddon name throughout her life in America, Betty asked, why did most people over the years (and through today) suppose that Haddonfield was named after her? This revelation produced other questions about the tale of Elizabeth Haddon. "Of the many legends concerning Elizabeth Haddon Estaugh," Betty Lyons argued, "some are outright fabrications, a few have partial glimpses of true incidents and others are based on slightly twisted facts." Lyons questioned traditional tales of Elizabeth Haddon's proposal of marriage to John Estaugh, her sitting on the knee of William Penn while playing with a doll of an Indian princess, her first residence with Francis Collins at Mountwell and many, many other accepted stories of her life.[26]

As her research into original documents and archival sources grew more extensive, Betty Lyons revealed a growing concern for the accuracy of the Haddon legend. She wondered why future generations named everything after Elizabeth Haddon, not Estaugh? In an interview with journalist Patricia Tice for the *Philadelphia Inquirer* in 1976, Lyons raised serious doubt about a "somewhat fictionalized account" that Haddonfield was founded by a "wonder woman named Elizabeth Haddon, who established a Utopia." However, this article seemed a bit too sensational for the Lyons research team, so Betty attached a cryptic note to a newspaper clipping of the article filed in the Historical Society of Haddonfield that read: "Pat interviewed us for this, but we didn't want our names used."²⁷

Betty and her brother continued to assemble boxes of notes, wrote outlines and eventually crafted the first of several rough drafts for a definitive Elizabeth Haddon Estaugh biography. They became increasingly critical of earlier historic accounts of Elizabeth Haddon, corrected many myths and debunked legends including that Indians (Native Americans) had attended the Estaugh wedding. "There are no marks on the [marriage] certificate as indicated by the romantics who put forth this theory," Elizabeth Lyons snapped. They discovered that Elizabeth's father John Haddon, her husband John Estaugh, cousin John Gill and nephew Ebenezer Hopkins and dozens of intimate female and male Friends from Delaware Valley Meetings held as much responsibility as Elizabeth for the founding and establishment of the Quaker community of Haddonfield, New Jersey. The Lyons desperately wanted "to bring Elizabeth Haddon's true story to light" and get the real Haddon-Estaugh-Hopkins story published by the end of the decade. As a forecast of a planned biography, in 1990 Elizabeth Lyons contributed the most accurate historical account of Elizabeth Haddon Estaugh to date in her short essay for the Women's History Project of New Jersey.²⁸

After her article, Betty and her brother struggled to write a complete biography. They labored through many manuscript drafts, each more detailed than the last. They searched for more and more documents and checked and double checked the accuracy of their work. Finally, Betty observed that these "documents yielded up their hoard of detail until the *ghostly* outlines of Elizabeth Haddon surfaced." The Lyons wrote that "as we worked, we felt her scrutiny upon us, her spirit with us." In the process, these twentieth century Haddonfield authors (Betty and Stuart Lyons) began to fall under the spell of the legendary and "elusive figure resistant to research." They kept researching, writing and revising, hoping to unmask the legend of this elusive and mysterious historic figure. However in 2001 as their final work began to take shape, Stuart Lyons passed away. Betty forged ahead alone, expecting to have a biography ready for a 300th Anniversary Celebration in 2013 of the traditional date that Elizabeth Haddon founded the town of Haddonfield.[29]

Betty Lyons's last draft, completed in 2008, showed great promise and offered hints that she had solved the riddles of the legend of the "Youthful Emigrant" Elizabeth Haddon. At this point, Betty Lyons, an inveterate traveler, decided to take a brief vacation to Norway, reprising the many trips abroad that she had once taken with her mother and brother. Betty planned when she returned from her European vacation to finish what she called the "definitive history" of Elizabeth Haddon Estaugh's life. Tragically, Betty Lyons died suddenly without warning in Oslo, taking with her in death yet another vision of the ghostly, elusive Elizabeth Haddon legend. Fortunately, Betty and Stuart Lyons left a great legacy of research and writing that we can now use as the basis for constructing that definitive biography that may put to rest once and for all the 300-year-old legend of the "Youthful Emigrant" Elizabeth Haddon.[30]

CHAPTER 1 NOTES.

[1] L. Maria Child, "The Youthful Emigrant: A True Story of the Early Settlement of New Jersey," in *Fact and Fiction: A Collection of Stories* (New York: C. S. Francis & Co., 1846), 48.

[2] Owen to Penn, May 8, 1702, *The Papers of William Penn*, eds. Mary Maples Dunn and Richard S. Dunn (Philadelphia: University of Pennsylvania Press, 1981–1987), *Penn Papers*, IV: 169.

[3] See Levenduski, *Peculiar Power*.

[4] Existing personal correspondence includes four letters from Elizabeth's sister, Sarah Haddon Hopkins, and fourteen letters from her parents, John and Elizabeth Clarke Haddon, on deposit in the Haddon-Estaugh-Hopkins Papers, Collection 1001, The Quaker Collection, Haverford College Library, Haverford, PA. (hereafter, cited as, HEHP).

[5] These stories started in 1845 with Lydia Child, "The Youthful Emigrant," in *Fact and Fiction*, 40–47; see, also Harriet O. Redman Willits, "Incidents in the Life of Elizabeth Haddon," in *Two Hundredth Anniversary of the Settlement of Haddonfield, New Jersey: Celebrated October eighteenth, nineteen hundred and thirteen* (Haddonfield, NJ:1913), 29.

[6] Willits, "Incidents in the Life of Elizabeth Haddon," 29.

[7] Lydia Maria Child, "The Youthful Emigrant," *Columbian Lady's and Gentleman's Magazine*, vol. 3, (1845). For the argument that Child created Elizabeth as an "Imaginary Friend," see Ryan, *Imaginary Friends*.

[8] Henry Wadsworth Longfellow, *Tales of A Wayside Inn* (Boston and New York: Houghton Mifflin, 1913 edition of 1873 work), 211–26, 265–66.

[9] C. E. N. Hartel, "The Mysterious Disappearance of Elizabeth Estaugh," (unpublished article, February 1954), file 75-58, Hartel Collection, HSHL.

[10] Clement, *First Emigrant Settlers*, 111–16.

[11] For a convincing argument on how the Estaugh name disappeared over time, see Hartel, "The Mysterious Disappearance of Elizabeth Estaugh," HSHL.

[12] Clement, *First Emigrant Settlers*, 9. As late as the 1970s, Edward T. and Mary James, *Notable American Women* (Cambridge: Harvard University Press, 1974) claimed that many Indians attended the Elizabeth Haddon and John Estaugh wedding.

[13] Rhoads, in *Camden Daily Courier*, July 1, 1907.

[14] John and Elizabeth Haddon to Dear Children, February 27, 1717. HEHP, folder 182.

[15] Edna L. Haydock, "Elizabeth and the Indians," in *This Is Haddonfield* (Haddonfield, NJ: Historical Society of Haddonfield, 1963), 262.

[16] Borough of Haddonfield Commission Minutes. Vol. 8: Jan. 15, 1917–April 7, 1921, 454.

[17]Samuel Nicholson Rhoads, "Address at the Unveiling of the Tablet to the Memory of Elizabeth Haddon," and Taylor, "Elizabeth Haddon: An Original Poem," *Two Hundredth Anniversary*, 33, 35–36. Historical Society of Haddonfield historian Carrie Hartel, who researched the Haddon, Estaugh and Hopkins family histories from the late 1940s through the 1960s, suspected in 1954 that descendants of Sarah Haddon Hopkins deliberately ignored the Estaugh name to keep the Haddon heritage alive, see Hartel, "The Mysterious Disappearance of Elizabeth Estaugh," HSHL.

[18]Harriet O. Redman Willits, "Incidents in the Life of Elizabeth Haddon," in *Two Hundredth Anniversary*, 28–32.

[19]Mary S. Wood to Hannah Sturge, 20 March 1880, Sarah R. Whitall to Mary S. Wood, 24 June 1880, and Wood to Sturge, 5 July 1880, all in Sturge folder, Biographical File, in box 3, Lyons Project Papers, HSHL. Though Sturge corrected Lydia Child's version of the romantic encounter between Elizabeth and John, she continued all the other legends in Hannah J. (Dickinson) Sturge, *Fragmentary Memorials of John & Elizabeth Estaugh, 1881* (Gloucester, N.J.: printed by J. Bellows, 1881.

[20]Rebecca Nicholson Taylor, "Original Papers Belonging to Elizabeth Estaugh in Possession of Rebecca N. Taylor," and "Business Papers of John and Elizabeth Estaugh," in *Friends Historical Association Bulletin* (1930), 92; (1931), 13. R. N. Taylor later donated these papers to the Quaker Collection, Haverford College Library, Haverford, PA.

[21]"Elizabeth Haddon," *Stories of New Jersey Prepared for use in Public Schools by the New Jersey Writers' Project*, Bulletin No. 1 (Newark, New Jersey: Work Projects Administration, 1940–41).

[22]*75 Years of Service: Borough of Haddonfield; Incorporated 1875* (Camden County, New Jersey, [1950]).

[23]*This Is Haddonfield*, iii.

[24]Elmer Garfield Van Name, "Elizabeth Haddon's First House," in The Historical Society of Haddonfield *Bulletin*, February 1963, 2.

[25]Lyons, "Search for Elizabeth," HSHL.

[26]See, Lyons correspondence, in box 5, Lyons Project Papers, HSHL.

[27]Patricia Tice, "Haddonfield: A Legend Grows in Suburbia," *Philadelphia Inquirer*, May 17, 1976; Lyons correspondence, in box 5, Lyons Project Papers, HSHL.

[28]Elizabeth and George Lyons, "Haddon, Estaugh Marry,"*Haddon Gazette*, December 6, 1990; Elizabeth A. Lyons, "Elizabeth Haddon, ca. 1680–1762," in Joan N. Burstyn, ed., *Past and Promise: Lives of New Jersey Women: the Women's Project of New Jersey Inc* (Metuchen, N.J: Scarecrow Press, 1990; paperback edition, Syracuse, NY: Syracuse University Press, 1997), 21–22.

[29]See, various drafts of Lyons's biography, Lyons Project Papers, HSHL.

[30]Lyons, "Search for Elizabeth," HSHL.

CHAPTER 2.
Observe the Pious and Godly Example of Tender Parents.

Be agreeable to that holy Path of Truth, in which their tender Parents walked, and for which some of them deeply suffered, and underwent many Cruelties, long and hard Imprisonments, from Men of dark and corrupt Minds.

—John Estaugh[1]

When and why Elizabeth Haddon sailed from Britain at the turn of the eighteenth century to the area now known as Haddonfield in present-day Camden County, New Jersey, stemmed directly from the tumultuous and historic era that defined her father John Haddon's life. It was a period of dramatic political and religious turmoil that led to an English Civil War and the beheading of King Charles I. It saw the rise of Oliver Cromwell's Protectorate, a short-lived Republican Commonwealth and Restoration of the monarchy that changed the entire fabric of British society and government. Parliament battled the king and nobility for political control. A rising pre-industrial middle class struggled for economic leadership against the landed aristocracy, while numerous Protestant reformist sects (including the non-conformist Religious Society of Friends known as Quakers) protested against the absolute authority of the Anglican Church of England.

Elizabeth Haddon also grew up in an era of English colonial expansion overseas, foreign wars and entrepreneurial capitalism. The religious, industrial and colonial movements became most significant for Elizabeth's future. Her father belonged to the dissident Protestant sect of the Religious Society of Friends, developed an iron mining business and invested in New World real estate. All, in one way or another, directly impacted on the Haddon family, particularly Elizabeth's life. The Quakers provided one of the most important networks of religious, social and economic connections in Anglo-American history. John Haddon used these Quaker connections to develop a prosperous blacksmith, anchor making and mining business in England and to accumulate a modest real estate empire in America. Moreover, these larger developments explained, in part, Elizabeth's role in building a Quaker community in Haddonfield, New Jersey.

Elizabeth Haddon's father was born in 1653 in the rural Northamptonshire village of Hardingstone some seventy miles north of London. John Haddon entered the world just as Oliver Cromwell became the Lord Protector of the Commonwealth of England, Scotland and Ireland. The English Civil War between 1642 and 1646 had created the opportunity for young middle-class members of the English Parliament, like Cromwell and Puritan Protestant reformers, to rise to prominence. They battled the king, old aristocracy and established Church of England for more political, religious and constitutional rights and freedoms. In the process, Cromwell became the leader of the Parliamentary forces (so-called Roundheads) by reorganizing a New Army to fight against the more professional Royalist (or Cavalier) military forces defending the king, nobility and Church of England. In the second and most violent phase of the English Civil War between 1648 and 1649, Cromwell's army emerged victorious, culminating in the beheading of King Charles I and establishment of the Commonwealth. Claiming that his Commonwealth was a republican government, Cromwell in fact ran Britain with an iron hand until his death in 1658, which led to the Restoration of the Stuart monarchy in 1660 under Charles II, who was then succeeded in 1685 by his brother James, the Duke of York.

The political, economic and religious developments during this Restoration and immediate post-Restoration period shaped John Haddon's life (and that of his daughter Elizabeth born in 1680). Between 1660 and 1689, the Stuart monarchs Charles II and James II launched major colonial enterprises in America. Their foreign policies helped found colonies in the Carolinas, New York, East New Jersey and the Quaker colonies of West New Jersey and Pennsylvania. After the Glorious Revolution deposed James and invited William and Mary to the throne in 1689, the British government more aggressively promoted English imperialism, colonization and trade under the Navigation Acts throughout the world. This policy led to wars with Holland, France and Spain but also great opportunities for entrepreneurs such as John Haddon to invest in overseas enterprises.

At the same time, though, Charles II and later his brother James II repressed dissident Protestant sects that threatened the absolute authority of the Church of England. The British monarchs worried that the Quakers, among the most troublesome Protestant non-conformist groups to come out of the Puritan Revolution, posed a serious threat to the Crown, imperial government and official Anglican Church of State. Founded in 1647 by dynamic preacher George Fox, his wife Margaret Fell and other religious reformers, the Religious Society of Friends, known somewhat derisively in England as Quakers for their reported propensity to make governmental officials quake in fear, continued to grow in numbers and influence throughout the British Isles and on the Continent, particularly in Holland. The Friends soon attracted converts from the poorer working folk, yeomen farmers and the rising middle-class of craftsmen such as John Haddon. Fox's teachings also convinced merchants, landowners and soldiers disillusioned with Cromwell's actions, as well as thousands of men and women searching for the Truth in the teachings of Christ. Fox taught that the inner light of the Lord revealed the Truth to every person, men and women, regardless of social or economic status, who accepted the teachings of the Friends. This appealed to those Protestant reformers who had long questioned why they must blindly submit to the aristocracy or pledge oaths and allegiance to only the King and the official Church of England.

Ignoring the formal structure of the Church of England, Quakers gathered in private houses, public places and village squares throughout the British Isles to pray silently with their Inner Light, or listen to visiting ministers testify to the Truth. Charles II tried to crush the Quakers with the Quaker Act of 1662 that made it illegal for anyone to refuse to take an Oath of Allegiance to King and Country. The king enforced this edict with the Conventicle Act of 1664 that forbade nonconformist religious dissenters to hold public meetings. The government deprived Quakers of all legal rights, overtaxed and condemned their property, tore down meeting halls and worse imprisoned, tortured, starved or executed many dissenters. This meant ever-increased persecution and suffering for members of the Religious Society of Friends, including Elizabeth Haddon's parents. Quakers faced confiscation of property, imprisonment and often death for practicing their religion in public meetings. The state called this rioting. Quakers also suffered for refusing to pay tithes or rates and assessments for building and repairing places of worship of which they did not approve. Quakers refused to use the established church rituals or ordained ministry for baptisms, marriages, burials and other religious ceremonies. They defied the traditional social order by not removing their hats in the presence of public officials. Worse, the Quakers seemed to sabotage governmental authority by refusing to support its wars or to swear oaths in order to conduct legal transactions.[2]

During this era of extreme persecution known as the Sufferings, John Haddon accepted the teachings of George Fox and found Truth and Unity with the Religious Society of Friends. His time of convincement remains uncertain. His father Matthew and mother Phillipiah Marriott Haddon had married in an Anglican church in 1651 at Harpole, a small Northamptonshire village four miles west of Hardingstone. However, sometime after their marriage, Matthew and Phillipiah Haddon became convinced members of the Religious Society of Friends. John Haddon's sister, Ann was born in Meeting in 1657 and later married noted Northamptonshire Friend John Gill in the Northampton Meeting House. The Haddon's Northampton neighbor Henry Gill was so active in pursing the Truth, and refusing to pay tithes to the Church of England, that officials dragged him to Southwark, London and committed him to the White Lion Prison for a year. County magistrates sent John Haddon's father Matthew to a "nasty stinking" prison for attending a Friends meeting at Mary Cooper's in Hardingstone and placed his aunt Elizabeth Haddon (not to be confused with his wife Elizabeth Clarke Haddon or daughter Elizabeth, later) in the county "Goal" that same year for attending Meeting. Members of John's mother's family, the Marriotts of Hardingstone, Northamptonshire, also suffered much at the hands of officials for attending Meeting. Moreover, John Haddon's future brother-in-law John Clarke was imprisoned for attending Friends Meeting in the streets of Southwark.[3]

Fox and other dynamic preachers in the region convinced the Haddon and Gill families. Both Northampton Quaker families suffered for their beliefs that the word of the Lord lay directly inside each person and through acceptance of the Truth; they "experienced an inward Peace and Tranquility of Mind." Undoubtedly this had a great influence on John Haddon. Haddon first showed unity with the Religious Society of Friends in 1670 when the government fined him £2.5 for attending a Quaker meeting at Anne Blackburn's, probably in Ellington, a tiny Yorkshire hamlet a few miles northeast of Hardingstone. The Cooper family and other dissident Quakers that later sailed to the Delaware Valley lived in the immediate vicinity. Young John Haddon attended this public meeting of Friends despite the government's Conventicle Act of 1670 that banned Quaker meetings. Defiance of the ban and the resulting imprisonment of some, convinced dissident groups of Yorkshire and nearby London Quakers to come to America between 1675 and 1681 to found Quaker communities in West New Jersey (and Pennsylvania). There was no evidence that John Haddon suffered imprisonment, but the preaching in Yorkshire probably moved him to accept the Truth of the Quaker teachings. It also may have introduced him during this interval to the Quaker movement to the New World.[4]

Soon after the Blackburn meeting, John Haddon and his brothers, Simon and Thomas, joined hundreds of other young men and women from rural towns like Hardingstone during the last decades of the seventeenth century to seek economic opportunity and perhaps religious and social freedom in London. Migration to the Southwark Borough of London seemed most active from the neighborhoods around Hardingstone, Northamptonshire. A large number of these Quaker families became friends and associates of John Haddon's family in London and America. These Haddon neighbors included the Marriott, Collins, Cooper, Hopkins, Hagen, Gove, Wright, Burrough, Warner, Ward, Clement, Wood, Chalkley, Bye, Dillwyn and Adams families among many others.

Once in London, John Haddon became a blacksmith. Possibly, he followed in his family's footsteps. His father Matthew owned some property and was taxed for two hearths, indicating that he either ran a bakery or more likely a smithy. Moreover, Matthew's older brother Roger Haddon, of Hardingstone, Northamptonshire, had been apprenticed to William Lee, a member of the Blacksmith's Company guild. Thus, the blacksmith's craft lay in the family. However, Matthew's youngest son

Simon, later opened a bakery in Cripplegate, St. Giles, London, suggesting the possibility that the Haddon family pursued that trade as well. Meanwhile, Simon's older brothers John and Thomas Haddon developed a blacksmith business in the early 1670s on the south bank of the Thames River in Rotherhithe, parish of St. George, Borough of Southwark, County of "Surry" (Surrey), City of London.

John (and later his brother Thomas) operated a blacksmith shop on Cherry Garden Pier along the south bank of the Thames riverfront in the London Borough of Southwark. The Haddon blacksmith forge soon expanded into an iron foundry that cast anchors for the many ships built along the Thames River. Such an operation required highly skilled training. The influential ironmongers' trade guild or the prestigious Blacksmith's Company where his uncle Roger had apprenticed most likely helped the Haddon brothers to establish their business. Moreover, John Clarke, probably John Haddon's future brother or father-in-law, was a noted blacksmith who resided in the same neighborhood where John Haddon first settled. Clarke may have apprenticed the Hardingstone young man and introduced him to Elizabeth Clarke. John Haddon would eventually marry Elizabeth Clarke, Elizabeth Haddon's future mother.

At the same time an enterprise of this importance had to have major financial backing, but no records remain that revealed the source of Haddon's first business loan. Possibly, the powerful Wood family of ironmasters that ran a great iron foundry in Southwark during the 1670s supported Haddon. Joshua Wood was a prominent witness at Haddon's marriage to Elizabeth Clarke in 1676.

More likely, Richard Matthews[5], a London goldsmith and factor (money lender) financed Haddon's business. Matthews invested heavily in the development of the iron mining business in Britain and became an original buyer of real estate in West New Jersey in America. During the 1690s Matthews became Haddon's major business partner in various British mining enterprises and in American real estate and land companies.[6]

By 1675, John Haddon resided in a row house on Jacob Street in the bustling industrial neighborhood of Bermondsey, in the London City Borough of Southwark. Overcrowded tenements lined narrow streets that were filled with busy coffee houses, inns, taverns, theatres (including the Globe, presenting plays by William Shakespeare), markets and craft shops. Tanneries, mills, breweries, dyers, lime burners and soap boilers shops filled the air with thick smoke from their fires of industry. Boatyards, ship repair facilities, including Howland's Wet Dock, (the largest in London, built in 1696), lined the riverfront just a few paces from Haddon's home and business. The centuries-old London neighborhood also contained ancient monasteries and historic churches some tracing their origins back to the early Middle Ages. It also proved a volatile neighborhood where Quaker dissidents struggled for freedom of religion against the dominant Church of England. At this time John Haddon accepted the call of the Horsleydown Monthly Meeting in Bermondsey, eventually becoming one of its most influential members. His future wife Elizabeth Clarke was already a member and treasurer of the Horsleydown Women's Meeting. All the Haddon children, particularly daughter Elizabeth, would become birthright Quakers, born in Meeting. The Meeting would largely determine every aspect of Elizabeth Haddon's life.[7]

The first concrete evidence that John Haddon belonged to the Horsleydown Monthly Meeting and lived in the Bermondsey neighborhood a few blocks from his Rotherhithe business came with the record of his marriage to his Jacob Street neighbor, Elizabeth Clarke of Bermondsey. "John Haddon of Southwarke In ye County of Surrey Smith, on ye 3d of ye 6th mo (August): 1676 did Solumnly [sic] take Elizabeth Clarke of the Same place Spinster, to be his wife In an Assembly at Horsleydowne In ye presence of" seventeen members of the men's meeting and ten from the women's meeting.[8] Witnesses to the Haddon-Clarke marriage included John's sister, Mary, and Elizabeth Carpenter, Anne Warner, George Rawlins and other Friends whose families participated in the Quaker settlement of West New Jersey and Pennsylvania. Rawlins was a respected Bermondsey blacksmith and possibly Haddon's master during his apprenticeship. Another possible source of his first apprenticeships was, as mentioned earlier, the Wood family since Joshua Wood also witnessed the marriage. Thomas Padley, owner of a Thames River pier; John Grove, another Southwark blacksmith; William Gibson, a waterman, and John Tiplady, a Bermondsey shipwright headed the men's delegation at the Haddon-Clarke marriage ceremony.

Family and business connections for John Haddon's new wife Elizabeth Clarke were not so clear. She was already a respected Quaker midwife and member of the Horsleydown Meeting when she met Haddon. Elizabeth Clarke may have been the sister of the brewer John Clarke (Clark) of London who invested heavily in West

Jersey land. Clarke was not among the witnesses to the marriage but later attended many Haddon and Hopkins family events. Moreover, noted Quaker dissident and essayist Thomas Lurting, who captained vessels to the Delaware Valley during this period and soon became one of John Haddon's closest friends in the Horsleydown Monthly Meeting, was related to Mary Clarke Lurting and may have been kin. Thus, John and Elizabeth Clarke Haddon were familiar with Quaker interests in American colonization from the very beginning of their marriage.

The newly-wed Haddons had no intention at the moment of joining the others in America despite continuing religious persecution, destructive fires, smallpox and other disease that in 1676 plagued their neighborhoods. Smallpox certainly impacted the development and growth of John and Elizabeth Clarke Haddon's family. Their first child William was born in 1677 and in 1678: "Aged about one year & a quarter Dyed [sic] of ye Gripes as p[er] Judgment of ye Searchers." Their second child Mary, born in 1678, "ye Daughter of John & Eliz: Haddon of ye parish of Magdalenes Bermondsey Aged about 2 years ½ Died of ye Small Pox as p[er] Judgmt of ye Searchers."[9]

John and Elizabeth Clarke Haddon's third child Elizabeth, was born in 1680. She was destined to live a long and blessed life, dying in 1762 at the age of eighty-two at her plantation house in Haddonfield, New Jersey. The Haddons had five more children over the next decade. Mary (II) was born in 1682 and died in 1688 of small pox. Sarah (I) was born in 1685 and died "Aged about fifteen weeks. It is thought she did die of ye Gripes and Teeth." Ebenezer (I) was born in 1686, and "Aged about 19 Weeks, Dyed of Convultion fitts as p[er] Judgiment of ye Common Searchers.[quoted as written]" Sarah (II), born in 1687, became, along with her older sister Elizabeth, the only Haddon children to live to adulthood.[10]

Ebenezer Haddon (II) was born in 1690 and it was hoped that he would be able to provide an heir to the family fortune, particularly by inheriting family properties in America. But, although an apparently healthy lad, Ebenezer died suddenly in 1706 at the age of sixteen of "convulsions."[11] So Haddon's future legacy now lay with his two daughters. Elizabeth would direct her father's affairs in America, while Sarah, who married into the Hopkins family, would remain in London and manage her father's businesses in England for thirty years. Sarah's son Ebenezer Hopkins (II), born in 1718, would one day be sent to Haddonfield, New Jersey, to live with his childless Aunt Elizabeth and her husband John Estaugh in order to carry on the Haddon-Hopkins line in America.[12]

John and Elizabeth Clarke Haddon's unity with the Horsleydown Monthly Meeting of the Religious Society of Friends during the last decades of the seventeenth century defined Haddon family life. It provided an unusual environment of equality between men and women (at least in Meeting) in which because their parents were members of Meeting, Elizabeth and Sarah Haddon were raised as birthright Quakers. All along, John Haddon's wife Elizabeth Clarke followed the teachings of her faith by sitting on many committees for helping the poor and suffering, particularly impoverished widows and persecuted women. She served as midwife for Quaker mothers and on committees to inquire into a woman's "clearness from all others" before receiving acceptance from meeting to marry. Elizabeth and her husband witnessed many

Quaker marriages at both the Horsleydown and London Meetings (particularly those at the Bull and Mouth Tavern that served as a place of the Friends Business Meeting, as well). More significantly, Elizabeth Clarke Haddon became treasurer of the Horsleydown Monthly Meeting carefully recording accounts and minutes. She most likely taught her daughters Elizabeth and Sarah to read the Scriptures and write beautifully hand-crafted sentences that appeared later in Elizabeth Haddon Estaugh's own business accounts and record books of the Newton and Haddonfield Women's Monthly Meetings in West New Jersey.[13]

Meanwhile, John Haddon served on numerous committees in his neighborhood weekly, monthly and quarterly meetings and often received a call to attend the London Yearly Meeting. Haddon collected donations to aid the needy, particularly maritime folk. The sturdy blacksmith carried coal to heat the houses of the poor in winter. At the same time he became one of the most important managers (overseers) of the local Friends Monthly Meetings at Horsleydown and Deptford, settled disputes and distributed Quaker funds to the poor and needy. John and Elizabeth witnessed and certified marriages including that of close friend Thomas Lurting. Lurting made many trips to the Mediterranean, where he was once captured by pirates and ransomed by John Haddon's Horsleydown Monthly Meeting. Naomy Lurting, probably Thomas's spinster sister, served in 1690 as midwife at the birth of the Haddon's son Ebenezer.[14]

The rugged Quaker anchor maker John Haddon enforced good order by keeping troublemakers away from the doors of Horsleydown Meeting Hall. He guarded

Meetings against "rude Boyes," who vandalized Friends properties. He directed repairs to the meeting hall when government patrols increased attacks on Quaker places of quiet worship most violently under Charles II, and for a time, with the ascension of James II to the throne. Catholic King James II, who succeeded brother Charles II in 1685, pretended to push religious toleration only to bring on a new wave of persecution against all dissident Protestant sects by the Church of England. During this period, John Haddon secured the land for a wall around the Long Lane Burial Ground for Quakers in Southwark to protect it against constant vandalism. John and Elizabeth Clarke Haddon, Captain Lurting, merchant botanist Peter Collinson, Haddon family attorney Jacob Hagen and other leading Southwark Friends would one day be buried next to each other in this secure Quaker cemetery.

Young Elizabeth Haddon's family felt the impact of both Charles II and his brother James II's religious policies. It cost John and Elizabeth Clarke Haddon in "Sufferings", as trained bands of government militia trashed the Horsleydown Meeting, causing over £40 of damages to the Meeting House and a Quaker-owned dwelling next door. In response, Haddon erected new shutters in 1690 to prevent further vandalism of Quaker properties. At the same moment, this increased persecution by Church of England and government militias led to fines and warrants against Haddon's personal property. As late as 1688, local magistrates fined Haddon £9.8s.5d for refusing to pay for the repressive trained bands of heavily-armed watchmen who were supposed to provide safety for his neighborhood's streets and alleys but instead destroyed Quaker property.[15]

As an anchorsmith and mining entrepreneur with major non-Quaker political connections in shipping, banking, real estate and finance, however, John Haddon did not suffer persecution as severely as his fellow Friends. During earlier decades of persecution following George Fox's founding of the Religious Society of Friends in the 1640s, thousands of Quakers suffered torture or starved to death, while the Crown and Anglican Church executed hundreds more. Many Quakers, including John Haddon's occasional business contacts William Penn and Thomas Story, as well as more intimate neighbors like Thomas Lurting, John Clarke, Henry Gill, Thomas Chalkley, Anthony Morris, Robert Fairman and Francis Collins, suffered imprisonment in nearby White Lion and "Marshalsea Prison[s]in the Parish of St. George, Borough of Southwarke and County of Surrey." Haddon's Horsleydown Meeting raised money to buy bedding for the Marshalsea prisoners. Eventually, many of these Haddon associates went to America where they founded Quaker communities in Pennsylvania and West New Jersey.[16]

John Haddon decided to remain in London during the last two decades of the seventeenth century and suffered some more discrimination at the hands of the British government and Church of England. The last phase of the Sufferings during the reign of James II, though, proved less virulent than the policies supported by his late brother Charles II. Nevertheless, the continued persecution disrupted the daily lives of Friends such as the Haddon family. Sometime around 1686 Haddon decided to leave his increasingly violent and unsafe Bermondsey neighborhood. Consequently, the Quaker blacksmith moved the family from a badly polluted and overcrowded

Jacob and Mill Street riverfront location, where sewage ran in a ditch behind his row house, to a better location in Rotherhithe nearer to his Thames Riverfront shop on Cherry Garden Pier. Fewer rowdy taverns and teeming row houses lined the streets of this more rural neighborhood, called "Redriff" by local residents that lay just east of Bermondsey. Less crime, prostitution and drunken thugs threatened Haddon's children. The Haddon's new house even boasted a garden in their new healthier, less crowded London neighborhood.

Elizabeth Haddon's father relocated to Rotherhithe not only to improve his family's living conditions but to increase his blacksmith and anchor making business. Rotherhithe held the first docks constructed for London. The docks and piers extended along the southern shore of the Thames River eastward as far as the neighboring borough of Deptford. Deptford boasted the great docks and shipbuilding facilities of the Royal Navy where Peter the Great of Russia and others came to study naval architecture and construction. Indeed, Peter the Great once visited the Deptford Friends Meeting, connecting with the Quaker shipbuilders, carpenters, merchants and anchor makers such as John Haddon. Though convinced of the Quaker peace testimony against war, Haddon probably held no qualms about providing anchors and anchor chains for the Royal Navy, Russian warships or ships of other navies. His contracts with the Royal Treasury, later, to mint coins to pay for war gave evidence that dealing with the government was simply good business and increased his wealth to comfort the Haddon family.

To facilitate his new religious and business contacts, Haddon supported the establishment of a Friends Meeting in Deptford. Thus, in 1691 Haddon helped the Religious Society of Friends to organize the Deptford Monthly Meeting. The following year, as trustee of a meeting house committee, he acquired land upon which in 1693 Friends erected a meeting house. Haddon continually promoted the Deptford Meeting. He purchased a book to record "the Monthly Meeting proceedings," and a copy of Religious Society of Friends founder George Fox's *Journals*. All this activity took Haddon away from overseeing his Horsleydown Monthly Meeting house. Horsleydown Friends expressed some dissatisfaction with Haddon, forcing him to give witness to a paper, calling for: "Every particular person to endeavour to preserve peace and unity in all our Meetings according to Truth."[17]

In the end, Haddon maintained peace and unity with both Horsleydown and Deptford Meetings from his new home in Rotherhithe. Moreover, John Haddon's eldest daughter Elizabeth, youngest surviving daughter Sarah and infant son Ebenezer (II) thrived in this more pleasant neighborhood. Elizabeth particularly grew into a well-educated, intensely pious Quaker teenager. She probably studied in the local Quaker school with life-long friend Thomas Chalkley, later a renowned traveling minister who moved to Philadelphia about the same time Elizabeth settled in West New Jersey. Elizabeth most certainly learned to write beautifully crafted, grammatically correct sentences from her mother, a clerk of the Horsleydown Women's Monthly Meeting. Young Elizabeth faithfully attended Meeting, served the poor in her community and according to tradition became deeply moved by a dynamic young visiting minister John Estaugh who testified during the 1690s at her Meeting.

Whether or not Elizabeth, her "worthy" parents and John Estaugh reached some sort of an understanding during this period that they would one day ask the Meeting for clearance to marry, Elizabeth would indeed marry this intensely pious Quaker minister a decade later in the Province of West New Jersey in America. At the moment, however, the teenaged Elizabeth Haddon gave up everything to serve her father John Haddon and their faith. The dutiful daughter became more familiar with her father's business affairs, most particularly his plans to invest in those West New Jersey properties in America where Elizabeth and John Estaugh would one day settle. As John Haddon's blacksmith and anchor making business expanded after his move to Rotherhithe, he started to look for wider business opportunities with Quaker-owned mining and colonial real estate companies. He possibly began to discuss the acquisition of New World properties as early as the 1680s, when mining partner Richard Matthews and Northamptonshire family friend Thomas Willis purchased large tracts of land in America. Beginning in 1698, John Haddon would purchase "Land, Messuages [dwelling house with adjacent outbuildings and land] Tenements Plantations and Hereditaments . . . situate lying and being in West Jersey aforesaid—in America." In order to secure legal rights and title to his new property, Haddon determined that his daughter Elizabeth stood ready and equal to any man to take actual possession of these new Haddon lands in America.[18]

CHAPTER 2 NOTES.

[1] John Estaugh, *A Call to the Unfaithful Professors of Truth* (Philadelphia: B. Franklin, 1744), 41.

[2] Joseph Besse, *Sufferings of the People called Quakers for the Testimony of a Good Conscience from The Time of their being first distinguished by that Name in the Year 1650 to the Time of the Act commonly called the Act of Toleration granted to Protestant Dissenters in the first Year of the reign of King William the Third and Queen Mary in the year 1689* (London: Luke Hinde, 1753).

[3] Besse, *Sufferings*, 462, 532, 690.

[4] Yorkshire and London Friends suffered heavy fines, seizure of property, livestock, and the greatest number of imprisonments in all of England, see Besse, *Sufferings*.

[5] In original sources, the spelling of his name is found both as "Matthews" and "Mathews." Matthews has been used throughout this text.

[6] See Arthur Raistrick, *Quakers in Science and Industry Being an Account of the Quaker Contributions to Science and Industry During the 17th and 18th Centuries* (New York: Augustus M. Kelley, 1968), 168–70.

[7] Members of a Quaker meeting comprise the smallest organizational unit in the Religious Society of Friends, called the meeting. The meeting is also known as a "Monthly Meeting" because they normally hold one meeting for business each month to discuss and consider issues in the life of the meeting including spiritual matters, community interests, work of committees, finances and property.

Most Quaker meetings for worship are unprogrammed, without clergy or liturgy. Quakers believe there is a "something of God in everyone" and worship is silent, unless someone is moved to speak, calling on what is referred to as their "inner light."

Quarterly meetings are gatherings of members and attenders of monthly meetings that are geographically close to one another. These meetings include worship, fellowship and business and are usually held four times each year, thus the name "Quarterly Meeting."

Yearly Meeting is an annual gathering of people from all the Quarters within its region as well as visitors from other Yearly Meetings.

In Elizabeth Estaugh's era, Quakers had separate, but largely equal, men's and women's meetings within the Monthly, Quarterly and Yearly Meeting. Having separate men's and women's meetings was discontinued around the turn of the twentieth century; Haddonfield Monthly Meetings merged in 1903. Otherwise, the Quakers' organizational structure today is essentially the same as in the eighteenth century.

⁸Southwark Monthly Meeting Records, Southwark, Surrey, England. Births, Marriages, Deaths and Deaths and Burials, 1648–1785 Society of Friends. Southwark Monthly Meeting (England), microform from the Family History Library, Salt Lake City, Utah; FHL Film #811790 (Births) and FHL Film #0811791 (Marriages, Deaths, and Deaths and Burials.) Transcriptions of items from the Southwark Meeting that pertain to the Hopkins and Haddon families, and to the families they intermarried, are also available online: http://home.comcast.net/~adhopkins/swkqrecs.htm (accessed 23 August 2013).

⁹Southwark Records. Deaths and Burials. August 12, 1678 and May 2, 1681.The Searchers hereupon (who are ancient Matrons, sworn to their Office) repair to the place, where the dead Corps[e] lies, and by view of the same, and by other enquiries, they examine by what Disease, or Casualty the Corps[e] died. Hereupon they make their Report to the Parish-Clerk, and he every Tuesday night, carries in an Account of all the Burials, and Christnings [sic], hapning [sic] that Week, to the Clerk of the Hall," John Graunt, *Natural and Political OBSERVATIONS Mentioned in a following INDEX, and made upon the Bills of Mortality* (London: Printed by Tho: Roycroft, for John Martin, James Allestry, and Tho: Dicas, at the Sign of the Bell in St. Paul's Churchyard, 1662), 11.

¹⁰Southwark Records. Deaths and Burials. January 28, 1688, December 12, 1686, July 7, 1685.

¹¹Southwark Records. Deaths and Burials, May 29, 1707.

¹²See Sarah Haddon Hopkins correspondence with her sister, Elizabeth Haddon Estaugh, HEHP, folder 184.

¹³Though some business records and meeting minutes in Elizabeth Haddon Estaugh's handwriting exist, not a single personal letter written to her family has been found.

¹⁴See *Books of the Monthly and Two Weeks Meeting of the People Called Quakers at "Horsleydown,"* Friends Library, London, copy of pages, in box 2, Lyons Project Papers, HSHL.

¹⁵Besse, *Sufferings,* 485.

¹⁶ Horsleydown file, in box 2, Lyons Project Papers, HSHL; also, see Besse, *Sufferings.*

¹⁷Horsleydown file, in box 2, Lyons Project Papers, HSHL.

¹⁸Indenture between Thomas Willis and John Haddon, 1698, folder 11; Indenture, Thomas Willis to John Haddon, 1700, folder 18; True copy of articles of Agreement between John Haddon (Blacksmith) and John Breach (Blacksmith), 1699, folder 22; Power of Attorney, John Haddon to Elizabeth Haddon, 1701, folder 123, all in HEHP.

CHAPTER 3.
That There Is Such a *Province* as *New-Jersey*, Is Certain.

We cannot but repeat our request unto you, that in whomsoever a desire is to be concerned in this intended plantation, such would weigh the thing before the Lord, and not headily or rashly conclude on any such remove; and that they do not offer violence to the tender love of their near kindred and relations.
—William Penn, Gawen Lawrie, Nicholas Lucas (1676)[1]

London blacksmith and anchor maker John Haddon had known for years about the land in America. This was the distant place where he was about to dispatch his daughter as his real estate agent and attorney. Haddon lived in a maritime, religious and commercial community along the Thames River that encouraged participation in such colonial enterprise. George Fox, founder of the Religious Society of Friends, had recently returned from a ministerial trip to the New World. It was "a tedious journey," Fox reported, "through bogs, rivers, and creeks, and wild woods where it was said never man was known to ride." However, he also testified that it was a marvelous land of natural beauty and filled with noble free Indians. "They were very tender and loving, seeking "a little entrance for Truth." Fox shared the message at many Meetings around London that God had chosen these new lands as a Quaker sanctuary where Friends could practice religious freedom and self-government, own farms and obtain great spiritual and material wealth. Fox particularly praised the fertile country along the Delaware River as a place for Friends to worship and prosper in peace. Fox's word influenced William Penn and other Quaker leaders to seek comfort and profit in America.[2]

A number of Quaker advertisers of colonial land purchases also visited John Haddon's riverfront neighborhood, urging Friends to look at the lands across the Atlantic Ocean to escape the Sufferings. Indeed, the most prominent of these promoters Gabriel Thomas received a loan from Haddon to purchase land along the Delaware Bay. Thomas vigorously promoted settlement of West New Jersey. His explanation of the cost of passage to the Delaware River undoubtedly interested Haddon. "The Price for every Passenger, (that is to say) for Men and Women, Meat, Drink and passage, with a Chest is Five Pounds sterling per Head," Thomas told prospective travelers. If London Quakers wished to develop Trade in this land, the real estate promoter continued, they only paid "For goods, Forty Shillings a Tun [sic] Freight, to be Landed at Burlington, or elsewhere upon Delaware-River."[3]

Delaware Valley Quaker Thomas Budd, related through marriage to Haddon's friend Francis Collins, published a tract in 1685 explaining that distressed Quaker families in England could escape poverty by settling in West New Jersey and Pennsylvania, where they might "reap great Profit" from the many economic opportunities afforded by the region. One of these enterprises that appealed to Haddon was Budd's observation that

"Iron may be here made, there being one Iron-Work already in East-Jersey."[4] Gabriel Thomas agreed that "as to Minerals, or Metals, there is very good Copper, far exceeding oars [ours] in England." Entrepreneurs such as Budd and Thomas promised potential settlers that in America they might own property free from all the tithes and restrictions placed on them in Britain.[5]

Meantime William Penn, who later received a large land grant in 1681 from King Charles II on the west side of the lower Delaware River and Bay, first vigorously promoted the sale of property and settlement across the river in West New Jersey. English and Irish Friends formed an extensive network of connections in order to build a Quaker community in the New World. More prosperous Quaker businessmen (and several wealthy women), merchants, ship owners and captains including John Haddon's close Horsleydown friend Thomas Lurting organized this late seventeenth century colonization movement to the Delaware Valley. Skilled craftsmen, like John Haddon, shopkeepers, poorer working folk and indentured servants soon purchased small shares in the Quaker settlements. Religious dissidents and missionaries (like Elizabeth's future husband John Estaugh), educated men and women, indentured servants and slaves added to the diverse social groups that became part of this Quaker experiment in the New World.[6]

Quaker interest in building a community in the Delaware Valley during the late seventeenth and early eighteenth centuries arose from many complicated land grants and real estate deals. Opportunity for acquisition of land followed the Restoration of the Stuart monarchy in 1660 after years of a bitter Puritan Revolution and

English Civil War. It coincided with the rising influence of a pre-industrial middle class, including the Quakers that defied the absolute authority of the Church of England. King Charles II sought to rebuild the Crown's and Church's fortunes and unify the British people by developing an overseas commercial and colonial empire. Intent on claiming New World territory from the Dutch, French and Spanish, Charles II conveyed to his brother James, the Duke of York, a vast tract of land occupied by the Dutch between the colony of New Netherland and the Delaware and Chesapeake bays. The Duke of York's agents soon wrested New Netherland from the Dutch renaming it New York. The Duke's men then sent a force to the Delaware River to assert British control over the handful of Dutch and larger group of Swedes and Finns who had settled along the river during the early part of the eighteenth century.

In 1664, the Duke of York transferred part of his grant that extended from the Hudson River to the Delaware Bay to loyal retainers Sir George Carteret and John, Lord Berkeley, who had both fought for the Royalists during the recent English Civil War. The tract of newly claimed land was called New Jersey after Carteret's home on the Isle of Jersey that had provided sanctuary to the Stuarts during the civil war. Carteret received the northern or East New Jersey portion and Berkeley acquired the southernmost section called West New Jersey. After a brief interlude in 1673, when the Dutch reclaimed the territory during the Third Anglo-Dutch War and then surrendered all claims in 1674 with the Treaty of Westminster after the hostilities had ended, Charles II issued a new patent for New Jersey to James, Duke of York, who confirmed his earlier gifts to Carteret and Berkeley.

Berkeley showed little interest in developing his southwestern half of the Jerseys. His English estates lay bankrupt, and consequently, Berkeley sold his shares for £1000 in 1674 to Edward Byllynge, Quaker brewmaster and former New Army cavalry officer. Byllynge also had money problems brought about, in part, by government fines for attending Friends meetings and refusing to take oaths of loyalty to the Crown and Church of England. At this moment, Quaker entrepreneur John Fenwick put up the money for the financially strapped Byllynge. Fenwick, like Byllynge a former officer in Oliver Cromwell's New Army, had commanded Monck's cavalry troop that beheaded King Charles I. Fenwick converted sometime during the English Civil War to the Religious Society of Friends. After the war Fenwick became involved with Byllynge in American real estate and loaned the financially strained fellow Quaker the money in 1674 to buy Lord Berkeley's West New Jersey proprietorship.

Fenwick insisted that his loan to Byllynge gave him the right to a governorship of all West New Jersey, to divide up and sell tracts of land and collect rents. Other Quaker investors in this Delaware Valley property balked at Fenwick's claim to the entire lower half of New Jersey and opposed Fenwick's conduct. This controversy threatened to disrupt the entire Quaker dream of a political, religious and economic sanctuary in the New World. Leading Quaker William Penn determined to arbitrate this dispute among Friends that might force the Crown to settle the affair. If a lawsuit against Fenwick ended up in court, Quakers would refuse to take oaths of loyalty in order to present their case and probably lose their New World property. "The present difference betwixt thee & E.B. [Edward Byllynge]," Penn wrote Fenwick, "fills the hearts of Friends with griefe [sic] [and] offers violence to the Award made or that will not End it without bringing it upon the Publique [sic] Stage."⁷

Penn joined London merchant Gawen Lawrie, Hertford maltster Nicholas Lucas and Fenwick's major creditors Edmond Warner, a London poulterer, and John Edridge, a wealthy tanner, as trustees over the West New Jersey proprietorship. The Trustees gave Fenwick ten shares of the property and reserved ninety shares in trust for sale to pay off all existing debts. In order to encourage renewed Quaker interest in West New Jersey, the Trustees and Edward Byllynge issued a frame of government in 1676 called the "Concessions and Agreements of the Proprietors, Freeholders, and Inhabitants of the Province of West New Jersey in America." This trail-blazing constitution ensured landowners a major role in their own governance, placed power in the hands of an annually-elected assembly of freeholders and granted every settler the right to freely worship God. "The Charter or Fundamental Laws of West Jersey agreed upon" also granted trial by jury and other legal rights. Most significantly, the Concessions and Agreements created a plan for the distribution, sale and leasing of land, which included granting indentured servants fifty-acres of their own property after their times of service. The Concessions called for "good understanding and friendly correspondence between the proprietors, freeholders and inhabitants of the said province and the Indian Natives thereof," when taking up of their lands for laying out towns, roads and farms. The Age of Reason's enlightenment-inspired document encouraged the surveying of property lines and the registering of titles and deeds in both London and West New Jersey so that: "the planting of the said Province be the more promoted." These provisions endorsed by the original Quaker proprietors, who one day sold land to John Haddon, would establish the legal basis for all of Haddons' (and the Estaughs') future land acquisitions, surveying, leasing, sale and registering of deeds and titles.[8]

The Trustees and a number of major investors signed the Concessions and Agreements in London. The original signatories included Richard Matthews, Francis Collins, Henry Stacy, William Peachee and Thomas Gardiner, all closely connected to the future Haddon real estate purchases in West New Jersey. The Trustees provided incentives for such investors to buy land with publication of the Concessions so that they might build "a Quaker community" in West New Jersey. London Quaker surgeon Dr. James Wasse carried the Concessions to West New Jersey as the Trustee's land commissioner. He arrived with detailed instructions to deal with the Quaker upstart, John Fenwick, and the problems he created for West New Jersey proprietors. Wasse also had orders to lay out two town sites: one at the Falls of the Delaware (present-day Trenton, New Jersey area) and the other between the Falls and Salem. Adding to the men who signed the Concessions and Agreements in London, Wasse secured the signature of most land-owning settlers in West New Jersey who had sailed in 1675 with Fenwick to found the Salem colony. Signatures on the Concessions by freeholders in Fenwick's colony and many of the original Swedish and Finnish settlers meant that they accepted English rule and pledged their allegiance to the British Sovereign.[9]

The convoluted process that enabled Quaker purchasers like Haddon to buy West New Jersey properties continued after West Jersey landowners had signed the Concessions. The Concessions and Agreements directed that West New Jersey be divided into ten equal parts, although only five of the tenths became a reality. Such arrangements convinced more than 800 Quakers between 1677 and 1678 to locate and purchase land in West New Jersey. Long suffering Yorkshire Quakers would settle the First Tenth, first identified as lying between the Falls of the Delaware River and the Rancocas Creek. The London Quakers would settle the Second Tenth, originally located between the Rancocas and Big Timber creeks. The bounds of these two tenths changed dramatically when the London and Yorkshire proprietors quickly agreed to join together in forming a new settlement named Burlington. High or Main Street in Burlington became the new division line between the First and Second Tenth, with the latter tenth now extending to the Pennsauken Creek. These two tenths later formed a portion of the landmass comprising Burlington County.[10]

During 1681, the Dublin Quakers purchased land in the Third or Irish Tenth (later the northern part of Old Gloucester County, now Camden County) between the Pennsauken and Timber creeks. The Fourth Tenth lay between the Big Timber and Oldman's creeks. Immediately below the Fourth Tenth, Fenwick staked his land claim, known as the Salem Tenth, located further downriver nearer the Delaware Bay. More than twenty years later, John Haddon would purchase several thousand acres of land in the Second, Third and Fourth Tenths, thus becoming an important West Jersey proprietor.

If William Penn and other Quaker leaders had not stepped in to arbitrate and settle affairs, future investor John Haddon and his daughter Elizabeth might not have become part of New Jersey and American history. John Haddon had known about these early Quaker colonization developments well before sending his daughter to America. Thomas Lurting and other Quaker ship captains brought New World intelligence back to his Thames riverfront neighborhood. Lurting was a member of Haddon's Horsleydown Monthly Meeting and a close friend. Moreover, Haddon had become intimate through his anchor smithy, maritime and mining connections with the Quaker entrepreneurs who founded the provinces of West New Jersey (and later Pennsylvania) during the last quarter of the seventeenth century. Haddon met regularly with commercial, business and financial leaders at Vernon's Coffee House on Bartholomew Lane near the Royal Exchange, the Bull and Mouth and other inns and taverns that crowded into nearby London neighborhoods and lay just across the Thames River from Haddon's Southwark home.

Haddon's contact with the wealthy goldsmith Richard Matthews, an original investor in West New Jersey real estate and signatory of the West New Jersey Concessions, seemed most important for his involvement in the enterprise that one day would send Elizabeth Haddon to America. Matthews became John Haddon's major partner in the Royal Mines Copper and Ryton stock company along with Haddon's Southwark neighbor Dr. Edward Wright, a glass grinder and innovator of a new furnace to refine lead. This company later formed the London (Quaker) Lead Company, and under John Haddon's guidance, affiliated with the Pennsylvania Land Company of London, later the holder of over 60,000 acres of William Penn's former land grant.[11]

Matthews also facilitated Haddon's connection to other major financial investors, particularly Thomas Gould and Grocer's guild member John Freame, a London goldsmith, and founders of the first Quaker owned bank in London that would become the great British banking firm of Freame and Barclay. They invested with Haddon and other Quakers in the British mining and American (Pennsylvania) real estate businesses. Quaker investors included Thomas Cooper, who had helped found Bucks County in Pennsylvania, and Francis Stamper, the Quaker minister who convinced Haddon's future son-in-law John Estaugh to join the Religious Society of Friends and probably to marry the potentially wealthy Elizabeth Haddon who might support Estaugh's traveling missionary work. Haddon's mining partners Stamper and Matthews connected the Southwark anchor maker (and later his daughter Elizabeth and her future husband John Estaugh) to dozens of other major Quaker investors in Delaware Valley real estate. These included Matthews's son Thomas and daughter Hannah, William Penn, Thomas Story, Francis Plumstead, Henry Goulding, Samuel Davies and James Logan among many other less well-known contacts. All of these entrepreneurial capitalists, in one way or another promised to influence John Haddon and his daughter's involvement in the Quaker religious, business and real estate enterprises in Pennsylvania and West New Jersey.

An astute business entrepreneur, Haddon certainly recognized the connection between mining, real estate and colonization for religious and economic reasons. Mining, banking and real estate associations, perhaps more than the desire to build a religious community in America free of the repressions suffered by Quakers in England, pushed Haddon toward investment in Delaware Valley land. He considered American property as a potentially lucrative business venture. However, at first, John Haddon hesitated to become involved in the Quaker experiment in the New World. He invested instead during the 1690s in real estate on the British Isles, where his mining company speculated in mineral-rich land purchases in Wales, northern England and probably Ireland. In that process, however, Haddon also bought stock in the London Land Company (of Pennsylvania) that ventured into American real estate. Eventually at the close of the seventeenth century and twenty years after the establishment of Quaker settlements in the Delaware Valley, John Haddon started to lease and purchase large tracts of land in Salem, Burlington and, most importantly Old Gloucester County, in the Province of West New Jersey in America. These transactions between 1698 and 1700 included land that Elizabeth Haddon one day occupied, developed and later would become part of the town of Haddonfield.

Haddon's procurement of large tracts of land in colonial America followed the complex course of purchase, sale and re-sale that defined the late seventeenth century settlement of West New Jersey. Richard Matthews first linked Haddon to West Jersey real estate. Matthews had signed the West Jersey Concessions in 1676 along with William Penn, Francis Collins and other Quaker investors familiar to John Haddon. Matthews's West Jersey acquisitions began in 1678 with the indenture between merchant Nicholas Lax, Matthews and Henry Stacy. This document conveyed "Land given by King Charles to his 'Dearest Brother,' the Duke of York, obtained by William Penn, Nicholas Lucas and Gawen Lawry, Trustees for Byllyngs, [sic] sold to William Ogle, William Roydon and Nicholas Lax, and then to Henry Stacy and Richard Matthews, One Ninetieth part of ninety equal and undivided parts of land called West New Jersey."[12]

Ogle, Lax and Richard Matthews never sailed to America. However, William Roydon, one of these proprietors, would come to America in 1681 and purchase with trinkets and other gifts Delaware Riverfront property near the mouth of Newton Creek from the local Native Americans. In 1688 the old Gloucester County Court issued a license to Roydon for the first ferry from West New Jersey across the river to Philadelphia. Meanwhile, Henry Stacy and his wife Mary settled in Burlington. Stacy became a West Jersey government official and served on the governor's council. Before returning to England in 1683, he deeded 490 acres near Newton Creek to his daughter Sarah. This Stacy property would later overlap land that Matthews sold to Haddon after Matthews also leased "one half part of the said one full, equal and undivided third part of the said one full equal and undivided ninetieth part . . . of the said tract of land" to Henry Stacy's widow Mary and daughters Hannah and Sarah Stacy.[13]

The Stacy transaction would cause Haddon, and later his daughter Elizabeth and son-in-law John Estaugh, many legal problems over actual ownership and title to this particular tract of land. Haddon wrote his daughter long after she had settled in America, that "threats about

Richard Mathewes [*sic*], his Land it cannot be sould [*sic*] to Stacyes widow deed, I sent you original." Other purchases by her father would hound Elizabeth as well. One tract that Haddon acquired had been sold (or leased) by Matthews in 1694 through his agent George Goldsmith to Nicholas Smith, a wealthy London tailor, in the "neighborhood of . . . Newton Creek, New Jersey." Again, the title to this tract of land remained unclear, and Elizabeth and her husband would one day have to clear the title in court.[14]

To further complicate actual ownership of Haddon's purchases, title to his new property conflicted with the sale of the estate of Richard Matthews's son, Thomas. Richard and Thomas Matthews had purchased land in West New Jersey from the Trustees for Byllynge sometime between 1676 and 1678. Thomas and his sister Hannah went to West New Jersey in 1678 as their father's agents and attorneys. Interestingly, Hannah Matthews's role shows that Elizabeth Haddon was not, as previous historians have claimed, unique as a woman holding the power of attorney "and operating as a general agent" in America for her father. Thomas died in 1695/96 and his sister Hannah and her new husband Thomas Gardiner, Jr., the land surveyor for the Burlington Court, transferred over 100 acres of land along the south branch of the Cooper's Creek to blacksmith William Lovejoy. Lovejoy most likely worked as the estate manager in the New World for Richard Matthews, who stayed in England. Once in the New World, Lovejoy served as an agent or indentured servant for Thomas Matthews much in the way that the Breach family would later serve John Haddon as manager of his estate in Old Gloucester County. After Thomas Matthews's death, his sister Hannah, and Thomas Gardiner Jr. now administered his estate and rewarded Lovejoy for his service with the Cooper's Creek property. Hannah and Thomas had little use for the land since they lived downriver on St. John's Creek estate (Oldman's Creek) that formed the southernmost boundary of the Fourth Tenth (Old Gloucester County) with Fenwick's colony, the Salem Tenth.[15]

The West New Jersey real estate maze that Elizabeth Haddon was about to enter became even more confusing when Richard Matthews decided to bring her father, John Haddon, into the process. Unaware due to the distance and uncertainty of communication with the New World that Hannah and her brother's "heir at law," Thomas Gardiner, had already granted the Cooper's Creek property to William Lovejoy, Richard Matthews sold the very same piece of property to his mining company partner Haddon. The Lovejoy connection complicated matters further when the Cooper's Creek blacksmith fell in love with his married neighbor, Anne Willis Penstone. Anne was the daughter of John Haddon's Rotherhithe friend Thomas Willis and the sister of Philadelphia and Newton Township landowner John Willis. Lovejoy first met Anne while managing her husband Stephen Penstone's land, after Penstone abruptly abandoned his West New Jersey lands and returned to England. Penstone's property, purchased by John Willis in 1686, adjoined the newly transferred Lovejoy tract and comprised part of the neighboring Willis tract that lay between the Newton and Cooper's creeks and ran along the south branch of Pennsauken Creek. The Willis family had granted one-third of this land to Penstone upon his marriage to Anne

Willis. When John Willis died in 1691, his portion went to his sister Anne and, through marriage, also to Penstone. This included "a plantation on Cooper's Creek, 80 a. on Southerly branch of Pensokin [Pennsauken] Creek, 90 a. plantation of South branch of Cooper's Creek, 210 a. other land."[16]

Lovejoy inventoried and served as the bondsman for the John Willis estate in America, and Anne Penstone served as "administratrix" and co-bonder. It was most likely during this interval that Lovejoy and Anne began their passionate adulterous tryst. The affair disturbed the West New Jersey Quaker community when Penstone brought a lawsuit against Lovejoy. "The [Old Gloucester County] grand jury present William Lovejoy, for that contrary to the order and advice of the Bench he doth frequent the house of Ann Penstone, and lodge there, none being in ye house but he and ye said Ann with the bastard child." The Burlington County Court then indicted the Cooper's Creek blacksmith. The adulterous couple's Quaker neighbors, including respected Newton Township surveyor Thomas Sharp, knew, however, that Penstone was suing for money from the sale of Willis family land and not for infidelity. After all, Stephen Penstone had abandoned his well-respected wife and returned to London. Anne and William's neighbors refused to testify against Lovejoy. Sharp actually paid a large fine levied by the Burlington Court for his refusal to testify. Nevertheless the case dragged on, confusing Haddon's land claims and creating property disputes. This situation would confront Elizabeth when she arrived in America.[17]

At this point, the so-called Lovejoy Tract became further entangled in legal ownership complications that affected John Haddon and his daughter. In 1698 Haddon's Rotherhithe friend Thomas Willis, father of Anne Willis Penstone of the Lovejoy affair, sold Haddon over one thousand acres of land in Waterford Township, Province of West New Jersey.[18] The following year, Richard Matthews released to Haddon one-third of one-ninetieth part of West New Jersey that included the disputed Stacy, Willis-Penstone and Lovejoy tracts. In November 1700 Lovejoy sold land to Willis, who immediately resold it John Haddon. To confuse matters further, this land was from the estate of the supposedly deceased Richard Matthews (probably Thomas Matthews, since Richard was still living in 1700). This land comprised "100 acres of land formerly belonging to Richard Matthews and then to William Lovejoy; and fifty acres of land formerly belonging to Thomas Matthews, bought from Edward Billings [sic] and others," and extending from Cooper's Creek to the property of Francis Collins.[19]

No wonder John Haddon wanted to have a personal agent in America to secure his perplexing real estate ventures. Soon after his first West New Jersey land purchase, Elizabeth's father signed "articles of agreement" with fellow blacksmith John Breach on May 8, 1699, indenturing Breach and his children, Simon and Ann, for six years. Haddon instructed his estate manager to oversee, manage and improve the recently acquired Cooper's Creek plantation. Elizabeth's father also expected Breach to carry on the trade of a blacksmith, and keep a "true and perfect account" of all transactions. For this service, Breach would earn half of what is the "net and clear profit, gains and overages to be gotten and obtained" from the blacksmith trade and plantation. The other half would be remitted to John Haddon twice yearly. The Breachs "shall and will forthwith imbarque [embark] on board such ship or vessel bound for West Jersey in America as the said John Haddon shall order and direct and therein proceed to West Jersey afore[sai]d (ye danger of the seas excepted) and being there arrived he then said shall and will repair to the plantation of said John Haddon."[20]

The sea conditions must have been favorable as John, Simon and Ann Breach soon set sail for America, although the exact date and ship are unknown. However, John Breach did not live long enough to "repair to the plantation of John Haddon." The records of the Philadelphia Monthly Meeting, under "Deaths of Persons Not Friends," list a burial of a John Breach on September 7, 1699. [21] Almost certainly this is the John Breach indentured by John Haddon and he must have died near the end of his trip across the Atlantic Ocean or very shortly after landing in Philadelphia.

After the Breach family left for America in 1699, John Haddon purchased more land in West New Jersey. Haddon's new land acquisition caused additional business complications for the Southwark blacksmith and hence for Elizabeth when she arrived in America the following year. In order to keep the "one hundred acres of land formerly part of the land of Richard Matthews, as the same is bounded with Coopers Creek on the one side and the land now or late of Francis Collins on the other side lying in the form of a triangle and late in the possession of William Lovejoy," Haddon or his "executors, administrators and attorneys," had to occupy it within six months. At the same time, his new properties required resurveying to define proper ownership, clear titles and establish boundaries with neighbors including those of Francis Collins, Joseph Cooper, John Kay, Jeremiah Bate, Mary Stacy and other Quaker families that had already built houses and farmed the surrounding Newton, Cooper's and Pennsauken creek regions.[22]

Dealing with overlapping boundaries, uncertain and unrecorded titles and other legal controversies in person meant that Haddon needed to come to America. But he lived more than four weeks' sailing distance across the Atlantic in England and expressed some anxiety about the impact of such a long sea voyage on his health. At the same time, complex family and religious meeting responsibilities prevented Haddon from rushing off to the New World. He currently performed vital service as overseer of the Horsleydown and Deptford (England) Monthly Meetings. Moreover, Haddon could not leave England at the moment because of his growing involvement in the reorganization of one of England's most important mining companies so that Quakers could hold positions on the managing board. Most significantly, Haddon observed William Penn's stricture that all prospective settlers in West New Jersey "obtain . . . the unity of friends [and family] where they live; that whether [he] go or stay, it may be of good savour before the Lord (and good people)."[23]

John stayed in England to comfort his "dearly beloved" family who, in 1700, comprised his wife Elizabeth Clarke, 20-year-old daughter Elizabeth, 16-year-old daughter Sarah and, most importantly, a still healthy 10-year-old son Ebenezer. His son gave promise to John Haddon of a male heir, so Haddon decided to preserve unity with family and Friends in Southwark. When he reached adulthood, Ebenezer would carry on the Haddon family name forward and secure its property rights in America. Yet Haddon needed to protect his real estate investments in West New Jersey now. It was simply a question of good business. Apparently Haddon did not consider his indentured servant Simon Breach capable of dealing with all the legal matters connected with his property rights. Moreover, Breach was not family. So with Ebenezer Haddon still too young to secure his interests in the New World, in July 1700 John Haddon turned to his eldest child Elizabeth to become his agent, with full power of attorney to handle affairs in the County of Gloucester, Province of West New Jersey in America.[24]

CHAPTER 3 NOTES.

¹"To Prospective Settlers in West New Jersey," September 1676, *Penn Papers*, I: 419–20.

²John L. Nickalls, *The Journal of George Fox* (Cambridge University Press, 1952), 619, 643–44; also, see Norman Penney, ed., *The Journal of George Fox*, 2 vols. (Cambridge: Cambridge University Press, 1911).

³Gabriel Thomas, "The Present State of West-Jersey," in Albert Cook Myers, *Narratives of Early Pennsylvania, West New Jersey and Delaware, 1630–1707* (New York: Charles Scribner's Sons, 1912), 194; Thomas-Haddon connection, in John and Elizabeth Haddon to Most Dear Children, March 9, 1718, HEHP, folder 183.

⁴Thomas Budd, *Good Order Established in Pennsilvania [sic] & New-Jersey*, Philadelphia: William Bradford, printer, 1685 (Ann Arbor: University Microfilms, 1966).

⁵Myers, *Narratives*, 321.

⁶See, Penn, "Prospective Settlers," in *Penn Papers*, I: 419–20; Harry B. Weiss and Grace M. Weiss, *The Early Promotional Literature of New Jersey* (Trenton, NJ: New Jersey Agricultural Society, 1964).

⁷Penn to Fenwick, January 20, 1675, *Penn Papers*, I: 384.

⁸*Penn Papers*, I: 388–408; also, see John E. Pomfret, *The New Jersey Proprietors and Their Lands, 1664–1776* (Princeton: D. Van Nostrand, 1964).

⁹*Penn Papers*, I: 410.

¹⁰http://jerseyman-historynowandthen.blogspot.com/2010/10/best-laid-schemes-o-mice-men-gang-aft.html (accessed 1 July 2013.) This blog will provide the details on the proposed settlement pattern for the Delaware River and how those plans quickly changed.

¹¹For Haddon's mining connections, see *Minute Book of the General Court of the Proprietor of the Royal Mines Copper, 1697–1709*, Library of Institution of Mining Engineers, Newcastle upon Tyne; Mining, and Pennsylvania Land company notes, loose leaf notebook in box 2, Lyons Project Papers, HSHL.

¹²Indenture between Nicholas Lax merchant of Wapping and Henry Stacy and Richard Matthews, 1678, HEHP, folder 4. Also, see collection of "Deeds and Indentures Relating to John Haddon's Purchases of Land in the Neighborhood of the Present Haddonfield, New Jersey," HEHP, folders 1–24.

¹³Lease, Richard Matthews to Mary Stacy, 1684, HEHP, folder 5; Isaac Mickle, *Reminiscences of Old Gloucester* (Philadelphia: Townsend Ward, 1845, reprinted by Gloucester County Historical Society, 1968), 56, 73; Clement, *First Emigrant Settlers*, 277–82.

[14] John Haddon and Elizabeth Haddon to Most Dear Children, October 15, 1713, folder 181; Indenture, George Goldsmith to Nicholas Smith, Property belonging to Richard Matthews, 1694, folder 8, both in HEHP.

[15] Thomas Gardiner, Administrator of the estate of Thomas Matthews, to William Lovejoy, 1696. HEHP, folder 10. This transaction most likely confirmed the original deed for a property between Cooper's Creek and that of Francis Collins already granted Lovejoy in 1691 by Elias Farr, the attorney for Thomas Matthews's father Richard.

[16] Will of John Willis, June 8, 1691, *Documents Relating to the Colonial, Revolutionary and post-Revolutionary History of the State of New Jersey* (Newark, Paterson, etc., NJ: 1880–1949) 1st ser., XXIII: 511.

[17] *Burlington Court Book: A Record of Quaker Jurisprudence in West New Jersey, 1680–1709* (Washington, DC: American Historical Association, 1944), 182; Mickle, *Reminiscences*, 52.

[18] Waterford Township, in Elizabeth Haddon's day, was much larger than today. Waterford Township was the northernmost township in Old Gloucester County, running from the Delaware River to the Egg Harbor/Galloway Township border in Atlantic County, including what today is Pennsauken, Cherry Hill and other political subdivisions.

[19] Indenture between Thomas Willis and John Haddon, 1698, folder 11; Indentures between Richard Matthews and John Haddon, 1699, folders 12 and 13; Indenture between Thomas Willis and John Haddon, 1700, folder 16; Indenture between William Lovejoy and Thomas Willis, 1700, folder 17; Indenture, Thomas Willis of Rotherhithe to John Haddon, 1700, folder 18; all in HEHP.

[20] True copy articles of Agreement, John Haddon (Blacksmith) and John Breach (Blacksmith) 1699. HEHP, folder 22.

[21] *An Abstract of the Records of the Births, Deaths and Burials of the Philadelphia Monthly Meeting 1688 to 1826* in Friends Historical Library, Swarthmore College, Swarthmore, PA. Many secondary sources, including John Clement, assumed that John Breach arrived in West Jersey and fulfilled his indenture to John Haddon. However, no record of John Breach appears in colonial documents. The date of burial for John Breach is listed, incorrectly, as September 7, **1698** in William Wade Hinshaw's monumental *Encyclopedia of American Quaker Genealogy* (Washington, [n.p.], 1948). John Breach's son, Simon, apparently fulfilled most of the terms of the indenture to John Haddon, acting as his estate manager, though unlike his father, he was not a blacksmith.

[22] Indenture, Thomas Willis to John Haddon, November 3, 1700. HEHP, folder 18.

[23] "To Prospective Settlers in West New Jersey" [c. September 1676], *Penn Papers*, I: 420–21.

[24] John Haddon Power of Attorney to Daughter Elizabeth as "general agent," July 25, 1700. New Jersey Archives: First Series. *Documents Relating to the Colonial, Revolutionary and post-Revolutionary History of the State of New Jersey*. 34 vols. Newark, Paterson, etc., N.J., 1880–1949, XXI, 676.

CHAPTER 4.
"My New and Lawful Attorney for Me in My Name," 1699–1701.

Be it known unto all men by these presents that I John Haddon of Rotherhith in the County of Surry, Blacksmith do hereby assign authorize make depute appoint and Constitute Elizabeth Haddon of the County of Gloucester in West Jersey in America, Spinster my Daughter my new and lawful attorney for me in my name.

—John Haddon[1]

John Haddon empowered his "Spinster Daughter [as] my new and lawful attorney for me in my name and stead and to my use to Grant Bargain Sell Convey and dispose for the most money as can be promised or gotten for the same all and every or any my Land, Messuages Tenements Plantations and Hereditaments as were taken up [&] not taken up situate lying and being in West Jersey aforesaid elsewhere in America."[2] Even for a Quaker community that treated women with more equality, or at least "spiritual" respect for female traveling ministers and as managers of their household space than any other segment of British society, John Haddon's selection in 1700 of a twenty-year-old, unmarried woman to conduct complex legal, business and real estate transactions in America revealed his incredible faith in daughter Elizabeth and her abilities.

Perhaps without an adult son ready to take over his new American estate, John Haddon had no other choice but to rely on his eldest daughter as his colonial business agent. But the London blacksmith saw that his daughter was ready for the task. Though a quiet, seemingly frail and slightly built woman, Elizabeth Haddon had a great inner strength derived not only from her religious beliefs but also acquired from her mother, the treasurer of the Horsleydown Monthly Meeting. As her father expected, young Elizabeth proved to be a highly successful real estate developer in America. Throughout the course of her sixty-year stay in Old Gloucester County, between 1701 and her death in 1762, Elizabeth accumulated more personal wealth than any other woman in West New Jersey. In the process, she helped to build the vibrant Quaker village of Haddonfield and establish the Haddonfield Monthly Meeting of the Religious Society of Friends. Elizabeth would employ an elaborate network of the Religious Society of Friends meetings, Quaker merchants, land owners and political connections to secure her place in the New World. Many of these connections were tied in one way or another to her father John Haddon and future husband John Estaugh.

John Haddon prepared for his daughter's journey in order to minimize any danger that might arise from her sailing across the Atlantic Ocean to West New Jersey. The crossing took four to six weeks and was often perilous in the 180 to 200-ton leaky, wooden merchant sailing ships that carried most Quakers to the Delaware Valley. Elizabeth Haddon's first biographer Lydia Child, writing stories about Quaker women as the "noblest of creatures" for nineteenth century "reading public," imagined in 1846 that Elizabeth had brought a complete household with her to America. "A poor widow of good sense and discretion accompanied her, as friend and housekeeper," Child wrote, "and two trusty men servants, members of the Society of Friends."[3] This account seems exaggerated and may be confused with the earlier voyage by Haddon's estate manager John Breach and family.

However, it is likely Elizabeth's father would have wanted her to have trusted and familiar companionship on the crossing. It is possible that the Haddons' Southwark neighbor Margaret Bye provided that assurance. Margaret's husband, Thomas Bye, and son John already were settled in Pennsylvania. The Bye men had received their certificate of removal to Philadelphia from the Horsleydown Meeting in August 1698 and by 1699 had established a home in Bucks County, Pennsylvania.[4] John and Elizabeth Clarke Haddon signed a certificate of removal from the Horsleydown Monthly Meeting in January 15, 1701 for Margaret Bye and her two daughters, who were planning to join their family in America.

Only an undocumented Bye family history written in 1956 mentioned that Elizabeth traveled with the Byes. In fact, no original record has been found of any contact between Elizabeth Haddon and Margaret Bye beyond the Haddon-Bye connection to the Horsleydown Monthly Meeting house in Bermondsey Parish. Yet, Margaret Bye and Elizabeth Haddon apparently arrived in America at the same time.[5] Quaker records reveal that Margaret Bye and her two daughters submitted their certificate of removal from Horsleydown Monthly Meeting to the Philadelphia Friends Meeting on June 27, 1701. Curiously, for reasons unknown, Elizabeth apparently was not issued a certificate of removal from the Horsleydown Friends Meeting. But one document from her father confirms that his daughter probably arrived in America the same time as the Bye women. John Haddon's grant of the power of attorney to Elizabeth Haddon in June 1701 was "between John Haddon of Rotherhith ... Blacksmith and Elizabeth Haddon of the County of Gloucester in West Jersey in America Spinster", indicating that his daughter was already living in West New Jersey.[6]

There also is no documentation on what ship brought Elizabeth to America. Elizabeth's father might have wanted her to sail with his close family friend and business partner Nathaniel Puckle, master of the ship BRISTOL TRADER, scheduled to leave England in late 1700 for the Delaware River. However, no evidence has been found that Elizabeth Haddon first came to America on Puckle's ship and her name does not appear on any extant passenger lists. When Elizabeth arrived in West New Jersey in spring 1701, she found (in a world described by many others) some meadowlands and thick woodlands of pine, oak and maple trees that covered most of the region. Nearly impassable wetlands infested with swarms of mosquitoes along the many creeks that emptied into the lower Delaware River created an inhospitable landscape for Elizabeth. The only roads to bring one overland from the river were well-worn Indian trails made by the Algonquin-speaking Lenape Native American peoples. These paths carried the semi-nomadic Lenape between their scattered small villages and winter camps along the many West New Jersey creeks that led to their summer hunting and fishing grounds along the shores and beaches of the Delaware Bay and Atlantic Ocean.[7]

Small bands or clans of Lenape, called Delaware Indians by the Quaker settlers, had lived for many years near the banks of every stream that Elizabeth Haddon needed to survey for her father. Early settlers often referred to part of the Haddon land purchase that would later be called Haddon's Fields as the Indian Fields, suggestive of the agrarian lifestyle common among the Late Woodland indigenous people.[8] By the time of Elizabeth's arrival, the original West New Jersey Quaker settlers most notably the Collins, Cooper, Matlack and Evans families had already purchased properties near Elizabeth's future home with gifts to the local Native American clans. In this, they followed the Concessions and Agreements that specifically urged Quaker buyers to treat the Natives fairly in their land purchases.

Despite the continuing legend that Elizabeth comforted the Indians "when they have gotten strong liquor in their head," no evidence remains that she had any extensive contacts with the Lenape. In fact, when Elizabeth Haddon first visited her father's land in America, only several hundred Native Americans remained in the entire region. "The Indians are but few in Number," West Jersey resident Thomas Budd, trying to promote European settlement of the area in 1685, assured settlers who feared the Native Americans. Smallpox, alcoholism and other diseases introduced by the Europeans, combined with settlers pushing into and fencing off the Indian hunting lands, had eroded the Lenape population over time. Instead, the region was starting to fill with European settlers.[9]

Elizabeth never wandered into an uncharted wilderness filled mostly with Indians as so many early

Detail from *A New Mapp of East and West New Jarsey* [sic] identifying "Haddon Feild," c.1706.[8] *Courtesy of the Library of Congress, Geography and Map Division*

chroniclers of her life claimed. Several thousand Europeans resided in the lower Delaware Valley region in 1701, although on widely scattered farms and in a few small clusters of houses. Europeans had been trading, settling and farming in the region for most of the seventeenth century. The Dutch erected the fortified trading post of Fort Nassau on the Timber Creek in 1626 (near present-day Gloucester City) and established several trading posts across the Delaware River and along the Schuylkill River in Pennsylvania. Swedes and Finns planted the small communities of New Sweden in the late 1630s on both sides of the Delaware River. A Swedish settlement existed in West New Jersey near Raccoon Creek (modern-day Swedesboro) long before John Haddon purchased over 1,000 acres of marshy meadow and woodland in this neighborhood that supplemented his earlier purchases upriver along the Cooper's and Pennsauken creeks.

Virtually no English settlement occurred along the Delaware River's eastern shore after the British seized first New Netherland from Dutch, in 1664. Some New Englanders and English émigrés arrived in what would become East New Jersey, including a number of Quakers. When William Penn established his colony on the Delaware River's west shore, he also obtained the three counties comprising the present-day State of Delaware as Pennsylvania's easy access to the sea. The Duke of York granted the town of New Castle to Penn and it became the principal port in these lower counties. Penn first stepped foot in the New World here at New Castle in 1682. Nearly twenty years later, New Castle was a busy riverfront port town that boasted docks, a market place, inns and several hundred permanent residents when Elizabeth

Haddon landed there. New Castle had been settled for over fifty years, and the Swedish (Fort Trinity), Dutch (Fort Casimir and New Amstel) and English all used the town as a seat of local government and port of entry for those coming up the Delaware River. Upriver, a vibrant Quaker community existed. Twenty-four years before Elizabeth's voyage to America, London, Yorkshire, and Irish-based Quaker families and their indentured servants had sailed to and settled in West New Jersey. A few slaves, most likely imported with their Quaker masters from Barbados, worked the larger Quaker-owned plantations in West New Jersey. These first settlers established the Delaware riverfront town of Burlington, located more than 100 miles up the Delaware from the sea. Quaker real estate promoters observed in 1698 that Burlington had become a "fine market-town . . . having several Fairs kept yearly in it," and exporting beer, bread, beef and pork to Barbados and other British West Indies islands.[10]

The original Yorkshire Quaker settlers sought land near the Falls of the Delaware while the London Friends would settle at present-day Gloucester City, but a change of plans caused the two groups to redraw their boundaries and settle together in Burlington. The First and Second Tenths extended from the Falls of the Delaware to the Cropwell Creek (Pennsauken). These two tenths comprised the landmass of Burlington County. Quakers emigrating from Ireland settled the lands between the Pennsauken and Timber creeks, including several hundred-acre tracts along the Cooper's and Newton creeks. This became the Third or Irish Tenth (then in 1686 established as part of Old Gloucester County), where Elizabeth Haddon ventured to secure her father's properties. Quaker proprietors had purchased land from the Lenape, and by the time of Elizabeth's entry, the new landowners had already surveyed their property, laid out farms, cleared the land for planting and grazing livestock, and built houses.

By 1701, when Elizabeth came to West New Jersey, a number of Quaker plantations and farms already stood on both sides of the Newton, Cooper's and Pennsauken creeks. Years before, Quaker carpenters had constructed sawmills and gristmills along several of these streams. Based on the terms of the Concessions and Agreements, the Quaker proprietors organized the Burlington Court in 1680 and the West Jersey Assembly in Burlington a year later. The Assembly established boundaries for dividing Burlington, Gloucester and Salem counties. They voted in 1681 for the construction of roads, particularly a highway between Burlington and Salem to join the two Friends Meetings and to promote commerce. The original road was operational the following year, but changes in population centers required a resurvey in 1686. Further route changes occurred in February 1689, when the Burlington Court established a new ferry service over the Rancocas Creek.[11] The Quaker leaders also urged the building of bridges across the creeks throughout the region, with Francis Collins receiving contracts for a number of the spans. In areas where waterways did not permit bridge construction due to being too wide, travelers used flatboat ferries or canoes to cross the many creeks.

When Elizabeth first set foot on West New Jersey soil, each county had built small courthouses and jails to provide law and order and to register deeds and cattle and hog earmarks. In fact, early on Elizabeth had her father's cattle earmark (acquired from Quaker surveyor Thomas Sharp) registered with the Gloucester County court. Most important for the young pious unmarried Quaker, Elizabeth Haddon's new place of residence contained a number of Friends meetings. The leading Quaker families received permission from the Quarterly Meeting of Friends at Burlington to hold "Indulged" meetings in their widely scattered farmhouses for worship and to conduct business for the local monthly meeting. Newton Township Friends met for Monthly meetings, alternating between their meeting house and the house of Thomas and Alice Shackle in Waterford Township (in present day Cherry Hill, near Chapel Avenue and King's Highway). Earlier, the Shackamaxon Friends Meeting in Philadelphia met briefly in the houses of Thomas Thackara and William Cooper on Pyne Poynt in present-day Camden City. Chester (later Moorestown) Friends held meetings at the home of Elizabeth and John Adams, while Evesham Friends received the Truth at the residence of William and Elizabeth Evans. Waterford Township Friends and those from the other nearby West New Jersey meetings most often met for worship at the Indulged Meeting in the house of John and Elizabeth Kay located on the north branch of Cooper's Creek (near the house known as the Barclay Farmstead). Eventually, West New Jersey Friends built meeting houses where they could gather each week on the first day (Sunday) to seek comfort in acceptance of the Truth. When Elizabeth arrived, log meeting houses stood in Salem, Chester, and Newton Township. John Haddon's old London associate Francis Collins had already built a hexagonal brick Friends Meeting house in Burlington. For years, the Burlington Yearly Meeting alternated with the Philadelphia Yearly

Meeting as the center of Delaware Valley Quaker leadership. Elizabeth's future husband had been accepted by both the Burlington and Philadelphia meetings and would link them to both communities.[12]

As Elizabeth Haddon arrived in America, the western side of the Delaware River, opposite Newton Township, boasted the Quaker city of Philadelphia. The Pennsylvania port city held an even larger Quaker community than West New Jersey directly across the river. This English and Irish Quaker settlement had started in 1681 after King Charles II granted William Penn a vast tract of land, there, that Penn named Pennsylvania. This grant settled the monarch's debt to Penn's father, Admiral William Penn for providing naval stores and service to the Stuarts (Charles II and brother James II) during the recent English Civil and Anglo-Dutch wars. Moreover, it gave Charles II, restored to the throne in 1660 after the English Civil War and Oliver Cromwell's Commonwealth, the opportunity to get rid of a troublesome religious dissident against the Church of England. Penn had the town of Philadelphia laid out between 1681 and 1682 on the Delaware Riverfront, some 100 miles from the sea as the center of his new Pennsylvania colony and Quaker experiment in America. It incorporated as a city in 1701, the same year Elizabeth Haddon arrived in America.

Penn advertised for buyers of his land and promoted settlement (much as he had earlier for West New Jersey), particularly among Quaker merchants, craftsmen and indentured servants. One of those promotional tracts, printed in 1698 by Haddon's fellow investor in Delaware Valley property Gabriel Thomas, mentioned the possibility of iron mining in Pennsylvania and West New Jersey. "As to Minerals, or Metals," Thomas wrote, "there is very good Copper, far exceeding ours in England." This feature must have interested mining expert and veteran ironsmith Haddon, who started to invest in New World properties the same year that Gabriel Thomas's book appeared in London. In any event, John Haddon began to acquire shares in the Pennsylvania Land Company of London properties about the same time that he purchased his West New Jersey real estate.[13]

Meantime, Penn's promotions convinced many others to sail to his Delaware River port town. By 1701, as Elizabeth settled across the river in West New Jersey, Philadelphia had grown into a bustling port city of shipbuilders, merchants, craftsmen and laborers residing in more than a thousand houses and many more small shops. Several riverfront wharves accommodated larger merchantmen sailing upriver to unload cargoes and take colonial products back to England or to trade with the British West Indies, particularly Barbados. A few brick mansions lined the waterfront. Wealthy Philadelphia Quaker merchant families of Samuel and Hannah Carpenter, David and Elizabeth Breintnall, Thomas and Sybilla Righton Masters and Anthony and Elizabeth Morris resided in these stately houses. These influential Philadelphia Quaker political-economic leaders and/or their wives would witness Elizabeth Haddon's marriage in West New Jersey to the then Philadelphia-based Quaker minister John Estaugh.

Philadelphia soon surpassed Burlington as the main port on the river and became the center of Quaker society in America. When Elizabeth Haddon first sailed into the Delaware Bay, forty Friends Meetings gathered in

Philadelphia and the surrounding rural Pennsylvania communities. Quakers established a Philadelphia Yearly Meeting, sharing responsibility for good order and unity among Friends with the Burlington Yearly Meeting. Friends from the Shackamaxon meeting met at the house of Thomas Fairman, one of William Penn's chief land surveyors. Fairman's house lay just upriver from Philadelphia (in the present-day Kensington section) and diagonally across the Delaware River from William Cooper's landing near his house. Shackamaxon Friends communicated frequently with Friends in the West New Jersey meetings, crossing the river to Cooper's house on Pyne Poynt. The Shackamaxon Monthly Meeting at the house of Thomas Fairman held special interest for the Haddon family. Fairman served not only as Penn's surveyor but as his father Robert Fairman's land agent and attorney in America. Robert Fairman was the clerk of the Horsleydown Monthly Meeting back in London and often worked with Elizabeth's father to oversee unity and peace within the Bermondsey Quaker community. Accordingly the Fairman-Haddon relationship revealed clearly how Elizabeth Haddon became part of a network of connections that built the Quaker society and economy in the New World.[14]

It is evident then that a well-established Quaker community already existed when Elizabeth Haddon arrived in America. Most importantly, Elizabeth found many strong independent Quaker women present in West New Jersey to offer their comfort and support to the younger Quaker woman. The widow Hannah Wood managed her late husband's large "Great Tree" plantation on Cooper's Creek near the Delaware River. Hannah Wood's house often served as the meeting place and site for marriage ceremonies for members of the Newton Monthly Meeting. The widow Esther (Hester) Spicer resided close by Hannah Wood's plantation near Cooper's Creek. These neighbors shared the Fast Landing property, where Esther operated her late-husband Samuel Spicer's ferry across Cooper's Creek. The ferry provided a flatboat pulled across the creek by ropes for the transport of horses, cattle and people. Esther Spicer and her daughters, Martha and Abigail, witnessed Elizabeth Haddon's marriage to John Estaugh. After Esther Spicer's sudden death when struck by lightning in 1703, Elizabeth formed a lifelong friendship with Abigail and Martha, who later married Thomas Chalkley, one of John and Elizabeth Estaugh's oldest and closest friends (and business associates).[15]

Other prominent Quaker women welcomed Elizabeth Haddon to West New Jersey, and most would witness her marriage. These included: Elizabeth Adams, founder of the local Chester Meeting; Alice Shackle, whose house often served as the meeting place for Newton Township Friends; and noted traveling minister Elizabeth Kay of Waterford Township, a founder of the women's meeting of the Newton Monthly Meeting. Elizabeth Kay not only led the Indulged Women's Meeting, accepted by the Burlington Yearly Meeting, in her Waterford Township house, but became a business partner with her husband John Kay in real estate sales and development of gristmills and sawmills. The Kay family would become intimately involved in Elizabeth's personal life, help locate her property, purchase tracts of her father's land from her and participate with her in the building of both the village and Friends Meeting of Haddonfield.

Elizabeth Adams and Alice Shackle comforted Elizabeth Haddon the moment that she landed in Old Gloucester County. Haddon witnessed the marriage of Elizabeth Adams' daughter at Adams's house in Chester in December 1701. Meantime, Shackle would warmly support Elizabeth's inquiry to obtain a clearness to marry, even though the young newcomer presented no certificate of removal from her Horsleydown Meeting in England. There were other prominent Quaker women who interacted with Elizabeth in the first months of her stay in West New Jersey. These included Francis Collins' daughter Sarah (later Dimsdale), who became Elizabeth's best friend, and the noted Burlington and Philadelphia inventor of herbal remedies, Sybilla Righton Masters, would also witness Elizabeth's marriage.

Not all Quaker women helped Elizabeth. Hannah Wood's and Esther Spicer's neighbor on the Cooper's Creek, Catherine Howell, claimed the same land grant that Elizabeth Haddon's father had sent his daughter to survey and occupy. Howell was a formidable competitor for choice real estate. She was one of only three women to pay the old Gloucester County poll tax in the 1690s and the sole woman in the entire county to record a cattle and hog earmark in her own name. Catherine Howell had placed her son Mordecai on the land that Elizabeth's father had purchased from Matthews and that Lovejoy now occupied. The Howells claimed that they had a legal title to the land from Lovejoy, but Elizabeth Haddon would eventually prevail and gain clear title to the contested Howell claim.[16]

Elizabeth Haddon entered a Delaware Valley world filled with strong, independent and acquisitive Quaker women who, in one way or another, helped her to settle in West New Jersey. She never became a traveling minister like the many "daughters of light" who preached the Word of God. She focused on managing her father's estate and building a new plantation house as a private and public place for other Quaker families and ministers to find comfort in worship or to conduct business, as well as supporting the ministries of her husband. During her life in America Elizabeth rarely ventured much beyond her beloved West New Jersey Friends Meetings or traveled across the Delaware River to the nearby Quaker community of Philadelphia. Elizabeth occasionally took dangerous sea voyages (usually accompanied by her husband or female friends) back across the Atlantic Ocean to her parent's home in Rotherhithe Parish. Here, Elizabeth reported on the condition of her father's estate and the sale of his lands in America. She would then receive instructions from John Haddon about how to conduct his American business. Thus prepared, Elizabeth then returned from each visit to London to serve her father's growing real estate enterprise in West New Jersey that soon would be recognized by West New Jersey neighbors as John (not Elizabeth) Haddon's Fields.

Elizabeth Haddon placed great faith in the Lord's inner light for guidance and like many Quaker "daughters of light" accepted her mission without hesitation as an agent and influential partner with her father and later her husband. After all, many other female Friends suffered much greater challenges and hardships in the New World as they traveled alone as missionaries, spreading the word of the Lord from Barbados in the West Indies to anti-Quaker New England. Intolerant Puritan

New Englanders particularly mistreated female Quaker preachers. They dragged Quaker women in chains behind horse-drawn carts, locking them in public stocks or prison, whipping and starving them. Indeed in one case, frightened and intolerant Massachusetts Bay Puritans executed Quaker missionary Mary Dyer for twice defying an ordinance banning Quakers from preaching in the colony.[17]

Elizabeth Haddon confronted no such threats of violent death or persecution from Puritanical religious fanatics when she arrived in West New Jersey. Her only real crisis was the very dangerous ocean crossing. She also needed a place to live in a still sparsely settled America while she dealt with her father's real estate holdings. Generations of historians have speculated on Elizabeth Haddon's first residence in America. Historical Society of Haddonfield member Carrie E. Nicholson Hartel, a respected local historian, and her son, Joseph Nicholson Hartel, a longtime society researcher, spent years trying to discover when and where Elizabeth first lived upon arriving in America. In the end they concluded that "Elizabeth's first location seems to be up for grabs." Joseph Hartel offered an informed estimate of where Haddon stayed, though, arguing that Elizabeth must have settled first near Cooper's Creek on the property purchased by her father from Thomas Willis. Hartel theorized that Elizabeth resided near a house or blacksmith shop possibly formerly occupied by Lovejoy. Hartel probably based his theory on a comment by Rebecca Nicholson Taylor. In her notes in the inventory of the Haddon-Estaugh-Hopkins papers at Haverford College, regarding the Lovejoy to Willis 1700 indenture, she wrote, "here it is supposed that Elizabeth Haddon found a small house." Willis immediately sold the former Lovejoy property to John Haddon. The Lovejoy house was ideally located for Elizabeth to travel on her business, since it stood near where the original poorly developed Burlington-Salem Road crossed Cooper's Creek. "I suspect that John Haddon got Willis to put this piece together for his daughter's protection," Hartel wrote. "Why would she have settled on land not covered by that deed?"[18]

What is overlooked in the Hartel theory is that John Haddon already owned a number of large parcels of land in West Jersey before he purchased the former Lovejoy property in November 1700. Elizabeth could settle on any of these properties, which would fulfill the conditions of the Concessions and Agreements that land purchased be settled within six months.

In fact, on one of those parcels, as will be discussed shortly, a substantial house already was built by 1700, a year before Elizabeth arrives. Surely a large and probably new dwelling would be where John Haddon would have his daughter reside, rather than in or near a blacksmith shop.

Historian John Clement wrote that Elizabeth first stayed in America at Mountwell, a house built by John Haddon's friend Francis Collins. According to this traditional view, repeated innumerable times in secondary sources, Elizabeth stayed in 1701 with Francis Collins at the Mountwell plantation, situated on a tract of land that Collins surveyed in 1682 several miles up the winding south branch of Cooper's Creek. However, there is no documented evidence that Elizabeth Haddon lived at Mountwell. Since Francis Collins was the first resident of the area that later became Haddonfield, undoubtedly many early historians assumed that Elizabeth would have first resided there.

Other researchers, including Betty Lyons, raised doubts about such residency. Before Elizabeth's arrival, Francis Collins had moved to Burlington, and his son Joseph and growing family filled his Mountwell estate. Francis Collins had given Mountwell in trust to Joseph in 1686 and if Elizabeth had resided at Mountwell on her arrival in 1701, it would have been with Joseph Collins and his family and it would have been only a temporary place to stay prior to moving to a more permanent residence.

There also is another possibility regarding Francis Collins. Captain Nathaniel Puckle, who may have brought Elizabeth to the New World, often debarked his passengers at Burlington. Puckle conducted business and carried correspondence and cargoes between Pennsylvania, West New Jersey and the British Isles for William Penn and frequently anchored off Pennsbury Manor. Penn's country estate lay above Burlington on the west bank of the Delaware River. If Captain Nathaniel Puckle brought Elizabeth Haddon to the Delaware Valley and sailed with her upriver past Cooper's and Pennsauken creeks to Burlington where she debarked, Elizabeth might have stayed briefly with Francis Collins, who had moved from his Cooper's Creek house to this vibrant market town. She could then travel from Burlington down a well-worn bridle path (Burlington-Salem road) near Cooper's Creek. This could account for the widely accepted tale of Elizabeth Haddon first staying with Francis Collins at Mountwell in Newton Township.

It also is possible that Elizabeth could have stayed for a short time with any of a number of Quakers already settled near her father's land. The Quaker families of

William Cooper, Hannah Wood, Esther Spicer, Simeon Ellis, John Burrough, Thomas Shackle, Samuel Lippincott, Edward Clemenz and Benjamin Stiles were farming land on Cooper's Creek. The Matlack, Haines, Heritage, Roberts and Hancock families lived nearby along the Cropwell (Pennsauken) Creek. The Robert Zane, William Albertson, Thomas Champion, Stephen Newby, James Grasebery, Jeremiah Bate, Thomas Thackera, Henry Stacy, and Thomas Sharp families were in residence along Newton Creek.[19] All these Friends would provide Elizabeth with the support that she needed to settle in this sparsely-settled rural neighborhood.

Samuel Nicholson Rhoads, a Hopkins family descendant and early twentieth century historian and researcher who also attempted the definitive biography of Elizabeth Haddon, thought it most likely Elizabeth lived in the New World initially in a house on her father's properties near the Cooper's Creek, possibly at Coles (Later Stoy's) landing, on present-day Coles Mill Road near Grove Street. This location was on land Haddon already owned (later known as Old Haddonfield) when he purchased in 1700 the additional 450 acres that would be known as New Haddonfield. In 1909 Rhoads had a photograph taken in which he points to the area near which he believed the first residence of Elizabeth Haddon stood near Cooper's Creek.

Betty Lyons presented other possible sites where Elizabeth Haddon lived first in America. An indenture dated 4 June 1701 between John Haddon and his daughter grants Elizabeth 931 acres of land along Pennsauken Creek and notes that the land is in Elizabeth's "actual possession." Lyons believed that this tract of land on

Map showing land owners and houses in Newton Township in 1700.
Thomas Sharp Map of Newton Township, NJ, 1700, Clement Collection #791, Historical Society of Pennsylvania

The land marked "John Haddons Land bought of John Willis" (1) shows an existing house on Cooper's Creek, Elizabeth's first home. The land marked "Smith's Shop, Richard Mathews" (2) is the land on which New Haddonfield was built in 1713. The small cabin in the upper left (3) and on the opposite page, is likely the site of the home of Simon Breach.

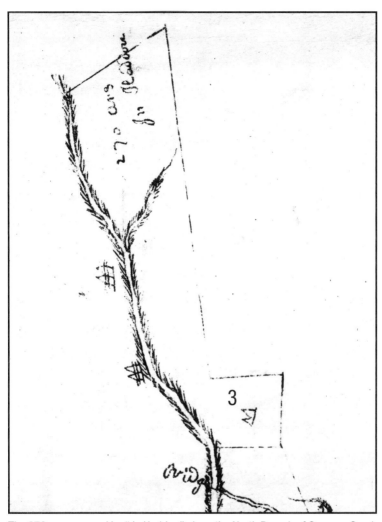

The 270 acres owned by "Jn Haddon" along the North Branch of Coopers Creek which shows a small, one story "cabin" type structure (3) is the likely site where Simon Breach, John Haddon's indentured servant originally lived.

Both, Thomas Sharp Map of Newton Township, NJ, 1700, Clement Collection #791, Historical Society of Pennsylvania

Samuel Nicholson Rhoads with his son Evan Lawrie Rhoads, pointing toward the area where he believed the first house Elizabeth Haddon lived in along Cooper Creek was located. It stood near what today is Coles Mill Road. *Rhoads Collection, Historical Society of Haddonfield*

Pennsauken Creek was the most likely location of Elizabeth's first residence, as well as the location of her marriage to John Estaugh in 1702.

However, Betty Lyons based her conclusions on the interpretation that "in the actual possession" means that Elizabeth already resided on this land. Looking at other deeds from the period, it appears that the phrase "in the actual possession" means simply ownership. South Jersey historian Paul W. Schopp believes John Haddon most likely gave this land along the Pennsauken Creek to Elizabeth as an investment property to be parceled out to others. John Haddon notes that he gave this land "in consideration of the Naturall [sic] Love and affection which he hath and beareth [sic] to and for the said Elizabeth his Daughter And for the promoting and advancing her fortune."[20]

The document that holds the key to the location of Elizabeth Haddon's first permanent residence is Thomas Sharp's 1700 map of Newton Township. The map shows three parcels of land already owned by John Haddon. By the end of 1700, John Haddon would purchase two additional parcels shown on the map. There are three structures on the properties owned by John Haddon. One structure is the former Lovejoy smith shop. The second structure is on the north branch of Cooper's Creek. This modest one story house almost certainly was the residence of Simon Breach, John Haddon's estate manager, who arrived in 1699.

The third structure stood along Cooper's Creek on land John Haddon bought from John Willis in 1698. The location of this structure corresponds to the site that Samuel Nicholson Rhoads correctly identified as Elizabeth Haddon's first home. Thomas Sharp, a meticulous and careful recorder, depicts a two-story house on this property in 1700, probably similar in size to the approximately two-dozen houses illustrated throughout his map of Newton Township. John Haddon likely had this house built in anticipation of the entire Haddon family emigrating, not just Elizabeth. At this house, Elizabeth Haddon and John Estaugh would marry in 1702 and reside until they completed the 1713 dwelling in New Haddonfield.

Once in West New Jersey, Elizabeth began to visit and survey her father's properties, most likely accompanied by Newton Township surveyor Thomas Sharp and her father's estate manager, Simon Breach. At some point, probably soon after her 1701 arrival, Elizabeth chose the site on which she would build her mansion home in 1713. She likely picked the location, today's 201 Wood Lane, because it sits on a prominent rise and was close to both Ferry Road (Haddon Avenue) and King's Highway, along which she envisioned the village of Haddonfield.

Here, again probably soon after her arrival, a modest, four room brick house was constructed. This most likely was constructed for estate manager Simon Breach. He would live here until the end of his indenture in 1706 after which the house would be used by Breach's successor. In frugal Quaker tradition, the small brick structure would be retained and would be attached to the much larger mansion house built in 1713.

Having answered the question of Elizabeth's first residence, however, leads to a further question. What happened to the house along Cooper's Creek after the Estaughs moved to their permanent house in 1713? There is no documentation about the Cooper's Creek house and its fate. Probably it was destroyed, most likely by fire, sometime between 1713 and 1737. Perhaps the Estaughs leased it out after the move to their new plantation house. In any case, had it been standing in 1737, when the Estaughs' heir Ebenezer Hopkins marries, it would have been the most likely place he would have resided. John Haddon, in his 1723 will, leaves the land on which the house stood, to then five-year old Ebenezer.[21] Instead, Ebenezer and Sarah Hopkins moved upriver on Cooper's Creek to the former Shivers house, which John Estaugh had purchased in 1735 and built a large addition to the about twenty-year old house.[22]

Once in West Jersey, Elizabeth began to nurture relationships with Friends in the Delaware Valley, many that had contact with the Haddon family back in London. The first evidence of Elizabeth's interaction with the Quaker community in West Jersey occurred in December 1701, when she witnessed the marriage of Deborah Adams of Judah Allen of Burlington at the Chester, New Jersey, Monthly Meeting. Before coming to America, Deborah Adams's parents, John and Elizabeth, lived near the Haddon family in Southwark, where, most certainly, they associated with John Estaugh and his friend John Richardson, the noted Quaker traveling preacher. Not incidentally, Adams had joined John Estaugh a few months earlier on a mission to Maryland and Virginia. John Adams, who Elizabeth Haddon called "an acceptable minister," and his wife Elizabeth Adams had helped to found the Chester (New Jersey) Monthly Meeting. Adams was also a prominent political leader for the West New Jersey Quaker community. When not traveling to preach the Truth, Adams served as a surveyor of roads and bridges and a justice of the Burlington Court.[23]

Elizabeth witnessed the Adams-Allen marriage on December 15, 1701. While Adams returned to his Chester Meeting in Burlington County in late 1701 to witness the marriage of his daughter Deborah, one of his nine children, John Estaugh did not join him in West New Jersey. When Elizabeth attended her friend's wedding, she still was, in the parlance of the day, a "spinster" in a West New Jersey community that expected every unmarried woman, if not traveling as a missionary, to marry in Meeting. Such marriages were deemed essential to keep the West New Jersey and Pennsylvania Quaker communities growing, and to ensure that their children would be able to inherit and retain title to the family land after their parents' deaths. This was particularly important because of the high mortality rate among children, who died from the smallpox and other diseases that ravaged the Delaware Valley. Two out of every three children died before the age of four, and of those that survived fewer still lived to adulthood.

Elizabeth was intimately aware of the importance of bearing a large number of children. Her mother Elizabeth Clarke Haddon served as a midwife in her community and wrote to her daughter about the birth of both healthy as well as stillborn children and about mothers "who died in childbed of her first Child." [24] Elizabeth knew that married women in Meeting gave birth to a new child, on average, every twenty-four months, so that they might carry on the family line. She saw large families all about her in West New Jersey, attending meetings together, opening their homes to comfort other Friends, intermarrying with other Quaker families and dividing up the land. Samuel Cole of Waterford Township had ten children. Francis Collins had nine children, including a daughter Sarah, who soon became Elizabeth's best friend and constant companion. The Evans family had ten children, Thomas Sharp sired eight and the John and Elizabeth Kay family had seven.

Undoubtedly Elizabeth's parents expected that their older daughter would marry and bear heirs to the Haddon estate in America. At the moment, though, Elizabeth bearing children was not as urgent as it became later since in 1702 her brother Ebenezer was a healthy ten-year old and in a few years could be expected to carry on

John and Elizabeth Clarke Haddon's lineage. Nevertheless, if Elizabeth expected to be fully accepted into the West New Jersey Quaker community she needed to marry in Meeting. An unmarried woman, even a Quaker, usually found it more difficult to carry on legal, business and social matters than a married Friend. Moreover, there was always the realization that many children (including Elizabeth's brother) would never live to adulthood. So, in the summer of 1702, Elizabeth asked the Newton Monthly Friends Meeting to inquire into her clearance from all others in order to marry her longtime acquaintance, the traveling minister John Estaugh, recently returned to Philadelphia and West New Jersey after months of ministering in America.

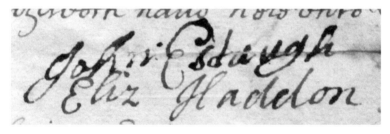

The signatures of John Estaugh and Elizabeth Haddon as they appear on their December 1702 wedding certificate. Unlike the majority of Quaker brides of the day, Elizabeth signed using her maiden name rather than her new married name of Elizabeth Estaugh. *Historical Society of Haddonfield*

CHAPTER 4 NOTES.

[1] Power of Attorney, John Haddon to Elizabeth Haddon, 1701. HEHP, folder 123.
[2] Release of John Haddon to Elizabeth Haddon, June 4, 1701. HEPH, folder 166.
[3] Child, "The Youthful Emigrant," in *Fact and Fiction*, 49.
[4] Alfred Cook Myers, *Quaker Arrivals at Philadelphia, 1682–1750* (Baltimore: Southern Book Company, 1957 reprint of 1900 edition), 20, 32; Ryan, *Imaginary Friends*, 22, 167–70.
[5] Arthur Edwin Bye, *History of the Bye Family and Some Allied families* (Easton, PA: Correll Printing Co., 1956), 286.
[6] Release of John Haddon to Elizabeth Haddon, June 4, 1701. HEHP, folder 166.
[7] Native Americans camped along the Assiscunk, Rancocas, Pensaukin [Pennsauken], Asoroches [Cooper's], Timber, Mantua and Raccoon creeks in Burlington and old Gloucester counties, see, Isaac Mickle, *Reminiscences of Old Gloucester*, 1–2, 21–30, 121–23.
[8] The earliest known reference to "Haddonfield" is a c.1706 map in the Library of Congress, Geography and Map Division. John Worlidge, *A New Mapp of East and West New Jarsey* [sic]: *Being an Exact Survey Taken by Mr. John Worlidge* (London: John Thornton, Hydrographer). Available at: http://hdl.loc.gov.gmd/g3810.ct000064.
[9] Budd, *Good Order*, 28; Clement, *First Emigrant Settlers*, 278–79.
[10] Gabriel Thomas, "An Historical Description of the Province and Country of West-New-Jersey in America" in Albert Cook Myers, *Narratives of Early Pennsylvania, West New Jersey and Delaware, 1630–1707* (New York: Charles Scribner's Sons, 1912), 345.
[11] *Burlington Court Book*, 96
[12] Frank Stewart, ed., *The Organization and Minutes of the Gloucester County Court 1686-7*, also, *Gloucester County Ear Mark Book, 1686–1728* (Woodbury, NJ: Gloucester County Historical Society, 1930); John M. Moore, ed., *Friends in the Delaware Valley: Philadelphia Yearly Meeting, 1681–1981* (Haverford, PA: Friends Historical Association, 1981); George R. Prowell, *The History of Camden County, New Jersey* (Philadelphia: L. J. Richards, 1886), 608.
[13] Gabriel Thomas, "Account of West New-Jersey and Pennsylvania" in Myers, *Narratives*, 30.
[14] See Will of Robert Fairman, brewer and citizen of Southwark, Surrey, England, 1716. HEHP, folder 202.

[15] The most notable marriages at Hannah Wood's house on Cooper's Creek were those of Daniel Cooper to Abigail Wood (1693), Joseph Nicholson to Hannah Wood, Jr. (1695), and Joseph Bates to Mercy Clement (1701), in Clement, *First Emigrant Settlers,* 330, 393; for "Great Tree" plantation, see *New Jersey Archives,* 1st ser., XXIII: 517–18; for ferry, Clement, 295.

[16] See Stewart, *Minutes of the Gloucester County Court 1686–7,* also *Gloucester County Ear Mark Book,* pages 10, 38. The other women paying the poll tax were "Hanna" Wood and Ann (Willis) Penston, both important to Elizabeth's earliest days in settling her father's lands in old Gloucester County, West New Jersey in America, see "Early Records: A Poll Tax List of 1692," *Year Book for 1929, The New Jersey Society of Pennsylvania,* 84.

[17] See Larson, *Daughters of Light.*

[18] Typescript of Hartel's notes (November 1978); C. E. N. Hartel, *"History of Haddonfield: Colonial Period,"* Hartel folder, in box 3, Lyons Project Papers, HSHL. Inventory prepared by Rebecca Nicholson Taylor, re: Indenture between William Lovejoy and Thomas Willis. HEHP, folder 17.

[19] Matlack came from the village of Cropwell Bishop in England, and left his name, temporarily, to what became known by its Indian name, Pennsauken Creek. See, William R. Farr, *Waterways of Camden County: A Historical Gazetteer* (Camden, NJ: Camden County Historical Society, 2002), 125–27; and Farr, *Place Names in and About Haddonfield* (Haddonfield, NJ: Historical Society of Haddonfield, 1979), 10–11, 18–19; Clement, *First Emigrant Settlers.*

[20] Release of John Haddon to Elizabeth Haddon, June 4, 1701. HEHP, folder 166.

[21] Will, copy of John Haddon's Will, 1723. HEHP and copy, in box 1, Lyons Project Papers, HSHL.

[22] Dennis G. Raible, *Haddon Township's Hopkins Plantation: The First Three Hundred Years* (Philadelphia: St. Joseph's Press, 1990), 11–18. Known as the Hopkins House, it still stands today in Camden County's Cooper River Park and houses the Camden County Cultural and Heritage Commission.

[23] Elizabeth Estaugh to John Smith, September 18, 1761, *New Jersey Historical Proceedings,* VI: 104; John Richardson, *An Account of the Life of John Richardson,* 5th edition (London: Edward Marsh, 1843, reprinted in Philadelphia, 1880), 201–202.

[24] John and Elizabeth Haddon to Dear Children, February 27, 1717. HEHP, folder 182; for large families, see "Calendar of New Jersey Wills," *New Jersey Archives,* lst ser., XXIII: 3–4, 102–103, 151.

CHAPTER 5.
A Faithful and Loving Wife, 1702.

Oh! He was a sweet Companion indeed! A loving tender Husband; an humble exemplary Man; a Pattern of Moderation in all Things; not lifted up with any Enjoyments, nor cast down at Disappointments. Oh! What shall I say of him, but that he was a Man endowed with many good Gifts, which rendered him very agreeable to his Friends, and much more to me, his Wife.
—Elizabeth Haddon Estaugh[1]

It would be easy to believe, as have so many followers of the romanticized Elizabeth Haddon story, that the lovelorn Quaker spinster proposed to the handsome Quaker minister John Estaugh while they rode through the dark forests of West New Jersey. However, the Haddon-Estaugh relationship that is central to understanding the building of Haddonfield and the larger Quaker community in America was far more complex. Elizabeth had known about John for nearly a decade, first meeting him when he preached at her Horsleydown Monthly Meeting in London. Estaugh's path to the Truth followed that of many young late-seventeenth century British men and women. Born in 1676 in Kelveden (Keldevon), an Essex County town fifty miles northwest of London, Estaugh became "uneasy with the religious Profession" of his parents that supported the Church of England.

"Being a Seeker," Estaugh "fell in with the Baptists, and liked them so well he was near Joining them." Then in 1693 he attended the burial of a "Friend, Neighbour," his wife Elizabeth later testified, "where that worthy Minister of the Gospel, Francis Stamper of London, being led to speak with Life and Power . . . made such deep Impressions on his tender Mind, that put him upon Search into the Principles of Friends."[2]

Convinced by the charismatic Stamper, the seventeen-year-old Estaugh, who witnessed Stamper's testimony, "came forth in the Ministry." Stamper probably brought Estaugh there because of his business connection to Elizabeth's father John Haddon. The dynamic traveling minister Stamper owned shares of land and mining company stock with Elizabeth's father and most likely chose this comfortable Meeting to initiate John Estaugh into his calling to spread the Truth. Possibly during this interval Stamper introduced Estaugh to John Haddon's daughter Elizabeth. Estaugh may have moved Elizabeth with his testimony at her Horsleydown Monthly Meeting and during several visits to the Haddon household. According to one tradition, it was during this sacred moment that the fourteen-year-old Elizabeth and eighteen-year-old John made plans with her parents to one day marry.

Whether or not such a proposal occurred at this time or that he received the necessary approval from her parents to marry, after his visit with the Haddon family, Estaugh left for a nearly six-year traveling ministry (between 1694 and 1700) through northern England, Ireland, Scotland and Holland. Itinerant minister John Estaugh returned to the Haddon's London neighborhood in late 1700, just as Elizabeth prepared to sail to the New World. Coincidentally, Estaugh sought a certificate of removal to America from the Quarterly Meeting at Cogshall, County of Essex. The Meeting immediately issued a certificate on September 26, 1700 that testified to the young traveling minister's great stature among Friends. Members of the Quarterly Meeting at Cogshall agreed: that "the Lord hath given a Gift of Ministry, which he hath for some years faithfully exercised amongst us." The Meeting certified that on his visits to the north of England and Scotland "he had Service and we believe was well accepted among friends in them [sic] parts." Members of the Quarterly Meeting continued that: "Since his return he hath laid before several Ministering friends & others who were solemnly well together, how for some months A Concern had been Upon him which he did believe was laid upon him by the Lord, To go forth in his Service to Visit ye Seed of God in America." The Meeting appeared "well satisfied" that Estaugh proceed to America and announced that "we have Unity with him."[3]

Thus Estaugh prepared to visit Friends in America just as Elizabeth's father appointed his daughter as the family's real estate agent and attorney to represent the Haddon interests in West New Jersey. Probably both sailed for America during the same year, and possibly the same month. As Elizabeth testified later, she prayed at this moment to become "the near Companion of this dear Worthy."[4] However, they sailed on different ships. While no record has been found of Elizabeth's certificate of removal or the name of the ship that she first sailed on to America, her future husband's journey was well documented. John Estaugh and fellow traveling missionaries from Yorkshire John Richardson, Josiah Langdale and Thomas Thompson left England in November 1700 for the New World on the ship ARUNDEL. They landed on March 5, 1701 in Pautuxent, Maryland after a stormy and unusually long sixteen week crossing. Estaugh and Richardson preached during early 1701 at Friends Meetings in Maryland, Virginia and the Carolinas. The Quaker missionaries "found great openness in these [colonial provinces] amongst the people, and a tender-hearted remnant of Friends scattered abroad in those wilderness countries." The Perquimans Monthly Meeting at the house of Francis Tomes in Albermarle County, North Carolina, seemed the most "acceptable," where in June 1701 they witnessed the marriage of John Newby to Elizabeth Nicholson. Interestingly, both families had kin in West New Jersey.[5]

Estaugh and Richardson next headed north to Pennsylvania where, according to Haddon-Estaugh family tradition, the traveling missionaries spent several days, in August, with William Penn at Pennsbury Manor on the west side of the Delaware River. Here, they apparently observed Penn signing a treaty of peace with the Susquehannock Native American people. At this moment, some accounts had John Estaugh forming his lifelong personal and business relationship with Penn's secretary and proprietary manager James Logan. The story of Estaugh's participation in the Native American conference may be flawed, however. Neither Logan nor Richardson recalled that Estaugh witnessed the treaty ceremonies. Furthermore, Penn had already signed articles of agreement with the Susquehannocks in April and then traveled to the Native American's Conestoga village in western Pennsylvania to express his friendship. Richardson claimed that instead of visiting Penn, "my companion [Estaugh] who I loved well, told me he must go back to Virginia." Indeed on the very month that Estaugh was supposed to be at Pennsbury Manor witnessing Penn's treaty with the Susquehannocks, he traveled south with prominent West New Jersey Quaker missionary John Adams of the Chester, New Jersey Meeting. Richardson's diary never again mentioned his "beloved companion" Estaugh.[6]

John Estaugh was not in the Delaware Valley for much of this period (March 1701 to March 1702) and it is not documented when Elizabeth Haddon and John Estaugh first met in America. In June or July 1701, soon after Elizabeth arrived, Estaugh was in West Jersey, recruiting John Adams of the Chester Meeting for another religious mission to Virginia and North Carolina. Most likely they met at this time. Estaugh then traveled during August of 1701 through Maryland and Virginia with West Jersey preacher Adams to comfort those in the southern Meetings. John appeared briefly in Philadelphia in October. He left the Delaware Valley again in November 1701. By the summer of 1702, Elizabeth and John began to seek clearance for marriage from the Newton Monthly Meeting.

According to Quaker traveling minister Thomas Chalkley, Estaugh had rushed off to join Chalkley and Thomas Story, a leading London and Philadelphia Quaker preacher, entrepreneur and William Penn's business agent, on a mission to "exhort Friends to love God and to be at unity with another" in Rhode Island.[7]

Chalkley was a reliable source for recalling the movements of John Estaugh before he married Elizabeth Haddon. The Quaker minister and businessman was not only an old friend of the Haddon family, but a lifelong companion of both Elizabeth and John Estaugh. Born five years before Elizabeth Haddon, Chalkley was raised in the same Southwark neighborhood and most likely attended the same Friends school as Elizabeth and the Horsleydown Monthly Meeting with the Haddon family. Here, he accepted the calling of "gathering people to faith and dependence on the inward teachings of Christ." After preaching in England and Ireland and suffering persecution and imprisonment, Chalkley planned to travel to America in 1698 on the ship JOSIAH, under the command of Thomas Lurting, another close associate of blacksmith John Haddon and a fellow leader of the Horsleydown Monthly Meeting. Lurting fell ill, however, and Chalkely had to sail with a most unpleasant non-Quaker replacement. Once in America, Chalkley spread the Truth to Meetings in Virginia, Maryland, Pennsylvania and New Jersey before returning to England. One of the most traveled Quaker ministers in history, and later a wealthy Philadelphia merchant ship-owner, Chalkley received certificates of removal with his wife Martha in August 1700 from the Horsleydown Monthly Meeting and returned to America. No sooner had Chalkely arrived in Philadelphia than he arranged to travel and preach with Thomas Story to Quaker communities in New England. The following year Chalkley and Story met Estaugh on their mission to the Rhode Island colony.[8]

John Estaugh appeared in Philadelphia after his journeys to the north with Chalkley, Story and other Philadelphia Friends during early 1702, and settled directly across the river from Philadelphia in Newton Township, Old Gloucester County. Soon after arriving back in Pennsylvania, however, John contracted a severe case of smallpox. Noted Philadelphia physician Dr. Griffith

Owen, who treated Estaugh, reported that "the smallpox hath much reigned here" and "it has been much in Chester County, New Castle County & this town & County [Philadelphia], and I hear it begins in Bucks County & the upper parts of Jersey." The young Quaker preacher survived the terrible smallpox epidemic of 1702, but according to Dr. Owen, the disease scarred John's face and body and caused headaches that plagued Elizabeth's future husband for the rest of his life. It probably left Estaugh sterile and, thus, incapable of producing offspring. John's illness, rather than as popularly believed, Elizabeth's slight build and supposedly frail nature, probably prevented the Estaughs from ever bearing heirs to the Haddon fortune in the New World.[9]

Elizabeth knew that her family wanted her to give birth to a Haddon heir in America, so undoubtedly she tried to have children during the early part of her marriage to John Estaugh. According to a biographical article, written in *The Friend* in 1857, after marrying "John was now comfortably settled, his wife's estate was ample for their need, she was in every way qualified to minister to his happiness, and his heavenly Father permitted him for nearly two years to remain at home with her, except on occasional absence at neighboring meetings."[10] Most likely, after two years, the Estaughs realized that Elizabeth would not bear John's children. Now John could resume his work as a traveling minister and Elizabeth, as she records after his death, "had given up her husband completely to the Lord, "leaving to the wife [a] disposing Hand."[11]

The extensive physical scarring from his severe smallpox caused Estaugh to question his intention to marry Elizabeth. Therefore, John seriously pondered returning to England rather than stay in the Delaware Valley to seek clearance to marry Elizabeth. During the early spring of 1702, the traveling minister went before the Philadelphia Monthly Meeting to seek a certificate of removal back to England. At the Philadelphia Meeting, Estaugh expressed satisfaction with his preaching in America and presented certificates to that effect from Meetings in Long Island and Rhode Island. He concluded that his mission in the New World had ended. He asked whether he should seek a clearance of removal, indicating that he planned to leave Elizabeth in America. Perhaps he planned to return to England in the 120-ton brigantine PHILADELPHIAN, Nathaniel Puckle, master, that had sailed from Bristol, England in April 1702 and was expected on the Delaware River off New Castle at any moment.[12]

The Philadelphia Friends Quarterly Meeting told Estaugh to obey his Inner Light, and the voice of God. Apparently, the Word of the Lord convinced him to remain in America and marry Elizabeth Haddon. Elizabeth recalled years later that Estaugh never considered leaving her behind in America. Moreover as future testimonies revealed, Elizabeth and John shared a genuine affection and deep spiritual bond with each other in their fifty-year relationship that had started long ago in Southwark. "Being then, and for some time after, freed from any Concern to travel in the Service of Truth," Elizabeth announced, "we were married to each other on the first Day of the Tenth Month [December] 1702."[13]

Many voices moved John Estaugh to marry Elizabeth Haddon. Perhaps his close friend Chalkley's description of "a suitable person" to serve as the wife of a traveling minister of God influenced Estaugh. Chalkley wrote that one should marry "a sober and religious young woman, and of a quiet natural temper and disposition which is an excellent ornament to the fair sex."[14] Or, Estaugh was convinced by Religious Society of Friends founder George Fox's instruction that marriage should provide "material security" to assist ministers on their journey toward spiritual salvation. Although a well-educated man, Estaugh held little wealth, probably disowned by his Anglican parents when he joined the despised Religious Society of Friends. At least one critic referred to him incorrectly as a "low born Irishman."[15] John knew that Elizabeth not only perfectly fit the acceptable vision of a Quaker wife, but that her father's proprietary estate gave Estaugh material security in order to continue his traveling ministry. Thus in the end, Elizabeth Haddon and John Estaugh, sufficiently recovered from the smallpox, began in the summer of 1702 to seek clearness to marry.

As was normal procedure, the Newton Friends Meeting appointed a committee to review the request to marry. The committee, consisting of Alice Shackle and Elizabeth Kay, perhaps the two most important women in the Newton Monthly Meeting, investigated Elizabeth in August. Shackle, who Elizabeth considered "a substantial Friend," had welcomed many Quaker business and religious meetings to her plantation house long before Elizabeth entered her neighborhood. For decades, the Shackle residence alternated with the Newton Meeting House as the location for the Friends' weekly worship and monthly meeting for business. At the same time, veteran Quaker preacher Elizabeth Kay also held meetings for worship and business in her plantation house (on what is now the Barclay Farms property in Cherry Hill). Almost at once, Shackle and Kay certified "clearness in marriage" for Elizabeth. The respected preacher of the Truth, John Estaugh, who had been accepted as a member of both Philadelphia and West New Jersey meetings needed no such inquiry. He brought a certificate of removal from England and had submitted it earlier to the Philadelphia Yearly Meeting. Thus, Elizabeth and John satisfied the Delaware Valley Quaker leaders and immediately received a certificate of "clearness from all others" attesting to the fact that neither were married to another and, therefore, possessed the necessary "unity" with Friends to marry in Meeting.[16]

The Haddon-Estaugh marriage on December 15, 1702 at Elizabeth's house in Newton Township, Old Gloucester County, New Jersey, provided a window through which future generations can understand the organizations and intricate network that supported and connected Friends in Pennsylvania, West New Jersey, Barbados and Britain. It also showed how these connections lay behind the establishment of Haddonfield. Marriage of the daughter of an absentee West New Jersey landowner to a widely respected Quaker traveling minister drew the most important Delaware Valley Friends to the ceremony. The thirty-five witnesses present as the pair of fervent Friends exchanged vows included leading Philadelphia and West New Jersey Quaker merchants, landowners and craftsmen, a notable Quaker ship captain, a celebrated visiting English preacher and major West Jersey political figures.

All the witnesses at the Haddon-Estaugh marriage were connected in one way or another to Pennsylvania proprietor William Penn and his inner circle of agents in Philadelphia, and to many of the most important Friends Meetings in West New Jersey, Pennsylvania, England

and Ireland. Nearly all knew and conducted business with Elizabeth's father John Haddon, the Thames River anchor maker, mining expert and real estate investor. Thus, the witnesses at the Haddon-Estaugh marriage reflected not only the complex religious, political and economic network that enabled the Quakers to dominate early settlement of the Delaware Valley, but how Elizabeth Haddon was able to begin building the Quaker community that would become Haddonfield. The type of people who witnessed the marriage also helps us to understand the motivation and methods that lay behind the founding of Quaker communities in America during the last decades of the seventeenth and early part of the eighteenth centuries. The prominent Friends at Elizabeth's marriage represented the search for religious freedom, self-government and ownership of private property and the overwhelming spirit of entrepreneurial capitalism to build economic security. Women, who held a certain amount of equality with men in Meeting, comprised nearly half of the group that signed the marriage certificate. They included several women traveling missionaries, wives of Philadelphia city officials and prominent members of every nearby West New Jersey and Philadelphia Friends Meeting.

The great early winter gathering of 1702 to witness the marriage of John and Elizabeth at Haddon's house revealed just how developed Delaware Valley Quaker society had become since 1675 when John Fenwick first planted the colony of Salem in the province of West New Jersey and six years later when William Penn founded Philadelphia and established the Province of Pennsylvania. Samuel Carpenter and John Jones represented Philadelphia Quaker leaders showing their unity with John

Estaugh, a fellow member of the Philadelphia Monthly (and Yearly) Meeting. Since moving to the area from Barbados in 1683, wedding witnesses Carpenter, a wealthy merchant, and Jones, a master carpenter, had developed Philadelphia waterfront properties that included wharves, taverns and coffee shops. Carpenter had built a magnificent brick house near the riverfront that his longtime business, political, and personal associate William Penn occupied before he left in 1701 for England. Carpenter had developed the first paper mill in America and speculated in frontier Pennsylvania lands and various risky merchant ventures that would eventually bankrupt him. At the time of the Haddon-Estaugh marriage, Carpenter served as a firm ally of William Penn on Philadelphia Common Council, as alderman and justice of city court. Penn had created these municipal governmental agencies a month before sailing for England. Then he had signed a city charter that established the city and borough of Philadelphia in the Province of Pennsylvania managed by eight aldermen, twelve common councilmen and a mayor. Carpenter held numerous Philadelphia political positions under this city charter, and later served briefly as mayor.[17]

Philadelphia merchants Carpenter and Jones held interests and connections to the West New Jersey Quaker community, as well. Carpenter purchased a 650-acre tract between the Timber and Cooper's creeks in Newton Township on the east side of the Delaware opposite the city of Philadelphia. In the process, he acquired the ferry house and landing owned by the first West New Jersey ferry operator and an original proprietor William Roydon. Carpenter also owned a large 1,100-acre plantation in Elsinboro, Salem County, worked by slaves that he may have brought with him from Barbados. As a local landowner, Carpenter had helped to finance the construction of a meeting house for the Salem Religious Society of Friends and in 1685 represented the Salem Tenth in the Burlington assembly. Carpenter also sat on many committees to review cases of dissatisfaction with West Jersey meeting members for the Burlington Yearly Meeting.[18]

Meanwhile, Carpenter's fellow Barbadian and now Philadelphia resident Jones also owned land on Pennsauken Creek in West New Jersey and held kinship connections to the Evans family formerly of Barbados and now of Evesham Township. William and Elizabeth Evans joined Jones to witness the Haddon-Estaugh wedding. William Evans had settled Evesham in 1685, purchased a large tract of land and built a great plantation worked by nearly a dozen slaves of African descent, possibly acquired from the Barbados trade. He soon served on the Traverse Jury in Burlington and sat on committees to survey West Jersey roads and to run the boundary dividing the townships of Evesham and Chester. Evans acted with another Haddon-Estaugh wedding guest, Henry Ballinger, as tax assessors for Evesham Township. Ballinger laid out roads with yet another Haddon-Estaugh intimate and traveling companion John Adams of Chester Township. For her part, marriage witness Elizabeth Evans, a traveling minister, became a supportive friend for Elizabeth Estaugh. Estaugh recalled years later that even though Evans left West New Jersey and moved to Philadelphia, she remained a very "serviceable Friend."[19]

Another "serviceable" Quaker couple, Philadelphia merchant Anthony Morris and his wife Elizabeth, a traveling minister, witnessed the marriage of Elizabeth

Haddon to John Estaugh, (and later, the marriage in Philadelphia of John's brother James Estaugh to Mary Lawson). Morris, too, had West New Jersey connections. A London Quaker and longtime associate of Elizabeth's father before moving to America , Morris had settled first in Burlington in 1678, established a brewery and speculated in real estate. He had removed to Philadelphia in 1686, opened a larger brewery and built a wharf next to that of Samuel Carpenter between Chestnut and Walnut streets on the Philadelphia riverfront that could accommodate large merchant ships. As a leading member of the Philadelphia Yearly Meeting and later clerk of the men's meeting, Morris oversaw establishment of the Quaker school in the city. He served as a Justice, alderman, judge of common pleas, provincial councilor and later mayor of Philadelphia under Penn's city charter.[20]

All along, Morris remained connected to the Burlington Yearly Meeting, visiting various West Jersey Meetings with Carpenter and other Philadelphia Friends to investigate differences and promote harmony across the river among their brothers and sisters in the Truth. His most important service for the Lord occurred in 1698 when accompanied by leading Philadelphia Friends Isaac Norris and Edward Shippen, Morris settled a terrible discord caused by George Keith's attack on established Quaker beliefs that threatened the very fabric of the Salem Monthly Meeting. Shippen's stepson Francis Richardson, a young Philadelphia silversmith also attended the Haddon-Estaugh ceremony in December 1702 with Anthony and Elizabeth Morris. Richardson later married Sarah Cooper and thus became related to many of those in the Haddon and Estaugh circle of Friends. Throughout his years spent in the Delaware Valley, Morris supported Carpenter, Shippen, Norris, James Logan and the Quaker political faction that tried to protect William Penn's proprietary interests in Pennsylvania. Many of these Quaker leaders and their wives and daughters would later visit the house that Elizabeth and John Estaugh built in 1713 near Cooper's Creek.[21]

Several other wealthy Philadelphia Quaker merchants were represented at the marriage ceremony in December, as well. These included David Breintnall, a tailor by trade, who owned several Philadelphia city lots, Pennsylvania land and businesses. He associated with Carpenter, Morris, Shippen and the others that comprised William Penn's proprietary faction. Breintnall signed the marriage certificate, probably representing his wife Jane Blanchard Breintnall, a Quaker traveling preacher of some note, then away on a mission to preach to the disaffected.[22] Richard Gove accompanied David Breintnall to the ceremony. Gove, a joiner, carpenter and traveling minister, lived on Chestnut Street near the other Philadelphia merchants who also witnessed Elizabeth Haddon's marriage. A much persecuted Quaker minister, Gove had decided in 1683, after imprisonment in Bridewell prison, to join William Penn in America. He purchased a tract of land from Penn in 1685 and four years later moved to Philadelphia. No sooner had he arrived in America than Gove was moved to accompany Thomas Chalkley on a mission to comfort Friends in Maryland, Virginia and the Carolinas. Then in 1699 Gove joined Thomas Story on a trip to London for unity with their former English Friends. More importantly, Gove met rising young minister John Estaugh in London and convinced him in 1700 to return with him to Philadelphia. The Gove-Estaugh relationship would continue for years. Not only did Gove witness the Haddon-Estaugh marriage in 1702, but in 1704 later joined John in a ministry to the West Indies where French privateers captured and imprisoned both.[23]

Prominent members of the Women's Meeting of the Philadelphia Monthly Meeting witnessed the marriage to show their unity with Elizabeth and John. Mary Stanbury and Sybilla Righton Masters were the most important Quaker women in Philadelphia. Mary was the wife of wealthy merchant Nathan Stanbury, an original purchaser of Penn's lands and city alderman under the Penn charter of 1701. Her presence further tied Elizabeth and John Estaugh to the Penn Quaker faction in the Delaware Valley. Stanbury, already a holder of notes of credit for other West Jersey Quakers, would later provide financing and building materials for the construction of John and Elizabeth Estaugh's 1713 plantation house near Cooper's Creek.

At the same time Sybilla Righton Masters, daughter of a Burlington sea captain and ship owner William Righton and once a leader of the woman's meeting of the Burlington Friends, represented her husband Thomas Masters at the Haddon-Estaugh nuptials. Thomas Masters was perhaps the wealthiest Quaker in Philadelphia, serving as alderman under Penn's charter of 1701 and later as mayor of the city. Not incidentally, Sybilla's father and husband drew the ire of the British government Board of Trade for carrying on illegal trade because he refused to pay import and export duties in violation of the Navigation laws. Masters joined Carpenter, Jones, Shippen, Stanbury, Story, Anthony Morris, Isaac Norris and other allies of William Penn's proprietary government in America as major investors in William Penn's Susquehanna Land Company that sought to build a Quaker city on the Susquehanna River to monopolize the fur trade.[24]

Sybilla Righton Masters was a significant person in her own right. She developed several new local medicinal remedies from Indian corn and other plants and herbs and obtained the first patents initiated by a woman in colonial British America for her inventions. Her presence may have influenced the Estaughs' lifelong interest with local herbal remedies. Moreover, Sybilla Masters connected Elizabeth and John to her husband Thomas Masters' real estate investments and to his attorneys and land agents Francis and William Rawle, who later became the Estaugh's family lawyers.[25]

The contingent of leading nearby Burlington and Old Gloucester County Quakers at the Haddon-Estaugh ceremony in 1702 proved even more significant for Elizabeth's future in America. It attested to these West Jersey neighbors' recognition of the promise Elizabeth and her new husband held for the advancement and preservation of Quaker religious and economic influence in West New Jersey. That influence was under attack during the same years that Haddon married Estaugh. East and West New Jersey had surrendered their proprietary government in 1702 to Queen Anne. Royal government combined the two Jerseys into the province of New Jersey under Queen Anne's hand-picked governor Edward Hyde, the Lord Cornbury. William Penn worried that the Jersey's surrender forecast the Crown's plan to take away his Quaker proprietary rights and privileges and make Pennsylvania a royal colony, as well. At the moment, though, Penn was in no shape to defend either West New Jersey or Pennsylvania against this new threat. He had returned to England in 1701 to defend his proprietary rights and pay off growing debts. Penn actually spent some time during this period in debtor's prison. So, he urged his loyal agents in America, James Logan, Samuel Carpenter and Isaac Norris of Philadelphia; and West New Jersey proprietor Samuel Jennings of Burlington, to protect Quaker interests in the Delaware Valley.

Penn expected Jennings, an original signatory of the West Jersey Concessions government charter now surrendered to the Queen, to recruit new allies to the Quaker mission to keep proprietary rights to the land. The Haddon-Estaugh wedding in late 1702 provided such an opportunity, and since Penn and his wife Hannah Callowhill could not attend personally, the absentee governor of Pennsylvania probably sent his New Jersey representative Jennings. Jennings had settled in Burlington during 1680 and in 1683 had become deputy governor for the absentee West New Jersey Governor Edward Byllynge. Between 1697 and 1701 Jennings had served as Speaker of the West Jersey Assembly. He often traveled on the Delaware to Pennsbury Manor just upriver and consulted with Penn, Logan, Samuel Carpenter and the other Pennsylvania Quaker leaders. They discussed how to divide up "unappropriated" land for sale to benefit Penn, develop exports of furs, cider, foodstuffs and the mining of iron ore to pay the proprietor's many debts. (Elizabeth's father later became involved briefly in Penn's iron mining enterprise).

New Jersey Deputy Governor Jennings was accompanied to the Haddon-Estaugh affair by an inner circle of

Burlington Court and Friends Meeting members. These included Burlington County Treasurer Peter Fretwell, Samuel Furnis, a wealthy Burlington saddler whose daughter married into the Collins family, and Francis Collins, himself. Both Jennings and Collins had signed the trail-blazing democratic constitution known as the West Jersey Concessions and Agreements. Thus, their presence at the marriage ceremony tied the Haddon-Estaugh relationship to the founding of West New Jersey.

Master brick layer and carpenter Francis Collins had first settled in Burlington but soon purchased two large tracts of land in the Cooper's and Newton Creek region south and east of the Burlington-Salem Road. He built Mountwell and joined the Newton Monthly Meeting. But after the death of his first wife, Collins had moved back to the vibrant Delaware Riverfront town and county seat of Burlington in 1686, where he built both the brick Burlington Friends Meeting House and the first Burlington County Court House. Jennings personally selected Collins for his governor's council. Collins also laid out the Burlington-Salem Road (that was re-routed later through the center of Haddonfield becoming the King's Highway) and selected sites for bridge construction over the many creeks that flowed westward across West New Jersey into the Delaware River. Most comforting to Elizabeth, Collins was a Haddon family friend in the old country and his daughter Sarah, who later married Burlington physician Dr. Robert Dimsdale, soon became Elizabeth's closest companion in America.[26]

While the powerful Penn associates from Philadelphia and Burlington overshadowed other West Jersey guests at the marriage ceremony, the presence of more local witnesses who were her immediate neighbors probably meant more to Elizabeth. Certainly this was true of Esther Spicer, widow of Samuel Spicer, owner of the first flatboat that ferried passengers over the Cooper's Creek, and her daughters Martha and Abigail. Although Esther died suddenly a year after the wedding when struck by lightning, her daughters became close friends with Elizabeth. Martha Spicer later married Thomas Chalkley. Spicer's daughter Sarah married into the prominent Cooper family whose lands adjoined John Haddon's properties. Indeed, many members of the West Jersey Cooper family also witnessed the Haddon-Estaugh vows. William Cooper settled at "Pyne Poynte" (present-day Camden City, New Jersey) at the mouth of the Cooper's Creek in 1682. William, his son Joseph and daughter-in-law Lydia and their son James appeared as witnesses. Elizabeth Haddon Estaugh wrote that William Cooper had a "small gift, but [was a] worthy exemplary man, early convinced, and much valued at home."[27]

Elizabeth Haddon and John Estaugh were connected to the Cooper family in many ways. William Cooper operated a ferry across the Delaware, which, among other things, brought Friends to Meetings at the house of Thomas Fairman in the Shackamaxon section of Philadelphia. The Joseph Cooper family lands bordered on Haddon real estate, and Elizabeth and John Estaugh later retained a surveyor to carefully establish the property lines to secure John Haddon's titles. But this marriage contact with the influential Cooper family helped to prevent future conflicts over land.

The Haddon-Estaugh marriage revealed a spiritual equality of women in the Quaker community. Leading West New Jersey Quaker women who had welcomed Elizabeth Haddon to their Meetings attended the 1702 marriage. Thomas Thackara's second wife Ann (his first wife Esther had drowned in the Delaware River while fishing) witnessed the marriage.[28] The Thackaras had conveyed land on the middle branch of Newton Creek in 1684 to construct the first Friends Meeting House in Newton Township. Mary Haines and her husband Richard (whose signature on the certificate of marriage was almost illegible and often mistaken for that of ship Captain John Annis, who never attended the marriage since he was in England at the time) joined Hope and John Wills at the Haddon marriage. The Haines and Wills families owned large plantations, several farmhouses and log cabins and like so many other West Jersey Quaker land owners used many slaves and indentured servants to work their farms. These prosperous farmers lived near the Pennsauken Creek and further north along the Northampton River (Rancocas Creek), and their presence at the marriage ceremony attested to the intimate connections between the larger Quaker communities in West New Jersey.[29]

Sarah Ellis also witnessed the Haddon-Estaugh marriage. Sarah and husband Simeon Ellis first surveyed land along Newton Creek before relocating on an 800-acre plantation between the north branch of Cooper's Creek and the south branch of Pennsauken Creek (near the present-day Ellisburg area of Cherry Hill, New Jersey). The Ellis family had developed land along Cooper's Creek, adjacent to that of William Cooper and Thomas Shackle. They served with the Cooper and Shackle families as founders of the Newton Quarterly Meeting.

Elizabeth Kay became the most notable Quaker woman to attend the Haddon ceremony. A "daughter of the inner light," who Elizabeth Haddon Estaugh recalled years later, had "a good gift in the ministry," Kay spread the Truth on missions to Maryland, England, Scotland and Ireland. When home in West New Jersey, Elizabeth Kay had acted as clerk of the Newton Friends Monthly Women's Meeting before Elizabeth Estaugh assumed that role in 1706. Kay and husband John operated a sawmill on the north branch of Cooper's Creek and later a gristmill on the south branch (Evans Mill). The Kay house near the sawmill functioned in 1685 as the place of Meeting "with whom Friends were much Comforted." The Kay family would become vital religious and business associates of the Estaughs in the future development of Haddonfield. As Elizabeth recalled, they were "well accepted."[30]

Ship captain Nathaniel Puckle seemed one of the most important witnesses at Elizabeth's marriage. As master at various times of the Quaker-owned ships BRISTOL TRADER, MESSENGER AND PHILADELPHIAN, Puckle sailed regularly between Elizabeth's parents' home in Southwark, England on the Thames River, and the Delaware River ports at New Castle, Philadelphia and Burlington. Puckle commanded ships owned by Philadelphia Quaker merchants, most notably James Logan, Isaac Norris, Samuel Carpenter, Thomas Story and the Pennsylvania proprietor William Penn. Captain Puckle operated until his death in 1706 as the Penn family's major conduit of information and cargo between Philadelphia and London. Puckle knew Elizabeth's father, the Thames River anchor smith John Haddon, very well and indeed became John Haddon's agent and business partner for locating possible mining lands along the Delaware Bay.

When he arrived on the Delaware in the spring of 1702 as master and commander of the merchantman PHILADELPHIAN, Nathaniel Puckle had carried the articles of agreement that Elizabeth's father John Haddon of Rotherhithe had signed with the Quaker merchant ship captain. This indenture granted Puckle one-half ownership with Haddon of the Bellamy plantation near "Prime Hook situate near Hore kills & town of Lewis (Lewes, Delaware) in Sussex Co., Pa."[31] Haddon had purchased the grant from Gabriel Thomas, publisher of promotional literature about settlement in West New Jersey and Pennsylvania, who did not have the money to complete the purchase. When Thomas threatened to take possession of the land without paying for it, Haddon contracted with Puckle to stake their claim to the land.[32] About the time of the Haddon-Estaugh marriage, Puckle took up permanent residency in Philadelphia and opened a merchant firm. Although Puckle would continue to sail regularly to England for Penn, Logan, Haddon and other Quaker merchants, he was known by the time of Elizabeth's December wedding as a Philadelphia merchant.

All of these witnesses at the 1702 Haddon-Estaugh marriage in West New Jersey played critical roles in a variety of ways determining Elizabeth and John's future life in America. The organizations and groups represented by the wedding guests largely defined how they would build the Quaker community of Haddonfield. However, in December 1702 the exchange of marriage vows overshadowed the social and political-economic importance of the gathering for Elizabeth Haddon's next sixty years in America. The Elizabeth Haddon-John Estaugh marriage during the early winter of 1702 in Old Gloucester County, West New Jersey was a glorious spiritual moment that joined their lives together. Following accepted Quaker doctrine, there was no formal wedding ceremony presided over by an ordained minister or civil official.

Moreover, Elizabeth's American marriage was not "recorded in the Scriptures of Truth," as her sister Sarah's marriage in London would be, later. Nevertheless, Elizabeth's American marriage was blessed "at the monthly meetings of Newton to which they belong according to truths order, and the Said meetings having received Satisfaction concerning their clearness both by due and orderly Enquiry made here and also by Certificates from Friends in England."[33]

The certificate of marriage recorded that Elizabeth and John had received "the consent of their Parents," suggesting that this marriage could possibly have been arranged long ago back in Southwark at the Horsleydown Monthly Meeting. In any case, in 1702 John testified before "Friends and Neighbors in the Presence of God and you his people Whom I desire to be my Witnesses I take this my Friend Elizabeth Haddon to be my Wife—promising through the Lords Assistance to be unto her A loving husband till ye Lord by death Shall separate us." For her part Elizabeth declared: "Friends in fear of the Lord and before you his people whom I desire to be my witnesses I take this my Friend John Estauge [Estaugh] to my husband promising through ye Lords Assistance to be unto him a Faithful and Loving wife until the Lord by death shall Separate us."[34]

It is interesting to note that Elizabeth chose to sign her marriage certificate "Elizabeth Haddon" rather than "Elizabeth Estaugh". Most Quaker women at that time signed their marriage certificate with their new name—their husband's surname. This marks the last time she signed her name "Elizabeth Haddon." From this point forward, she always used the name "Elizabeth Estaugh."

CHAPTER 5 NOTES

[1] Elizabeth Estaugh's "Testimony To the Memory of her beloved Husband John Estaugh," Preface to John Estaugh, *A Call to the Unfaithful Professors of Truth* (Philadelphia: printed by B. Franklin, 1744), v–vi.

[2] Elizabeth Estaugh's "Testimony," in John Estaugh, *Call to the Unfaithful*, iii–v.

[3] John Estaugh Certificate of Removal to America, September, 28, 1700, in Book 352, Friends Library, London, copy, in box 1, Lyons Project Papers, HSHL. The certificate was received by the Philadelphia Monthly Meeting on June 26, 1702, shortly before John Estaugh and Elizabeth Haddon, sought clearance to marry, Myers, *Quaker Arrivals*, 30.

[4] "Elizabeth Estaugh's Testimony," in John Estaugh, *Call to the Unfaithful*, iii.

[5] Richardson, *Life of John Richardson*, 62–65.

[6] Richardson, *Life of John Richardson*, 69–70, 128, 137.

[7] Thomas Chalkley, *The Journal of Thomas Chalkley, A Minister of the Gospel in the Society of Friends* (Philadelphia: Friends Bookstore, 1890), 30.

[8] Chalkley, *Journal*, p. vii. Estaugh received his certificate of removal to America, a few weeks later, but probably traveled on a different ship.

[9] Owen to William Penn, May 8, 1702, *Penn Papers*, IV: 169. An examination of the two capes and apron worn by Elizabeth, now displayed in the Historical Society of Haddonfield museum, show not the clothing of a diminutive person but of a woman of average size for the early eighteenth century.

[10] *The Friend: A Religious and Literary Journal* (Philadelphia: Robb, Pile & McElroy, 1857) 30: 108.

[11] "Elizabeth Estaugh's Testimony," in John Estaugh, *Call to the Unfaithful*, xii.

[12] Puckle's warrant to sail in 1702, Institute of Historical Research, *Calendar of Treasury Books*, vol. 17 (London: 1702).

[13] Elizabeth Estaugh's "Testimony," in John Estaugh, *Call to the Unfaithful*, v. Under the Quaker calendar the Tenth Month was December, since Friends employed the Julian calendar until 1751 that started the New Year on 25 March. The Quakers rejected the pagan names for the months and substituted numbers, calling March the First Month, April the Second Month and so forth, ending the year in February or the Twelfth Month.

[14] Chalkley, *Journal*, 109.

[15] Samuel N. Rhoads, "Haddon Hall of Haddonfield," *Bulletin of Friends' Historical Society of Philadelphia* (1906–1910), 61.

[16] Elizabeth Estaugh to John Smith, September 18, 1761, in John Clement, "Elizabeth Estaugh and some of her Contemporaries," *Proceedings of the New Jersey Historical Society*, 3rd ser. (1912–1913), VII: 103–105.

[17]See, Larry Gragg, *The Quaker Community on Barbados* (Columbia: University of Missouri Press, 2009), 68, 70, 95–96, 129, 150.

[18]Stewart, *Gloucester County Court Minutes*, 25; Clement, *First Emigrant Settlers*, 18.

[19]Elizabeth Estaugh to John Smith, September 18, 1761, *New Jersey Historical Society Proceedings*, VI: 104; William Evans will, "Calendar of Wills," *New Jersey Archives*, 1st ser., XXIII: 157; Gragg, *Quaker Community on Barbados*, 70.

[20]For John Haddon-Anthony Morris connection, see John and Elizabeth Haddon to Dear Children, February 27, 1717. HEHP, document 182; *Penn Papers*, IV: 90n13.

[21]"Haddon Hall had almost a monopoly in the hospitalities given to Public Friends visiting that neighborhood," Samuel N. Rhoads, "Haddon Hall, of Haddonfield," in Frank Stewart, ed., *Notes on Old Gloucester County, New Jersey* (Camden, NJ: Sinnickson Chew, printer for The New Jersey Society of Pennsylvania, 1917), I: 302; Also, see "The Quaker Home as Private and Public Space," in Stoneburner, *Influence of Quaker Women*.

[22]Breintnall, in *Penn Papers*, IV: 662n1.

[23]Richard Gove biography, *The Friend: A Religious and Literary Journal*, vol. 28, no. 16 (Philadelphia, 1854), 125.

[24]Bill of John Estaugh to James Johnson, 1717. HEHP, folder 98.

[25]See Memorandum that Thomas Masters purchased a certain piece of land from John Estaugh, 1720. HEHP, folder 116.

[26]Francis Collins biography, in Clement, *First Emigrant Settlers*, 71–84.

[27]Estaugh to Smith, *New Jersey Historical Society Proceedings*, VI: 103–104.

[28]Drowning, in *Gloucester County Court Records*, I: 34.

[29]*New Jersey Archives*, 1st ser., vol. XXIII: 200, 513–14.

[30]Elizabeth Estaugh to John Smith, September 18, 1761, *New Jersey Proceedings*, VI: 104–105; Larson, *Daughters of Light*, 311.

[31]Articles of agreement between Nathaniel Purkle [Puckle], Mariner and John Haddon Blacksmith., 1702. HEHP, folders 23 and 24.

[32]Gabriel Thomas role in John and Elizabeth Haddon to Most Dear Children, March 9, 1718, folder 183; both in HEHP.

[33]Marriage Certificate: John Estaugh and Elizabeth Haddon, 1702, HSHL. Elizabeth's sister, Sarah Haddon's marriage vows with Benjamin Hopkins made in 1706 before a large public gathering at the Horsleydown Friends Monthly Meeting, by contrast, were far more solemn, see Benjamin Hopkins and Sarah Haddon Marriage certificate August 29, 1706, copy transcribed by Samuel W. Rhoads from original, 1907, box 1, Lyons Project Papers, HSHL.

[34]Marriage Certificate: John Estaugh and Elizabeth Haddon, 1702, HSHL.

CHAPTER 6.
The Search for Unity, 1703–1713.

Be it Known unto all men by those presents that I, John Haddon of Rotherith in the County of Sussex, Blacksmith, have made, ordained, authorized and appointed, and by those presents do make, ordain, authorize, constitute and appoint John Estaugh and Elizabeth Estaugh of New Jersey in America Planters, jointly or severally and the survivor of them my true and lawful attorneys and attorney in my name and behalfe [sic], to sell and dispose of all or any my lands tenements and hereditaments whatsoever and wheresoever in the province of New Jersey aforesaid.

—John Haddon[1]

Elizabeth Haddon and John Estaugh began married life in a world torn by perpetual wars. Britain, Holland, France and Spain battled continually for power and empire. Much of this century-long imperial struggle involved the New World. The current War of the Spanish Succession (1702–1713) brought enemy privateers up the Delaware River close to their new West New Jersey home in America. At the same time, the Estaughs now lived in a New Jersey united as a royal colony in 1702 and governed by the debauched and venal governor Edward Hyde, the Lord Cornbury. The Royal governor manipulated the Quakers in Burlington for control of West Jersey politics and money. He instituted fines on the Quakers who refused to serve in militias or take oaths of office. Pennsylvania Proprietor William Penn, for one, considered the New Jersey governor and his gang of corrupt courtiers the "most dishonorable shirking neighbors." Eventually Lord Cornbury's cousin Queen Anne removed him from the Jersey governorship, but not after years of plundering Quaker settlers to support his depraved lifestyle.[2]

Across the river Philadelphia and Pennsylvania suffered from constant political controversy that had forced William Penn to grant more authority to non-Quaker, anti-proprietary factions. He also had to block the governor of Maryland, Lord Baltimore, from seizing Pennsylvania's Lower Counties of Sussex, Kent and New Castle on the west banks of the Delaware Bay and river (later the colony and state of Delaware). Penn lived in England from 1701 on where he battled legal and financial crises that removed him from intimacy with Delaware Valley politics. His agents James Logan, Samuel Carpenter, Thomas Story and Samuel Jennings, all connected closely to Estaugh and Haddon, maintained Quaker control over the region, but suffered severe financial and political setbacks. The great Quaker New World experiment in developing a community where Friends might practice freedom of worship, maintain self-government and gain economic opportunity was everywhere under assault.

The newlywed Elizabeth and John Estaugh seemed immune to these threats. Tucked away in the relatively remote rural farming neighborhoods of Newton, Chester and Waterford Townships in Old Gloucester and Burlington Counties, they established their identity as part of the West Jersey Quaker community rather than with the more prominent Philadelphia Friends. However, John and Elizabeth received constant help from Philadelphia Friends Thomas and Mary Chalkley. Thomas, a former member of Elizabeth's Horsleydown Monthly Meeting in England now receiving unity with the Philadelphia Monthly (and Yearly) Meeting, often crossed the Delaware and joined the Estaughs to build the Quaker community in West New Jersey. John Estaugh along with Thomas and Mary Chalkley attended the John Mickle-Hannah Cooper marriage in November 1704 held in William Cooper's house at Pyne Poynt (present-day Camden city). Inexplicably, Elizabeth failed to attend. In the future, Elizabeth often avoided traveling any distance from her beloved house and meeting. But this time, she had other obligations. That month, she provided lodging at her home to Susanna Freeborn and Esther Champion Palmer, two of the most-traveled Quaker women ministers. Freeborn fell ill and perhaps Elizabeth attended to her needs as she did for so many other Quaker women over the years, rather than traveling to the Mickle-Cooper marriage ceremony.[3]

After a few years of marriage, John Estaugh began to seek clearance for removal from Meeting to travel and spread the "Spirit of Truth" to distant Friends. Attachment to a propertied woman now gave him the material base that allowed him to carry on the work of the Lord. In 1704 John accepted another call to accompany Philadelphia traveling preacher Richard Gove to minister to Friends on the West Indies island of Barbados. Thomas Story had intended to go instead but had not returned from his mission to New England, where he found "acceptance" of his Truth and established the first Friends

Meeting on Nantucket Island. So, Estaugh sought a certificate of removal from his new home in West New Jersey to accompany Gove. Consequently, the Yearly Meeting of Ministering Friends held in Burlington gave its blessing for John to travel to Barbados in 1704, praying that the Lord "may keep and preserve him in the dangerous voyage from the hands of unreasonable men."[4]

As the Burlington Meeting's testimony to comfort Estaugh revealed, it seemed a very bad time for ocean travel. French and Spanish privateers roamed at will off the Delaware Bay and down the Atlantic Coast into the Caribbean where they battled Britain for possession of West Indies trade and colonies in Queen Anne's War (1702–1714), the American phase of the War of the Spanish Succession. James Logan (one of John Estaugh's emerging business partners) wrote Penn, that "Martinico Privateers" had already seized "150 sail," including a large sloop owned by leading Philadelphia merchants Logan, Norris and Samuel Carpenter. "Two weeks ago," Logan continued, "we had advice of the best ship belonging to our river being taken . . . Capt. Puckle's brigantine." Logan worried, "if so, it will be the greatest blow this Country has received of the Kind," because the fast merchantman carried gold coin and goods badly needed by leading Quaker merchants in Philadelphia.[5] Indeed, a heavily armed privateer seized an unarmed Quaker-owned Philadelphia merchantman carrying Gove and Estaugh, took the two missionaries to the French Caribbean stronghold of Martinico (Martinique) and threw them into a goal. They languished in the dank island prison for two months until a prominent English Quaker administrator on the nearby island of

Antigua negotiated with French officials for the traveling ministers' release.

After a quick visit in June 1705 to comfort Barbados Friends with "the Truth," Estaugh and Gove sailed back to Philadelphia. When he returned to West New Jersey after being abducted and held hostage in a Caribbean jail, Estaugh resumed building unity with local Friends. In November 1705, John and Elizabeth, accompanied once again by Thomas Chalkley, witnessed the marriage of Josiah Southwick of Springfield, Burlington County, to Francis Collins's daughter Elizabeth at Joseph Collins' Mountwell house in Newton Township (part of present-day Haddonfield). Several months later, John and Elizabeth joined again by their most faithful friend Thomas Chalkley, attended the marriage of Benjamin Wood of the "Hopewell" plantation to John and Elizabeth Kay's daughter, Mary. The ceremony was held at John Kay's house in Waterford Township near where the Barclay Farmstead stands today in Cherry Hill. This marriage united two powerful and wealthy Gloucester County Quaker families. Next, Chalkley and the Estaughs witnessed the marriage of John and Elizabeth Kay's son John Kay Jr. to Sarah Langston at the Newton Monthly Meeting.

The Estaughs' contacts with the John Kay family proved of particular significance for the eventual development of Haddonfield. Kay owned land on the east side of the winding Burlington-Salem Road, which was later replaced by King's Highway, located to the west of the original road. John Haddon held title to the land on the west side of this old Indian path directly opposite Kay's property. In fact, Kay grew corn on Haddon's land near the gristmill. Perhaps of more significance, John Kay was the most powerful political figure in Gloucester County when Elizabeth and John settled there permanently. Kay represented the old Gloucester County Quaker community in the Burlington Assembly and protected the interests of landowners such as the Estaughs, who never participated in local political affairs.[6]

The most important marriage witnessed by John and Elizabeth during this defining period in their young lives occurred in March 1707 at the Philadelphia Monthly Meeting. Here they witnessed the marriage of John Estaugh's brother James to Mary Lawson. James had received a certificate of removal from the Felsted Division Monthly Meeting in Essex County just east of London in April 1702 but had not submitted it to the Philadelphia Monthly Meeting until several weeks before his marriage to Mary Lawson, a noted English traveling minister. Lawson had received a certificate of removal to the Philadelphia Monthly Meeting on August 27, 1700 from the Monthly Meeting upon Pardsay Crag in Cumberland County, England. This Meeting was one of the oldest in Britain, and was often attended by George and Margaret Fell Fox, the founders of the Society of Friends. From Philadelphia, the Quaker stronghold in the New World, Mary Lawson had joined another important English female preacher, Esther Palmer, in 1704 and 1705 on a missionary trip through Maryland, Virginia and the Carolinas. Palmer (and possibly Lawson) stayed with the Estaughs during their mission to comfort Friends by preaching the Word of God at a Friends meeting held at James Whitall's plantation house, located at Red Bank near Woodbury Creek in Old Gloucester County, West New Jersey.[7]

The James Estaugh-Mary Lawson marriage proved the only recorded time that Elizabeth Haddon Estaugh witnessed such a ceremony in Philadelphia. Moreover, it was one of the few times that she traveled from her quiet Newton Township sanctuary down Cooper's Creek or along the Indian trail that became Haddon Avenue to one of the primitive Pyne Poynt ferryboats that crossed the Delaware River to the bustling Pennsylvania city. Elizabeth had to attend this Philadelphia marriage ceremony not only for the sake of her husband and his brother but because members of the most important Quaker families in the region witnessed the marriage (many that had attended her own marriage in 1702). The Estaugh-Lawson connection provided yet more evidence of the powerful network of Friends that built the Quaker community in the Delaware Valley. It revealed further the intimate association that the Estaughs and Haddons developed with British, Pennsylvania and West New Jersey Quakers.[8]

Renowned preacher and William Penn's confidant, Thomas Story, witnessed the Estaugh-Lawson marriage at the Philadelphia Monthly Meeting. Story often conducted real estate and religious business with James's brother John Estaugh (and after Story removed to England became a partner with Elizabeth's father in the Quaker mining and land companies of London). John Fothergill (1676–1745) also witnessed the James Estaugh marriage. A Yorkshire traveling minister and intimate of William Penn and the Barclays (also Haddon associates), Fothergill had recently moved to Philadelphia and by 1706 oversaw the Philadelphia Monthly Meeting. Fothergill visited the Haddon-Estaugh house from time to time, probably for spiritual and business interests, particularly matters regarding William Penn's property in America. Traveling minister Richard Gove, recently released along with John Estaugh from French prison in Martinique, witnessed the important Friends marriage as well. Most significant for the Estaughs, Philadelphia merchant builder Nathan Stanbury attended. Stanbury soon became involved in the construction and probably financing of the new Haddon-Estaugh plantation house in West New Jersey.

Philadelphia merchants John Jones, Henry Willis, Clement Plumstead and the ubiquitous Samuel Carpenter signed the marriage certificate for the Estaugh-Lawson union. Caleb Pusey, who was Carpenter's manager for William Penn's mills on Chester Creek, joined the Estaugh-Lawson affair. Nicholas Waln, a wealthy landowner, overseer of the Philadelphia Monthly Meeting, Pennsylvania assemblyman and traveling minister originally from Yorkshire, also witnessed this marriage. Waln became an intimate at the Haddon-Estaugh household between 1713 and 1722 despite the criticism of fellow Estaugh intimate and business partner James Logan. Logan called Waln a "Worthless man," because he opposed Penn's proprietary interests in America. Nevertheless, John Estaugh had to develop unity with Logan, Waln and other wealthy Philadelphia Quaker merchant entrepreneurs in their development of Pennsylvania real estate.[9]

Once again, the presence at the Estaugh-Lawson marriage of some of the most influential Quaker women in America attested to Elizabeth Estaugh's growing significance in the community. After all, Elizabeth had just been accepted as the recording clerk for the Women's Meeting of the Newton Monthly Meeting, replacing the well-respected Elizabeth Kay. Elizabeth Estaugh's friends Esther Palmer, Martha Chalkley, Jane Breintnall, Elizabeth Morris and Susannah Marriott represented the Philadelphia Monthly Women's Meeting. Susannah Marriott appears of particular interest. She had married into the prominent Burlington, New Jersey Quaker Marriott family and was most likely related through marriage to Elizabeth Haddon's grandmother Phillipiah Marriott of Hardingstone. Other Philadelphia Monthly Meeting women leaders, some well acquainted with Elizabeth attended the marriage. These included Grace Lloyd and Hannah Lloyd Hill, Margaret Jones and Hannah Carpenter. Margaret and Hannah's husbands had witnessed Elizabeth Haddon's marriage in 1702 to John Estaugh. In addition, Philadelphia traveling Quaker women ministers Elizabeth Durborow, Elizabeth Janney and Grace Harker witnessed the Estaugh-Lawson marriage to express their unity with the "daughter of light," Mary Lawson, and at the same time with the increasingly important West New Jersey Quaker business woman and member of Meeting, Elizabeth Estaugh.[10]

The James Estaugh-Mary Lawson marriage at the Philadelphia Monthly Meeting confirmed the growing importance of John and Elizabeth Estaugh to the development of the Quaker community in America. The Estaughs' emerging circle of influential Philadelphia Friends, who attended the Estaugh-Lawson marriage, required that John and Elizabeth establish a permanent place in West New Jersey for comforting Friends and to conduct business. Founder of the women's meeting Margaret Fell Fox taught that those Quaker women not traveling on missionary work needed to develop a public space in their houses where Friends might stay in their travels to spread the Truth. The permanent Estaugh house, completed in 1713, would be designed and built to be large enough to accommodate traveling preachers, both men and women and to conduct their real estate and merchant business with other Friends.

Moreover, Elizabeth fully expected to have her mother, father, sister, brother-in-law and brother come to America and settle on John Haddon's land in West New Jersey. In England, in 1706, her fifteen-year-old brother Ebenezer (II) had died, her sister Sarah had married Southwark vintner Benjamin Hopkins and had given birth to her first child in 1707. Thus, despite the changing situation in England that might tie her family more closely to their London home and Friends Meetings, Elizabeth expected that one day the entire family would ultimately join them in Haddonfield.[11]

As Elizabeth Estaugh developed plans between 1705 and 1708 for the plantation house on her father's land, her husband assumed direction of John Haddon's real estate transactions and trading connections in America. Haddon's business dealings largely guided John and Elizabeth Haddon Estaugh's daily life in America, perhaps as much as their deep devotion to and leadership in the local Religious Society of Friends meetings. After Elizabeth first moved to Old Gloucester County, her father had continued to invest in West New Jersey lands along Cooper's and Pennsauken creeks. Haddon also purchased several thousand acres of land along Oldman's Creek in Salem County. At the same time, Elizabeth's father became involved in East Jersey land deals.[12] Quaker banker Robert Barclay of Scotland and London, probably expecting Haddon to remove to America, had appointed the West Jersey proprietor Haddon to administer Barclay's proprietary possessions in East New Jersey, and to sign releases for investors in Barclay's 1/40th part of the former province of East New Jersey. Furthermore, John Haddon had become deeply involved in the Pennsylvania Land Company of London affairs and would soon ask the Estaughs to represent the company's extensive real estate interests in America. To this end, John Haddon "ordained, authorized and appointed John Estaugh and Elizabeth Estaugh of New Jersey in America Planters, jointly or severally and the survivor of them my true and lawful attorneys." The Southwark Quaker entrepreneur John Haddon instructed his daughter and son-in-law "in my name and behalfe [sic] to sell and dispose of all or any my lands, tenements and hereditaments whatsoever and wheresoever, in the province of New Jersey aforesaid, to any Person or Persons whatsoever for the most money or other advantage of me."[13]

John Estaugh, assisted by Gloucester County surveyor and an overseer of the Newton Friends Monthly Meeting, Thomas Sharp, began to resurvey, clear and record titles to properties acquired earlier by John Haddon from Richard Matthews and Thomas and John Willis. Estaugh and Sharp first surveyed Haddon's new 2,400-acre Oldman's Creek proprietary grant purchased in 1705 from the estate of Richard Matthews' late son Thomas. The tract of land extended from John Hugg's Gloucester County property below Timber Creek southwesterly to the Oldman's Creek properties of Isaac and John Davis of Salem County.[14]

The most important job for Estaugh, though, lay with the need to resurvey an 838-acre tract on the south branch of the Cooper's Creek in Waterford Township that John Haddon leased in 1706 to his nephew John Gill Jr., probably the "Kingsland" grant recorded on Thomas Sharp's 1700 map of Newton Township. Clearing this uncertain title, ownership and boundaries for Gill was most important to Haddon. Young Gill was the son of John Haddon's sister Ann Haddon and John Gill Sr. The Gills and Haddons had a long history together. Elizabeth's grandfather Matthew Haddon and the elder Gill had been longtime Northamptonshire neighbors and close friends who shared some of the same sufferings and trials against Quakers during the 1670s in their region. Sometime before 1708, the younger Gill had arrived in America where he was expected to assist his cousin Elizabeth in her business dealings and perhaps marry a member of the Newton Women's Monthly Meeting in order to provide a Haddon family heir in the New World. To this end, Gill immediately became involved in local affairs. He witnessed in Philadelphia court on September 4, 1708 the recording of the 1702 Haddon lease of Delaware Bay property to Nathaniel Puckle. A few months later Gill served as the principal creditor and administrator for the estate of William Higgs of Newton Township.[15]

Gill's most interesting service for the Haddon family occurred in late 1708 when he joined James Estaugh and Joseph Cooper in witnessing John Estaugh's transfer of his power of attorney for John Haddon to Thomas Sharp and Joseph Kay. This was in response to John Estaugh's clearance in 1708 to leave with Elizabeth for London to visit the Haddons. With all this real estate activity since her marriage in 1702, Elizabeth decided in 1708 to bring recent legal documents to her father in London. She would then return with legal papers, such as new power of attorney for her husband. Undoubtedly, Elizabeth held out the hope, as well, that she might convince her parents to remove to the bucolic and increasingly profitable and secure West New Jersey Quaker sanctuary in the Delaware Valley. Therefore, Elizabeth and her husband conducted "an honest, orderly and exemplary conversation" with the Newton Friends Monthly Meeting to obtain a certificate of removal to the Monthly Meetings of Friends in London.[16]

Their Newton Monthly Meeting approved certification of John and Elizabeth's first clearance of removal together for travel to London. Members of every leading Gloucester County Quaker family signed the certificate, including members of the Cooper, Shackle, Collins, Kaighn, Evans, Mickle and Kay families. Most signatories came from the Newton Monthly Meeting, but significant regional Meetings also were represented, demonstrating their growing unity with the Estaughs. James Whitall signed for the Red Bank Meeting, Joshua Lord for the Woodbury Meeting and Thomas Ballinger and Francis Collins for the Burlington Meeting. All testified that John and Elizabeth Estaugh "had a Unity with them in their staying with us." Elizabeth, now clerk of the Women's Meeting, "hath been a very serviceable member," while John had been "faithful in his Testimony." Most important, John had a "gift in the Ministry to the glory of God."[17]

A few months after Elizabeth and John received the Newton Meeting's blessing for their trip to England, John Estaugh applied for an additional certificate of removal for himself from the "Ministering Friends of the Provinces of Pensilvania [sic] & New Jersey in America held at Philadelphia the 5th [day] 4th mo. [June] 1708" to the

"Ministering Friends at London in Great Britain & others whom it may Com[fort?]." The Philadelphia Meeting's certificate of removal, signed by Thomas Story, Nicholas Waln, Griffith Owen and other influential Friends who conducted business with Estaugh, stressed that John Estaugh planned to expand his traveling ministry in Britain as well as to promote trade with America. They likened him to "a fresh, green & Living plant . . . growing [in his] Condition in the Gift of the Ministry, in which he hath been Servic[e]able among us." Estaugh expected that while his wife Elizabeth conducted their business affairs in Britain, he would minister to Friends in the Truth.[18]

The separate certificates suggested that John did not sail with Elizabeth in early 1708 after they had received the Newton Meeting certificate of removal in February. Further evidence lay in the fact that John Estaugh alone witnessed the marriage of their good neighbors Samuel Mickle and Elizabeth Cooper in April. If Elizabeth had been in the area, she would never have missed this marriage. Moreover, John received another certificate from Newton Meeting in June. In any case, Elizabeth Estaugh (possibly with female traveling companion Sarah Collins who was about to marry Dr. Robert Dimsdale) arrived in England in 1708 and submitted her certificate to the Friends Meetings in London in August. Elizabeth would stay there for nearly four years.

Much had changed for the Haddon family when Elizabeth Haddon Estaugh returned in 1708 to her parents' house in Rotherhithe. Her brother Ebenezer (II), her family's hope for a male heir, had died in 1706 of convulsions. Also, her only living sister Sarah had married in 1706 and given birth to a daughter in 1707.[19] Sarah

Haddon had married London wine merchant Benjamin Hopkins of St. George Parish, Southwark. This marriage united two influential London Quaker families. The entire Haddon family had witnessed the Haddon-Hopkins marriage, except for Elizabeth who was still in America. Elizabeth's father and mother Haddon, her uncles Simon, William and Thomas Haddon and John Clarke attended the marriage. John Haddon's major business partners in the mining industry Enoch Floyd, Dr. Edward Wright and his wife Kathryn had also signed the certificate of marriage. Most of the Hopkins family of the Southwark borough of London represented the husband. This connected the newly married couple intimately to their Southwark neighborhoods and to the Horsleydown Monthly Meeting. It also brought together two rising middle-class Quaker entrepreneurial families. Haddon, of course, operated an increasingly influential mining and anchor smith business in Southwark. Concurrently his new son-in-law Benjamin Hopkins held membership in the Mysterious Company of London Vintners, one of the twelve most powerful, ancient merchant trade guilds. Hopkins conducted his business from the Vintner's Company Hall that was located on the Southwark Bridge that crossed the Thames River into the center of London, a few streets from the Haddon's and Hopkins's houses and places of business.

Sarah and Benjamin Hopkins bore twelve more children between 1707 and 1722 although only five—Sarah, Mary, Haddon, Elizabeth and Ebenezer Hopkins—survived to adulthood. It would be Ebenezer, born in 1718, who one day would come to West New Jersey with his Aunt Elizabeth and eventually found the Hopkins, Haddon and Estaugh line in America. During this visit to her London birthplace, Elizabeth grew closer to her sister. She served in 1709 as midwife at the birth of Sarah Haddon Hopkins' daughter Mary and in 1711 for an unnamed stillborn child. All along the childless Elizabeth helped with management of the Haddon-Hopkins family. It soon became apparent to Elizabeth that her Sister Sarah and husband Benjamin Hopkins would never leave England for America. Each day as she interacted with her family, Elizabeth saw that they remained comfortable in their own London Quaker community. Her mother became more deeply engaged in serving the Horsleydown Monthly Meeting as treasurer and member of committees to ensure unity within the women's meetings. She served as midwife for her daughter Sarah's growing family and for other Quaker mothers in Southwark.[20]

The attachment of her family to their London community became clearer when Elizabeth witnessed another Haddon family marriage ceremony in 1710 that united two important Quaker families in the region. Interestingly, Elizabeth attended alone since her husband had returned to America where he received yet a third certificate of clearance from the Newton Monthly Meeting to return to London. In any case, Elizabeth joined Sarah and Benjamin Hopkins, her parents John and Elizabeth Clarke Haddon and other London Friends at the Bull & Mouth Monthly Meeting in London on July 5, 1710 to witness the marriage of Samuel Lloyd, a wealthy London grocer, to Mary Haddon, daughter of her Uncle Simon, the Cripplegate meal man. The Lloyd family held a number of real estate, banking and business interests in Britain (and the Delaware Valley) that further extended John Haddon's business network.[21]

It was John Haddon's expanding enterprises, perhaps more than family and the Religious Society of Friends Meeting, that convinced Elizabeth that her dear parents might never immigrate to America. Elizabeth Estaugh learned about the many new business and political connections developed by her father since her removal to America more than six years before. Her father had become deeply involved in the complex industrial, mining, financial and colonial real estate enterprises that defined early eighteenth century British entrepreneurial capitalism. Haddon typified late-Stuart Restoration England's rising middle-class of merchants, bankers and industrial guild and company craftsmen that associated with the older landed aristocracy and moneyed interests. He met at the Bull and Mouth Inn or Vernon's Coffee House with major mining entrepreneurs, colonial land owners and financiers of colonial properties, including William Penn, Richard Matthews, John Freame, Thomas Gould, the Barclays and Lloyds of London; and when they journeyed to England, Haddon conducted business with Thomas Story, Isaac Norris and other visiting Philadelphia merchant entrepreneurs.

The mining industry became Haddon's main enterprise at the turn of the eighteenth century. He held a major share with Quakers Richard Matthews, Thomas Cooper, Samuel Davies and Dr. Edward Wright in the Royal Mines Copper and Ryton Company. Between 1700 and 1704, when the first Lord of the Treasury allowed Quakers to substitute an affirmation for the shunned loyalty oath to Crown and Church of England in order to become officials in joint stock companies and corporations, John Haddon became active as a member of the Committee of Ten and then Court of Assistants in management of the mining company. In 1704 Haddon, Wright and Cooper took the affirmation in lieu of oaths and became members of the General Court of the mining company, reorganized in 1705 as the London (or Quaker) Lead Company. This new Quaker-run firm obtained contracts to mint silver coins for the Royal Treasury, and Queen Anne gave Haddon's company a warrant in 1706 to officially stamp all silver refined from company mines with a crest of two roses and two feathers, indicating the Welsh and English roots of the company. Haddon directed the shipment of lead ore from Wales to Bristol and London. Meanwhile, he worked with Dr. Wright to perfect a new more efficient smelting process, obtaining the patent for an innovative German reverberatory furnace to separate silver from ore. Haddon traveled extensively with Wright, Enoch Floyd and Peter de Launoy to visit mines in Wales, often walking miles when company coaches broke their axles and traveling by foot over nearly impassable mountain roads to the widely scattered mines.[22]

When not traveling, Elizabeth's father conducted mining business, settling accounts and recording shares as the clerk for the managing committee of the Mining Company's General Court. Freame and Gould lent the company £500 at six percent interest to invest in overseas trading enterprise and discounted bills of exchange. Such expanded company business brought long hours of meetings for Haddon at Jonathan's Coffee House, White Lion Tavern and most often at Vernon's Coffee House in Bartholomew Lane near the Royal Exchange in London. Haddon held twenty shares of mining stock, valued at £50 per share. Only financial giant Richard Matthews with 100 shares and Dr. Edward Wright with thirty-six shares held more company stock. In the end Haddon earned substantial stock dividends and gratuities for his work.[23]

With his leadership of the Quaker Lead Company, Haddon began to guide it toward acquisition of land in the New World particularly for the mining rights. In May of 1707 he asked the board of directors to investigate the financial state of the Pennsylvania Land Company of London. The Quaker Lead Company directors found that though primary owner William Penn was in deep financial trouble that led to debtor's prison, the Land Company itself appeared clear from debt in both Pennsylvania and Britain. It promised a sound investment. The London Lead Company purchased a majority share of land company stock and though retaining separate boards of directors merged with the Pennsylvania Land Company. The new joint stock company promptly purchased 60,000 acres of Pennsylvania land from the William Penn family. John Freame, a goldsmith and founder of the Quaker bank of London, backed the enterprise. London (Quaker) Lead Company directors Haddon, Wright, Davis, Cooper and Floyd sat on the new company's board of directors. This transaction brought Haddon into personal contact with William Penn.[24]

Now in 1708, struggling to get out of debt and stay out of prison, Penn expressed concern not only in selling land to the Lead Company, but in developing mines on his Pennsylvania land in conjunction with Haddon and Wright. Penn's interest in mining peaked when Isaac Norris brought the absentee proprietor in London an ore sample from Pennsylvania. Norris was one of Penn's closest confidants. He had come to Philadelphia from Jamaica in 1690 after his parents had died in the Port

Royal earthquake. Soon, Isaac Norris became one of the wealthiest Philadelphia merchants, particularly in the West Indies and African trade and purchased a great tract of land from Penn (around present-day Norristown). Norris had rushed to England to help get his proprietor and friend William Penn out of prison and in the process brought samples of Pennsylvania iron ore mined from Penn's properties that promised great profit from American mining enterprises.

Penn asked Dr. Edward Wright and John Haddon to evaluate this material. Wright simply agreed to work with Penn on the importation of ore for refining to extract silver in his English smelting furnaces. Haddon proved more forthright, noting that the American ore lacked the quality of that produced in the Welsh mines. "The Black sand mined that came with Is. Norris in the leather Bag proved no better than Iron as a notable [s]melter tells me, Jon Haddon, whose Daughter," Penn mistakenly explained to James Logan, "is married to old Anthony Sharp's son in Jersey."[25] Of course, Elizabeth was married to John Estaugh, not to Sharp's nephew and her land surveyor Thomas Sharp. Indeed, Dr. Griffith Owen had informed Penn several years before that Estaugh planned to marry Haddon's daughter. But Penn now had other things on his mind.

Penn ignored Haddon's advice and still hoped to profit from his Pennsylvania mines. Mired in debt and facing lawsuits against his proprietary and governmental rights brought by the Board of Trade, former business associates and purchasers of his lands. Penn searched for any way possible to escape financial ruin and imprisonment. He begged Logan to ship some of his ore to Dr. Wright's smelting furnace. "Pray," Penn wrote his agent in Philadelphia, "send us some Barrels of it, w[hich] may be better, & perhaps more expeditiously separated here than there, w[hich] would be a good and cheaper as well as better Cargo than any other you can raise."[26] Penn's loyal retainer James Logan, who was developing iron forges in Bucks County, wanted to help but warned his proprietor that they confronted too many problems to risk entering the mining business with the Quaker Lead and Pennsylvania Land companies. For one thing shipping between Pennsylvania and England had become too risky with the War of the Spanish Succession (1701–1714) spreading to American waters as Queen Anne's War (1702–1714). Heavily armed French privateers seized dozens of ships sailing off the Delaware Capes each month.

Another problem for Penn stemmed from the suspicious activities of Swiss mining expert Francois Luis Michel who had been hired by Penn and Logan to find ore deposits in Pennsylvania. Reportedly, Michel failed to locate sites for mines on Penn's properties in the Susquehanna Valley. Logan believed that Michel refused to reveal the sites of the mineral deposits because he had gone off to England to negotiate directly with the Crown for purchase of Penn's claims. Such a deal would deprive Penn of any profit from New World mining enterprises. Logan suspected that Michel also colluded with Pennsylvania Governor John Evans and investors from the neighboring Maryland and Virginia colonies who continually disputed ownership of their borders with Pennsylvania in order to squeeze Penn out of the mining lands. Penn ordered Logan to examine if his mines had "not been worked, embezzled, by and for persons of other colonies."[27] Logan concluded in early 1709 that Michel "has tricked us all" into believing that no mines had been discovered and that only the Shawnee Native Americans lived on the alleged mining lands.[28]

Most likely Penn had given up on the mining project by 1709 and no longer consulted with Wright or Haddon. Haddon was too busy to worry about Penn. He was involved in increasingly complex business dealings. All his intricate industrial and real estate operations took Haddon away from his Southwark home for weeks at a time. Indeed when Elizabeth arrived in London, her father was off to Scotland, Ireland, the Isle of Man and Orkney Islands to investigate mining lands. Nevertheless, Elizabeth, her husband and her father, whenever they all gathered together in London, continued to review the family's business affairs, particularly Haddon's expanding real estate empire in the New World. During this visit Haddon connected John Estaugh firmly to his mining business, selling him in 1710 "five shares in a company for melting down lead with pit-coal and sea-coal."[29] As the Estaughs became more deeply immersed in John Haddon's business affairs, they began to encounter flawed titles and other disputes surrounding earlier land acquisitions that would have to be presented to proprietary officials at the Burlington and Philadelphia surveyor's offices and county courts when they returned to America.

Finally, John and Elizabeth Estaugh requested a certificate of removal to Pennsylvania from the Horsleydown and London Meetings. They arrived back in West New Jersey in 1712, whereupon the Newton Monthly Meeting immediately appointed John an overseer of the meeting where he joined six other elders. Elizabeth returned to her service as recorder of the minutes for the Newton Women's Meeting, attesting to her complete unity with the women of her Quaker community. The big news for the Estaughs, though, came from the progress on construction their fine Jersey brick house that Quaker carpenters and brick layers had constructed for John and Elizabeth. The large new plantation house would serve as the cherished public and private space for the rest of the Estaughs' lives. It also became the center for the building of the Quaker community of Haddonfield, New Jersey.

CHAPTER 6 NOTES.

[1] Power of Attorney, John Haddon to John and Elizabeth Estaugh, September 7, 1705, recorded May 19, 1707, copy in Gloucester County Historical Society, Woodbury, NJ, and in box 1, Lyons Project Papers, HSHL.

[2] William Penn to James Logan, September 14 and 21, 1705, *Correspondence between William Penn and James Logan*, 2 vols. (Philadelphia: J. B. Lippincott, 1872), II: 73–75.

[3] Freeborn-Palmer Diaries, *Journal of Friends Historical Society*, v. 6, no. 1 (London, 1909), 39.

[4] John Estaugh's Certificate of Removal 1704, in box 1, Lyons Project Papers, HSHL.

[5] James Logan to William Penn, July 14, 1704, *Penn Papers*, IV: 291; Logan to Penn, February 5, 1705, *Logan-Penn Correspondence*, II: 1.

[6] Clement, *First Emigrant Settlers*, 167–79

[7] Mary Lawson and James Estaugh's certificates of removal, in Myers, *Quaker Arrivals*, 27–28, 38. For Lawson's importance as a traveling woman minister, see Larson, *Daughters of Light*, 4, 9, 116–18.

[8] For roads and creeks, see Dennis G. Raible, *Down a Country Lane* (Camden,NJ.: Camden Country Historical Society, 1999).

[9] Logan to Penn, October 2, 1702, *Penn Papers,* IV: 190.

[10] James Estaugh-Mary Lawson Marriage Certificate, January 19, 1707, Monthly Meeting of Friends of Philadelphia, Book 284B: 55, Quaker Collection, Haverford College Library, copy in box 1, Lyons Project Papers, HSHL. Also, see Rebecca Larson, *Daughters of Light*.

[11] See "The Quaker Home as Private and Public Space," in Stoneburner, *Influence of Quaker Women*, 22.

[12] Map for John Haddon made by Richard Bull, containing 650 acres on banks of Oldman's Creek, 1704. HEHP, folder 58; Resurvey for John Estaugh, in right of John Haddon, north side of Oldman's Creek, 1,000 acres, 1708. HEHP, folder 62.

[13] Power of Attorney, John Haddon to John and Elizabeth Estaugh, September 7, 1705, recorded May 19, 1707, copy in Gloucester County Historical Society, Woodbury, NJ, and in box 1, Lyons Project Papers, HSHL.

[14] Survey, copy made for John Haddon, for 2400 acres adjoining John Hugg's land, 1705. HEHP, folder 59.

[15] Articles of Agreement between Nathaniel Purkle [Puckle], Mariner. Purckle (Puckle), Mariner, and John Haddon, Blacksmith, 1702. HEHP, folder 23, and in box 1, Lyons Project Papers, HSHL; William Higgs will, May 3, 1709, *New Jersey Archives*, 1st ser., vol. XXIII:228.

[16] Power of Attorney, John Estaugh to Thomas Sharpe and Joseph Kay 1708. HEHP, folder 125.

[17] Monthly Meeting held at Newton in Province of New Jersey, February 12, 1707 to the Monthly Meetings of Friends in London, Friends Reference Library, file 12, Quaker Collection, Haverford College Library, copy, in box 1, Lyons Project Papers, HSHL.

[18] Certificate from meeting of ministering friends to John Estaugh, June 5, 1708, copy, in box 1, Lyons Project Papers, HSHL.

[19] Southwark Records. Marriages: August 29, 1706; Births: December 1, 1707.

[20] Sarah (Haddon) and Benjamin Hopkins children: Elizabeth I (1707–1711), Mary (1709–1786), Sarah (1710–1759), unnamed? (1711–1711), Elizabeth II (1712–1764), Haddon I (1713–1714), Haddon II (1715–1757), Benjamin (1716–1719), Ebenezer (1718–1757), Hannah I (1719–1719), twins John and Benjamin II (1721–1721), Hannah II (1722–1728), "The Family of Benjamin Hopkins," http://home.comcast.net/~adhopkins/benjamin.htm (accessed 23 August 2013).

[21] Monthly Meeting held at Newton to thy Monthly Meetings of Friends in London, certificate of clearance for "our Well beloved Friend John Estaugh," July 13, 1710, Quaker Collection, Haverford College Library, copy, in box 1, Lyons Project Papers, HSHL.

[22] General Court Minutes, The Society of Royal Mines Copper and the Ryton Company, 1695–1704, Library of the North of England Institute of Mining Engineers, Newcastle-on-Tyne; also, see Raistrick, *Quakers in Science*.

[23] General Court Minutes, 1702; also, see Margaret Ackrill and Leslie Hannah, *Barclays: The Business of Banking 1690–1996* (Cambridge: Cambridge University Press, 2001), 11.

[24] There was no evidence that John Haddon and Penn met earlier, and not as the Lydia Child story goes, when Elizabeth sat on Penn's knee at the Haddon house, playing with the straw doll of an Indian princess.

[25] William Penn to James Logan, May 3, 1708, *Penn Papers*, IV: 600–601.

[26] Penn to Logan, May 3, 1708, *Penn Papers*, IV: 600.

[27] Penn to Logan, Sept 29, 1708, February 3 and March 3, 1709, *Penn-Logan Correspondence*, II: 295, 315, 319.

[28] *Penn Papers*, IV: 602n.38.

[29] Receipt signed by Edward Wright, Treasurer, to John Estaugh, for payment for five shares in a company for melting down lead with pit-coal and sea-coal, 1710. HEHP, folder 138.

CHAPTER 7.
"Most Dear Children ...
We Cannot Come to You," 1713–1719.

I am glad you have lett the Plantation to make your Selves Easy—I am Persuaded that Country is the Place god has apointed your Services in and that If Nothing Else will do we must be Removed to make way for itt—So I would have my dear Child to give Due weight to the Consideration of these things in the meekness of the Everlasting truth of our God—you are amongst our Kindred in the faith of Christ Jesus though wee are Separate in Body wee are near Each other in Spirritt and can truely Rejoyce in heareing of Each others Prosperity.[quoted as written]
—John and Elizabeth Clarke Haddon[1]

Sometime before leaving for England, Elizabeth and John Estaugh had contracted with several leading Quaker carpenters and bricklayers from Philadelphia and West New Jersey to build a grand plantation house. The Estaughs envisioned that this large structure would house Elizabeth's parents, her sister Sarah Hopkins and her family, as well as serve as a retreat for the many Quaker traveling ministers passing through the Delaware Valley. Probably the elderly Francis Collins, a master carpenter and mason, designed the mansion. He was the region's leading builder, with the great hexagonal Burlington Monthly Meeting House and the County Court House among his architectural legacies. Moreover, Collins had been close to the Haddon family for many years, witnessing Elizabeth's marriage and constantly supporting the Estaughs in meeting and business. On their part, Elizabeth and John Estaugh witnessed the marriages of Francis Collins's daughter Elizabeth to Josiah Southwick at Joseph Collins's Mountwell plantation house. Sarah Collins (who married Dr. Robert Dimsdale, a prominent Burlington County landowner and London physician) became Elizabeth Estaugh's lifelong friend and personal companion both in West New Jersey and on trips to London, where both women conducted family business.[2]

However, Francis Collins had grown too old to work on this new Haddon-Estaugh house and probably contracted his grandson Benjamin Collins, a young carpenter, and other apprentices to construct the frame. Receipts for work on the new plantation house indicate that Philadelphia master carpenter and building supplier Nathan Stanbury participated in construction. Stanbury and his wife Mary had attended the Haddon-Estaugh marriage in 1702, the Estaugh-Lawson marriage in 1706 and remained close to John and Elizabeth. William Matlack, who purchased 200 acres from Haddon in the late 1690s and moved from Philadelphia to West New Jersey, seems the most likely builder of the Haddon-Estaugh plantation house. Matlack worked closely with local brick makers Isaac Kay, Joshua Evans and Jonah Scroggins. These local craftsmen extracted yellow clay from pits dug in front of the Estaugh house during construction and molded the yellow clay into bricks used to finish the structure. "The House was brick, rough-cast and yellow," a last resident of the original Haddon-Estaugh plantation Rebecca Reeve recalled, "the Kitchen part also brick and rough-cast."[3]

Though the original Estaugh plantation house burned down in 1842, three sources help us to reconstruct the original house and surrounding grounds. John Evans Redman, noted Philadelphia illustrator and collateral descendant of the Haddon-Estaugh-Hopkins family, painted a watercolor of the house as he remembered it appearing in the early 1830's, standing just 100 yards north of the Ferry Road (present day Haddon Avenue). Later, Rebecca C. W. Reeve, daughter of Elizabeth Cooper and Isaac Wood, the last residents of the house before it burned down, shared her memories of the place with noted Haddonfield historian Samuel Nicholson Rhoads, a distant collateral descendant of Elizabeth Estaugh. Rebecca Wood Reeve had lived in the house for eight years before the fire, and though her conversation with Rhoads occurred more than fifty years after the event, her recollection of the place remained clear. It allowed her to draw a detailed sketch of the interior of the Haddon-Estaugh house. The inventory of Elizabeth Haddon Estaugh's 1762 will also provided detailed evidence of the estate. It recorded much of the plantation house's interior fixtures, furnishings and outer buildings.[4]

These sources show a spacious two-and-one-half story yellow brick house attached to a two story structure. The smaller house, also yellow brick, built after Elizabeth's arrival in 1701, most likely housed John Haddon's estate manager Simon Breach. The older section was a square, four-room house with low ceilings and no basement. In contrast, the new house attached to it had

John Evans Redman's original 1830s painting of "New Haddonfield" house before its fiery destruction in 1842. *Courtesy of Judith Clement Hensel and Diane Clement Jondahl*

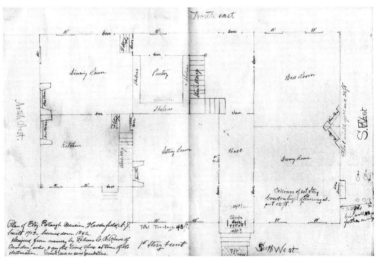

Floor Plan of the first floor of New Haddonfield done by Rebecca C. W. Reeve who was eight years old and lived in the house when it burned in 1842. *Rhoads Collection, Historical Society of Haddonfield*

twelve-foot-high ceilings, large rooms and a deep stone basement. The Redman painting and the Reeve drawings and descriptions revealed a house less majestic than the stately residences of the Philadelphia Quaker elite like Pennsbury Manor, yet more elaborate than any of the neighboring West New Jersey plantation houses. One entered the Haddon-Estaugh house through a magnificent covered porch and main hallway leading to a parlor, Elizabeth's sitting room and library where over the years the Estaugh's assembled a great collection of Quaker books. The Haddon-Estaugh library featured a rare eighteen-pound *Treacle Bible* published in 1566, bound in English oak and leather and embellished with Elizabethan-era religious wood cuts. Most copies of this Bible published during the reign of Elizabeth I had been destroyed by her vindictive Stuart successor Charles I after the Tudor Queen Elizabeth's death in 1603. Elizabeth Haddon's father probably purchased the *Bible* secretly and sent it with his daughter to the New World on one of her voyages. The *Treacle Bible* would comfort John and Elizabeth Estaugh and their many guests over the years with daily reading of the scriptures.[5]

Elizabeth's parents shipped many other books to their daughter and son-in-law for their new library that in some ways provided a West New Jersey version of James Logan's famous Philadelphia Quaker library. Books shipped to America by John Haddon included the most important turn-of-the-century works on Quaker doctrine and history by Robert Barclay, William Penn, Joseph Pike and William Sewell. Barclay's *Truth Triumphant*, published in 1692, and An *Apology for the True Christian Divinity*, published in 1710, contained what most Friends considered the definitive testimony of Quaker belief. William Sewell's English translation of his popular Dutch-language work *A History of the People Called Quakers,* published in 1662, provided the basic reference history for the founding of the Religious Society of Friends for the Estaughs and their many visitors. The Haddons also sent Thomas Ellwood's book *Sacred History: or, the historical part of the holy scriptures of the New Testament* in two volumes and Joseph Pike's *A Treatise Concerning Baptism,* published in 1710. Haddon wrote that these books "will be good Company for you." Perhaps the most significant addition to the Estaugh library came from Richard Claridge's controversial epistle *The novelty and nullity of dissatisfaction: Or, The Solemn Affirmation Defended.* Claridge's study would assist John Estaugh, twelve years later when he presented a testimony of appreciation from Philadelphia Yearly Meeting to King George I for acceptance of the affirmation. During this meeting the West New Jersey traveling minister and other Quaker leaders would thank the monarch for accepting the solemn affirmation that Quakers might use, rather than the hated oath of loyalty to church and state, in order to conduct all legal affairs in Britain and the colonies.[6]

The Estaughs' library also held William Salmon's *Botanologia; or the English Herbal or History of Plants,* published in 1710. One of the most successful "Professors of Physick" in post-Restoration London, Salmon revealed in his treatise on herbs and plants, the medicinal value of the New World tomato heretofore considered a poisonous plant.[7] John and Elizabeth, thus, knew that the tomato was edible, 100 years before Colonel Robert Gibbon Johnson was said to have eaten a tomato in front of a horrified

Salem County, New Jersey crowd to prove that the tomato was safe to grow and eat.[8]

Over the years, John and Elizabeth used their extensive medical library, practical experience with the plants and herbs that grew around them and had a household pharmacy stored in the great "Doctors Cupboard"[9] to treat the sick and suffering in their neighborhood. The cupboard contained not only local remedies but highly alcoholic (90 proof) bitter drops. Her father sent bottles of these bitters and other medicines to his daughter from London. "I have shipped you two hundred Bottles of Bitter Drops instead of fifty and also sent John Kaighn['] s things," John Haddon wrote his "Dear Children" from London.[10] It was unclear what Haddon wanted his children to do with such a large shipment of drugs. As someone who marveled at the 1715 eclipse, perhaps Elizabeth's father expected his daughter, her husband John or their close friend John Kaighin (Kaighn), who studied the "astrological practice of physick" with Dr. Christopher Witt, to use them medicinally.[11] More likely, though, Haddon knew that the Estaughs would employ the alcoholic spirits to treat their own medical needs as well as others in the community.

The library of spiritual, business and medical books adjoined a sitting room, parlor and study that formed John and Elizabeth's public space for religious meetings and business dealings. The Estaughs clearly modeled their new house after the teachings of Margaret Fell Fox, founder of the Women's Meeting of the Religious Society of Friends, who believed that a Quaker home must serve as both public and private sanctuaries shared equally by men and women. The public rooms in the Haddon-Estaugh house featured not only the great Elizabethan-era *Bible* and more recent Quaker religious tracts but held writing desks, ledger books, money scales, weights and hammers to measure coins and gold used in their many transactions. While public space dominated the Estaughs' life, they had a very private space in their plantation house as well. These more private rooms held Queen-Anne furniture, a marble-top claw foot parlor table, mirrors, vases and tall-case clocks much of the furnishings shipped from England by Elizabeth's parents. Elizabeth's father expended sizable sums to furnish his New Haddonfield plantation house. He paid over £24 in custom house duties, freight charges and other costs to ship furniture on the Mary Hope, John Annis, master. This shipment included thirteen chairs, two looking glasses, one walnut desk, chest of drawers, earthenware, drinking glasses, sewing silk and quilts.[12]

Biblical scenes of Delft figures, possibly crafted by the Daniel Coxe pottery in Burlington, decorated the great fireplaces located at each end of the mansion. The ground floor contained, in addition to the sitting room, library and parlor, a downstairs bedroom and dining room. Servants entered the large kitchen, slightly detached from the dining room to prevent fire in the main house, through a back door. Traveling ministers and other Friends who spent the night at the Estaugh's climbed to the second floor by a great center staircase that emptied onto a landing that led down a hallway with two large bedrooms on either side. These bedrooms featured great feather beds, night tables and "sundry bedpans."[13]

All the many visitors to the Haddon-Estaugh plantation house found a beautiful walled herb and flower garden that extended on the north and east side of the West New Jersey plantation house. A wooden fence and gate secured the front yard. A partly bricked walkway and dirt lane extended from the front gate directly to the Ferry Road (present-day Haddon Avenue). Some accounts had this lane ending at the corner of the Tanner's Road (Tanner Street) and the King's Highway. Either way, the lane gave Elizabeth direct access to the emerging Quaker village and later to the Meeting House nearby.

Native plants, trees and herbs as well as some English yews and other plants provided over the years by John Haddon's Southwark friend Peter Collinson, a merchant of hats and woolens and an amateur botanist, filled the gardens surrounding the Haddon-Estaugh plantation. On his travels to America, Collinson brought seeds and plants for the gardens of John Bartram and other Philadelphia botanists (and to Benjamin Franklin). Collinson also supplied plants, trees and seed for Elizabeth and John Estaugh. It helped that John Estaugh served as Collinson's attorney in America to collect money owed the London plant merchant. The intimacy of Collinson and the Haddon family can be seen by the fact that he would be buried in Long Lane Quaker cemetery in a grave next to Elizabeth's parents John and Elizabeth Clarke Haddon and near that of the Quaker essayist and sea captain Thomas Lurting.[14]

The Haddon-Estaugh plantation not only became a comfortable meeting place and retreat for the Delaware Valley Quaker community, but soon became an active and profitable farm. It provided the wealth for the Estaughs, bringing assurance to their parents who prayed that their children might "live most comfortably." The profitable enterprise also sustained the traveling minister John Estaugh on his many journeys to spread the Truth. A small outbuilding contained two stills, which produced spirits. Commonly referred to as the "brew house," it is the only surviving structure of the original Haddon-Estaugh plantation.[15] The farm also produced hard cider and wine, some of which was exported to Elizabeth's father and possibly to her brother-in-law Benjamin Hopkins, a noted vintner back in London. The plantation had numerous farm buildings including stables and a carriage house for Elizabeth's four-wheel "chaise." There also was

John and Elizabeth Estaugh's "Brew House," the last remaining building on the site of "New Haddonfield." Originally built as a one-story building, addition of the second floor occurred after the main house burned in 1842.
Rhoads Collection, Historical Society of Haddonfield

a large outhouse, a smoke house, and a blacksmith forge containing "bellows, shovels, tongs [and] Smith's Tools." Orchards, corn fields and pastures for horses, cattle and hogs surrounded the plantation house. Thomas Sharp's earmark for; "John Haddon: Both ears crop'd and slitt [sic] and Thomas Sharp[']s mark to be void" branded the Haddon-Estaugh plantation's livestock.[16] Elizabeth dedicated much of her time to managing her great estate while her husband was away on frequent business and missionary trips. She kept plantation business records, purchases and sales. She employed local gardeners, farm hands and African slaves, including Primus Marsh (the only Estaugh slave whose name is known), to help work the farm, gardens, smoke house and brew house associated with the main house. The house servants most likely lived in the old Breach residence attached to the main house, while slaves and indentured laborers probably stayed in small out buildings nearby. Indentured servant Sibill (Sybil) Grimes, though, probably stayed in the plantation house. Elizabeth's father sent Sibill over to West New Jersey in 1713 (from the Horsleydown Monthly Meeting) to be Elizabeth's maid. Haddon assured his daughter that he had paid her passage and provided her with "a pretty good bed & bolster and Rug and Blankett [sic]" for her own room.[17]

A letter from John and Elizabeth Haddon to his "Most Dear Children"—Elizabeth and John Estaugh—dated October 15, 1713, brought the devasting news that the Haddons would not be leaving London and joining the Estaughs in America. John Haddon's letter recognizes that the news would bring them great sorrow and also recognizes that the newly completed mansion was designed to accommodate the entire extended family. "Wee wrote you by Thomas Emblin in the Petter brow [a letter that evidently did not arrive in America], an account that wee Cannot Come to you to Enjoy your company, nor the other felicityes wee Promised our Selves, but however wee are Resigned to the will of God in Enjoying and hope you are also, Especially Considering your Sorrow will be of all one in Enjoying what Provisions were made for us . . . . Now Dear Children you know how wee have Straighted our Selves in Drawing our Effects to that Side, wee desire you to sell Land to make your Selves Easy, and furnish your Selves with such things as you want for wee now grow old and must take care to goe through that little Space wee have to stay heare [in London] honourably & comfortable, the house and the orchard and Whatsoever you desire is yours, and hope you will be made Comfortable . . . [quoted as written]"[18] Apparently John Haddon's health played a major role in the decision to remain in England. He wrote that "Dorcas Shelton [who] Lived with us till Shee came over [to America] She Can give you an account how my humer [health] was, it is not now Soe bad butt am advised the Sea would Kill mee, to Say noe more of the other Difficultyes that attend us.[quoted as written]"[19]

Elizabeth's sister and brother-in-law, Sarah and Benjamin Hopkins, also did not come to West New Jersey in 1713 to live in the new mansion house. It is quite possible that Elizabeth's parents did not come in large part because the Hopkins deciding to stay in London. That Elizabeth had lingering disappointment and perhaps even bitter feelings is evident in a 1714 letter from her father. John reports that Sarah and Benjamin Hopkins

Letter from John and Elizabeth Clarke Haddon in London to John and Elizabeth Estaugh in Haddonfield dated 1713 in which Elizabeth's parents tell them that they cannot come to West New Jersey as they had all originally planned. *Collection 1001, Quaker Collection, Haverford College, Haverford PA.*

"are well, and remember their love to you. I desire you not to leave him [Benjamin] out of yours. Do not place our not coming to his [Benjamin's] door . . . say, 'the Lord hat done it,' for what He only knows, who is the only wise disposer of all things."[20]

John and Elizabeth Estaugh set out immediately to sell additional tracts and lots of Haddon land. John joined Newton Township surveyor and close family friend Thomas Sharp in carefully defining the boundaries of his father-in-law's original purchases from Richard Matthews and Thomas Willis (known later as the "Old Haddonfield" tract). Elizabeth's cousin John Gill, most likely assisted them. In the first transaction made July 26, 1714, Estaugh sold Gill part of the large former Willis tract (sold to Haddon in 1698) and "already surveyed and laid forth" and adjacent to that of Joseph Cooper and Joseph Bates. Gill had leased this property since his arrival in West New Jersey, and now received title to the 260-acre tract for £65 "of Lawfull [sic] Mon[e]y of America."[21]

Haddon wanted "his dear Children" to sell off even more property for a larger profit, both to make his daughter and her husband comfortable and to get out of his own growing debt in England. So, the Estaughs sold tracts of Haddon's Waterford Township land to Samuel Cole, Samuel Burrough and John Roberts. They paid Estaugh (for John Haddon) the sizeable sum of £75 for each of these real estate transactions. Next, Estaugh surveyed and sold 1,288 acres of land to his neighbors Joseph Collins and John, George and William Matlack. Estaugh established the boundaries for another 2,000 acres of Haddon land along Oldman's Creek in Salem County. He also bought land, purchasing a 2,000 acre tract in 1716 above the Falls of the Delaware River in Old Hunterdon County, New Jersey. At the same time, Estaugh purchased 1,020 acres of lands probably in Burlington County from Dr. Daniel Coxe, who had obtained the Byllynge proprietorship in 1687 and had served until 1692 as the absentee governor of West New Jersey. Estaugh began to sell off portions of this land to some of his neighbors. John Haddon also expected the Estaughs to offer for sale the land held in America by his wife's brother John Clarke. This tract as with most early surveyed properties in West New Jersey involved conflicting claims. In 1716, Sharp finally resurveyed and thus secured legal title to this new property for Estaugh. The survey showed that Haddon's land (that actually overlapped that purchased by Estaugh from Coxe) extended from the southerly branch of Cropwell (Pennsauken) Creek to Joseph Cooper's land along Cooper's Creek. The neighboring lands of Friends Samuel Cole, William Ellis, Thomas Shackle and Samuel Burrough formed the boundaries of the new purchase.[22]

All this real estate activity disturbed Estaugh. Some of the titles and boundaries for the Haddon land in West New Jersey remained uncertain. Haddon's original deed

(1698) with Richard Matthews for West New Jersey property conflicted with that of the late Henry Stacy family's claim that they held the original deed (1684) to the lands that Haddon now owned. The Stacy family insisted that it owned: "One half part of the said one full, equal and undivided third part of the said one full equal and undivided ninetieth part and being one ninetieth part of the aforesaid equal and undivided hundredth part of the said tract of land called New Jersey." John Haddon instructed Estaugh to clear this convoluted original land grant and the Matthews title with the deed that "[I] sent you being the original deed, you may depend on it, he never sold it to none but my self [sic]."[23]

Estaugh confronted even more difficult problems in the management of John Haddon's share of the Pennsylvania Land Company of London's real estate empire in America. Not only had Elizabeth and John Estaugh served as personal real estate agents for John Haddon's West Jersey properties, but his son-in-law also operated as the American attorney and land agent for the Pennsylvania Land Company. Land Company directors (that included Haddon) sent Estaugh elaborate instructions in 1714 on how to do his job of surveying, selling and recording all legal documents for the British corporation's American real estate business. The directors particularly wanted Estaugh to settle the much disputed ownership of the late Richard Noble's plantation in Bucks County, Pennsylvania. The great London real estate firm put its deed to the Noble property in the custody of "Thy Father Haddon" in Estaugh's name and prepared to send the document to America. The Pennsylvania Land Company's council of managers warned Estaugh to collect only "good bill of exchange or money" when selling property "for it often happens American bills prove bad." Estaugh's employer urged him to move quickly in the settling of land deals because the end of the War of the Spanish Succession in 1714 promised to bring many families "flocking over to the New World" in search of land.[24]

While Estaugh hurried to conclude deals for Haddon and the Land Company, he received yet another assignment. James Logan employed Estaugh to survey, sell, collect back rent and monies owed William Penn from purchasers of his land (not owned by the Land Company), and including that purchased long ago by original buyers. Logan also wanted Estaugh to help him locate mining lands. This brought Estaugh into intimate contact with wealthy Quaker landowners Nicholas Waln, Isaac Norris, Thomas Story, trustees of the Thomas Fairman property, creditors of the Noble estates and other investors who owed Penn money. At the same time, Logan expected Estaugh to remove squatters from Penn's proprietary lands. All these tasks meant that Estaugh had to frequently leave his wife Elizabeth back in West New Jersey, cross the Delaware River and travel by horseback or on foot into the largely uncharted Pennsylvania wilderness. Here Estaugh directed surveying, collected rent from tenants and probably evicted squatters from William Penn's Indian treaty lands.[25]

Traveling in the Pennsylvania frontier proved particularly uncomfortable for Estaugh not because of the surveying business, but because he greatly feared the rattlesnakes that hid in the thick underbrush of the wilderness forest lands through which he had to travel. These were probably the snakes studied by his plant merchant

Peter Collinson.[26] Apparently, Estaugh saw the "serpent" as a Biblical symbol of the devil that "hath beguiled some Innocent Ones." Moreover, such dangerous work took him away from what he saw as his true calling as a traveling Quaker minister. Estaugh worried that pursuing profit threatened to extinguish his Inner Light and plunge him into Darkness. "A man cannot serve two Masters, as said our blessed Lord; for either he will hate the one and love the other," Estaugh wrote, "or else, he will hold the one, and despise the other." The traveling minister and busy land agent concluded that; "We cannot serve God and Mammon."[27]

Estaugh continued to attend two masters, both in the meeting house and the counting house. However, he sought assistance in the secular sphere. Estaugh employed Isaac Taylor, deputy surveyor of Chester County, Pennsylvania to survey tracts for Irish Quaker buyers of the New Garden subdivision of London Grove. Taylor surveyed for Estaugh the former Penn property along the Mill and Conestoga Creeks in the Susquehanna River Valley sold to Mennonite purchasers by the Pennsylvania Land Company. This land that in 1729 became part of Lancaster County, Pennsylvania formed a portion of the 60,000 acres that the company had acquired from William Penn. Taylor could not survey all this land, so John Estaugh hired his brother James, then a Philadelphia wheelwright, to assist him in surveying and dividing into lots these vast tracts of land. James Estaugh concentrated on resurveying the 2,000-acre Rocklands Tract in Pennsylvania for his brother.[28]

In the end, John Estaugh bore most of the burden for conducting business for James Logan and the Pennsylvania Land Company. It forced him to travel alone. Estaugh often disappeared into the thick forests of the Pennsylvania frontier inhabited by many sometimes hostile Native Americans and unpleasant European squatters. No one heard from him for weeks, and rumors circulated in England that Estaugh had died in the wild New World forest lands. We heard a "report we had about town," Elizabeth Estaugh's parents wrote from London, "that Dear John was dead." Elizabeth assured her parents that her husband was very much alive. John and Elizabeth Haddon responded with "unexpressable joy" for the news of Estaugh's survival. The Haddons also expressed relief in the same letter, that since their son-in-law was alive, he could continue the land business for them. They urged their children "to sell as much as we can or all and as soon as may be" possible. To facilitate business, Elizabeth's parents dispatched a new letter that strengthened Estaugh's power-of-attorney. John Haddon praised his "most Endeared" children for contributing to his recent business successes in Pennsylvania real estate that led to a twenty-five shilling per share dividend that greatly pleased the Land Company's directors and not incidentally began to get Haddon out of debt.[29]

But this was not enough. Driven by the need for cash, John Haddon suggested that while working in the Pennsylvania woodlands, Estaugh ought to join James Logan and other Quaker merchants in the lucrative fur trade. The London blacksmith, businessman and real estate entrepreneur claimed that good deer hides and bear skins would bring a profit in the London market. The Haddons also wanted Elizabeth to contribute to their growing American business ventures. She shipped some agriculture products from the West Jersey plantation to England. John Haddon wrote in 1717 that the "ap[p]les and Wine did well [but] the cranburyes [cranberries] would not Keep."[30]

It was clear that during the first years in her new house, Elizabeth quietly managed the plantation without much help from her husband who was constantly away doing Land Company business or traveling to comfort distant Friends. The farm prospered and the family wealth increased through the sales of family landholdings.

Throughout these years, Elizabeth still retained hopes that her parents would come to America. In 1714 John Haddon writes: "as to our nott comeing, I am more and more Satisfyed its for the better one [on] all hands"[31] and again in 1717, "as to our comeing cannot see it possible to be Ever accomplished.[quoted as written]"[32] The 1717 letter also indicates that Elizabeth considered leaving America and returning to England, at least through her parent's lifetime. John Haddon strongly urged Elizabeth to stay in West Jersey. "I am persuaded that Country is the Place god has apointed your Services in and that If Nothing Else will do we must be Removed to make way for itt—So I would have my dear Child to give Due weight to the Consideration of these things in the meekness of the Everlasting truth of our God—you are amongst our Kindred in the faith of Christ Jesus though wee are separate in body wee are near Each other in Spiritt and cann truely rejoyce in heareing of Each others Prosperity.[quoted as written]" However, if she decides to return to England, he notes that she "must gett [sic] the Land Company[']s business pretty well over."[33]

In the end, instead of the Haddons coming to America, Elizabeth would travel twice more to visit her parents in England and they maintained a frequent correspondence across the ocean. The Haddons regularly wrote to Elizabeth about of her sister's growing family, including the news that her nieces Mary and little Sarah could already read the *Bible*. More compelling, John and Elizabeth Haddon, now in their sixties, noted their declining health and that their time on earth was coming to an end.[34]

Elizabeth received a certificate of removal in August 1715 for travel to London. Her husband booked passage (probably as usual on the Philadelphia Quaker-owned merchant ship MARY HOPE, John Annis, master) for his wife Elizabeth and her best friend Sarah Collins Dimsdale. John Estaugh did not travel with them since the Newton Monthly Meeting minutes show that he witnessed, without Elizabeth, the marriages in April 1716 of Thomas Robinson and Sarah Low and in August that of Job Whitall to Jan Siddon. And while Elizabeth was in England, the Newton Meeting sent her husband to attend the Salem Quarterly Meeting and the Burlington Yearly Meeting in order to obtain unity throughout the Quaker community. Elizabeth stayed in England less than a year, returning in July 1716 with Sarah Dimsdale and Elizabeth's six-year-old niece Sarah Hopkins, a potential heir to the Haddon fortune in America. When she arrived back in her West New Jersey home, Elizabeth Estaugh resumed her place as clerk of the Women's Meeting of the Newton Monthly Meeting. "At a monthly meeting of women friends held at Newton, ye 9th day of ye 5th month 1716, our Friend E. Estaugh, being returned from England, ye meeting requests her to accept ye book again, which she complied."[35]

Soon after Elizabeth settled back into her old Gloucester County plantation house and Newton Friends Meeting, her husband sought clearance yet again from the Meeting to travel to the West Indies. The Meeting provided a certificate of removal in October 1716 for Estaugh to visit Friends on the islands of Antigua and Barbados. Estaugh transferred his power of attorney to his wife and prepared for his West Indies mission.[36] The following month, the local Meeting issued another certificate for travel to the Caribbean islands to Estaugh's next-door neighbor John Kay. It was not clear whether Kay actually traveled with Estaugh since the Barbados Friends Meeting certified only "their great unity with John Estaugh and his ministry."[37] Estaugh ventured into the Caribbean once again, despite an increase in piracy off the Jersey coast and in the Delaware Bay where heavily-armed corsairs plundered ships sailing out of Philadelphia nearly every week. He had already been seized in 1704 by privateers while on a missionary trip to the West Indies and thrown into prison on the French West Indies island of Martinco (Martinique). Estaugh's willingness to constantly sail on the increasingly dangerous seas attested to his lifetime commitment to spreading the Word of the Lord, wherever Quakers gathered. This time, though, Estaugh held other motivations to visit the islands, as well, and ignored his father-in-law's belated entreaty that he should delay his trip until "that time the Pirrates [sic] I hope will be subdued."[38]

John Estaugh had been involved for some time in the West Indies trade with Philadelphia merchant and traveling minister Thomas Chalkley, James Logan and other Quaker traders. In April 1716, John Haddon and the committee of directors of the Pennsylvania Land Company of London urged Estaugh to increase company business by selling wheat, flour and bread and "other Commodities" to its agents in Barbados, Jamaica and Antigua. Haddon took special interest in this business, writing his "dear children" in 1717, that "I hope to hear of the little venture from Antigua." At the same time, Elizabeth's father wrote his "Dear Children from London, that "Our ships from Guinea are not arrived so that can give no account of their Success." Guinea ships dealt in many commodities, including the African slave trade with the British West Indies and North American colonies. Since Quaker-owned merchantmen from Philadelphia sailed directly to the Guinea coast of Africa to pick up slaves in what some considered to be "by farr [sic] the most profitable trade," Haddon's brief mention of "our Guinea ships" indicated a possible involvement in the slave trade.[39] Also, Estaugh had close connections to business partners James Logan and Issac Norris, Philadelphia's most active Quaker slave traders.

John Estaugh's frequent absences left Elizabeth, as usual, to deal with spiritual and secular matters in Haddonfield. In fact, no sooner had John Estaugh returned from his 1717 trip to the West Indies than he sought yet another certificate of removal in May 1718 to visit Friends in Barbados. This seemed to be a voyage taken entirely to spread the Truth to suffering Friends since Barbados Quakers attested in June that John Estaugh had formed, during his six week's ministry, a great unity among Friends on the island. John Estaugh returned home to West New Jersey in time to join Elizabeth in witnessing the marriage of her cousin John Gill to Mary Heritage at the Chester, New Jersey, Monthly Meeting on August 23, 1718. However, Elizabeth appeared increasingly anxious to go back to England one more time to say goodbye to her parents. She had recently received a letter from them reporting that they had just buried her four-year-old nephew Benjamin Hopkins (I) in Long Lane burial ground. Father Haddon sighed that this death was such a great burden upon "your sister Sarah."[40] John and Elizabeth Clarke Haddon worried that they were not in the best of health and planned to draw up their wills. In response, Elizabeth Estaugh resolved to journey back to her familiar Rotherhithe neighborhood and Horsleydown Monthly Meeting to say goodbye to her beloved Haddon family.

CHAPTER 7 NOTES.

[1] John and Elizabeth Haddon to Dear Children, February 27, 1717. HEHP, folder 182.

[2] Power of Attorney from John and William Dimsdale (Chirurgions) to John Estaugh, 1722. HEHP, folder 134.

[3] Rebecca C. W. Reeve to Samuel N. Rhoads, February 11, 1908, in Rhoads, "Haddon Hall," 58–69, 65; also, see Stewart, *Notes on Old Gloucester County*, I: 299–300.

[4] Inventory of Elizabeth Haddon Estaugh's Goods and Chattel, attached to will, April 13, 1762, HEHP; Reeve to Rhoads, 11 February 1908, in Rhoads, "Haddon Hall;" copies of the Reeve floor plan of the Haddon-Estaugh plantation house in Haddonfield, in box 2, Lyons Project Papers, HSHL.

[5] Walter Irving Clarke, "Found—Elizabeth Haddon's Bible," *New Era Magazine*, vol. XXVI (November, 1920), 760–67, illustration, 762.

[6] John and Elizabeth Haddon to Most Entirely Beloved Children, September 17, 1714. HEHP, folder 181; Richard Claridge, *The novelty and nullity of dissatisfaction: Or, The Solemn Affirmation Defended, Against the Unwarrantable Attempts of a Nameless Author* (London: Philip Gwillim in Austin-Fryars, near the Royal Exhange, 1714); Thomas Ellwood, *Sacred history: or, the historical part of the holy scriptures of the New Testament; gathered out from the other part thereof, and Digested (as near as well could be) into due Method, with respect to order of Time and Place* (London: J. Sowle, in White-Hart-Court, in Gracious-Street, 1709).

[7] William Salmon, *Botanologia; or the English Herbal, or History of Plants* (London: I Dawks for H. Rhodes and J. Taylor, 1710).

[8] Historians today believe this story is legendary. See, Andrew F. Smith, "The Making of the Legend of Robert Gibbon Johnson and the Tomato,"*New Jersey History* (New Jersey Historical Society) vol. 108 (Fall/Winter 1990), 59–74.

[9] Inventory of the goods and chattels, rights and credits of Elizabeth Estaugh. HSHL, Manuscript collection, 1913-001-1642.

[10] John and Elizabeth Haddon to Dear Children, February 27, 1717. HEHP, folder 182.

[11] Copy of Kaighin's medical diploma, Biographical File, in box 3, Lyons Project Papers. Astrological medicine is an ancient medical system, which associates zodiac signs and planets with parts of the body, certains diseases and organs.

[12] John and Elizabeth Haddon to Most Entirely Beloved Children, September 17, 1714. HEHP, folder 181.

[13] See Inventory of Goods and Chattel, Elizabeth Estaugh Will, April 13, 1762, HSHL; "The Quaker Home as Private and Public Space," in Stoneburn-

er, *Influence of Quaker Women*, 22. Daniel Coxe had business relations with John Estaugh, see folders 33, 64 and 65, HEHP.

[14] Power of Attorney—Peter Collinson to John Estaugh, 1711. HEHP, folder 130.

[15] Although the small outbuilding commonly has been referred to as the "brew house," there is no documentation that beer was brewed on the Haddon-Estaugh plantation.

[16] Stewart, *Gloucester County Earmark Book*, 35, 40.

[17] John and Elizabeth Haddon to Most Dear Children, London, October 15, 1713. HEHP, folder 181.

[18] Ibid.

[19] Ibid. Nothing is known about Dorcas Shelton, nor is it known what were the "other Difficultyes that attend us."

[20] John and Elizabeth Haddon to Most Endeared [John and Elizabeth Estaugh], August 10, 1714. HEHP, folder 181.

[21] Indenture, John Haddon to John Gill through attorney John Estaugh, July 26, 1714, file 14-00-045 P1, copy, in box 1, Lyons Project Papers, HSHL.

[22] Survey and map of property purchased by John Haddon of London, 1228 acres afterwards sold to Matlacks [sic] and Collins, 1716, folder 69; Deed, Daniel Coxe, of Burlington, to John Estaugh, 1715, folder 33; Survey and map of land purchased by John Estaugh from Daniel Coxe, 1714, folder 65; Survey, "The courses of a Tract of upland & meadow ground Lying on Oldman's Creek, Oct. 7, 1716, folder 67; all in HEHP.

[23] Lease, Richard Matthews to Mary Stacy, 1684, folder 5; Release, Richard Matthews to Mary Stacy, 1684 folder 6; John and Elizabeth Haddon to most dear children, October 15, 1713, folder 181, 1713 folder 181 all in, HEHP.

[24] Letter from the Pennsylvania Land Company to Friend John Estaugh enclosing Power of Attorney to sell land from, John Freames, Jos. Grove, Daniel Quare, John Haddon, Henry Gouldney, and others, September 14, 1714. HEHP, folder 83.

[25] Letters written by James Logan to John Estaugh, regarding land, 1731, 1735/6. HEHP, folder 198. For Penn's problems with land sales, see *Penn Papers*, IV: 61n, 148n.

[26] C. Witt to Peter Collinson, n.d., in "On the Bite of the Rattle Snake," *Gentleman's Magazine*, v. 38 (January 1768), 10.

[27] Estaugh, *Call to the Unfaithful*, 32, 38, 72.

[28] Instructions from Priscilla and Mary Benthall to John and James Estaugh, concerning land recovered for debt, 1723. HEHP, folder 105; Receipt signed by Jacob Taylor To James Estaugh, on account of London Land Company, 1717/8. HEHP, folder 143; "The John Estaugh and Company Tract," in *Historical Papers and Addresses of the Lancaster County Historical Society*, vol. 28 (1924), 8–9.

[29] John and Elizabeth Haddon to Most Endeared, August 10, 1714. HEHP, folder 181.

[30] John and Elizabeth Haddon to Dear Children, February 27, 1717. HEHP folder 182.

[31] John and Elizabeth Haddon to Most Entirely Beloved Children, September 17, 1714. HEHP, folder 181.

[32] John and Elizabeth Haddon to Dear Children, February 27, 1717. HEHP folder 182.
[33] Ibid.
[34] "Family Letters," John and Elizabeth Haddon to John and Elizabeth Estaugh. HEHP, folders 181–183.
[35] Minutes of the Newton and Haddonfield Monthly Meeting, 1710–1731, on microform at the Quaker collection, Haverford College Library.
[36] Power of Attorney from John Estaugh to Elizabeth Estaugh, 1717. HEHP, folder 133.
[37] Copies of certificates of removal, in boxes 1 and 2, Lyons Project Papers, HSHL.
[38] John and Elizabeth Haddon to Dear Children, London, July 7, 1717. HEHP, folder 182.
[39] John and Elizabeth Haddon to Dear Children, February 27, 1717. HEHP, folder 182. Also, see Steven Deyle, "By farr [sic] the most profitable trade," *Slavery & Abolition*, vol. 10, Issue no. 2 (1989): 107–125.
[40] John and Elizabeth Haddon to Dear children, January 4, 1720. HEHP, folder 183.

CHAPTER 8.
"Lett the Plantation to Make Yourselves Easy," 1720–1726.

> *These are to Give you to under stand that our well Esteemed friend Elizabeth Estaugh (whose Husband is Intending to visit Friends in Barbados & then to Return home In order to Visit Friends In those Parts) made aplication to the meeting for a Certificate Giving us to understand of her Intentions once more to Visit her aged Parents having Such an opportunity And hoping there to meet her husband Againe. [quoted as written]*
> —Newton Monthly Meeting[1]

Elizabeth Haddon Estaugh, now thirty-nine years old, faced the winter of 1720 as she had many others before without the constant companionship of her husband John. Elizabeth admitted that she often willingly gave up this "dear Worthy" so that he might "travel in the Service of Truth." Consequently, she witnessed, without John, the February 1720 marriage of Elizabeth Tindall of Waterford Township to Joseph Gibson of nearby Deptford Township at the Newton Monthly Meeting house. John returned briefly in early March and accompanied Elizabeth to the Newton Meeting House to witness the marriage of Thomas Eayre of Burlington County to Priscilla Hugg, daughter of one of the leading Gloucester County land owners, general store owner and local government official, John Hugg. Soon after this ceremony John Estaugh left again to visit Barbados. Elizabeth thus witnessed without John by her side the marriage of Timothy Matlack of Waterford to Mary Haines at the Evesham Meeting.[2]

The Haines-Matlack marriage united two of the more wealthy West New Jersey Quaker landowning families and intimates of the Estaughs, so John's absence attested to his continued attention to religious and business matters in the West Indies. Indeed, when John returned in June, he almost immediately sought yet another certificate of removal for travel to Barbados. In August 1720, John sailed from Philadelphia with West New Jersey neighbor and confidant John Kaighin (later spelled Kaighn) to comfort Friends (and to conduct business) in the Caribbean. This time, though, Elizabeth asked her husband before he left on his latest mission to meet her in England after he finished his business in the West Indies. In response, John's certificate for travel included not only Barbados but Bristol, England, where he planned to meet his wife.

Elizabeth had wanted to visit her parents for some time and finally in June 1720 applied to her Newton Monthly Meeting for a certificate of removal to travel home to her London birthplace. Twenty Newton Monthly Meeting women and fifteen men attested to Elizabeth "being of Good Report among all sorts of People [that] know her being also very Servic[e]able in [that] Church and Very deare [sic] unto us." The "friends, Brethren & Sister in ye Truth" who signed this important document defined the vibrant West New Jersey Quaker farming and craft shop community where Elizabeth had lived for her entire adult life. Women leaders of the Monthly Meeting who signed the certificate included members of the Kaighn, Haines, Cooper, Sharp, Evans, Hollinshead, Lord, Hooten, Ladd, Heritage, French, Lippincott, Allen, Adams, Borton and Albertson families. The male members from the same families also signed the certificate. John Estaugh's signature was on the top of the sacred document that sent Elizabeth to London alone and "hoping for her Safety & Deliverance . . . from ye hands of Vile & Wicked Men."[3]

Elizabeth took her last trip back to London in 1720 accompanied by her now ten-year-old niece, little Sarah Hopkins. Sarah was very happy in America, including riding a pony; a letter from grandfather John Haddon refers to her as "the little maid who wants a Round Side Saddle."[4] However, the young girl had no choice in the matter, since the Haddon family wanted a male heir to reside with their daughter in West New Jersey. She knew that her sister had given birth to a healthy son in June 1718, so apparently an exchange of a female for a male ward as a potential heir was planned before Elizabeth's trip home to England. Sarah Collins Dimsdale agreed as usual to accompany Elizabeth and little Sarah on the trip across the Atlantic. The widow Dimsdale traveled to settle the estate of her late husband Dr. Robert Dimsdale, who had died in 1718, with her stepsons who resided in London. The Quaker women arrived in England in October 1720, and Elizabeth turned in her Newton Monthly Meeting certificate of removal to the Horsleydown Monthly Meeting. Elizabeth's husband arrived a few months later, landing in Bristol, England on the ship BETTY and making his way to his wife's Southwark birthplace.[5]

John and Elizabeth Estaugh would stay in London for three eventful years, during which time they purchased a house in the London Borough of Southwark near Elizabeth's parents. Elizabeth later leased the house to her mother's relatives John and Susanna Clarke.[6] Elizabeth helped her sister Sarah Hopkins with her surviving children. She particularly cared for two-year-old Ebenezer Hopkins, who the Haddon and Hopkins families determined to send to America and live with John and Elizabeth Estaugh as their ward, when they chose to return to the Haddon-Estaugh plantation in a neighborhood that by 1717 was commonly called Haddonfield after Elizabeth's father John Haddon. The families expected that Ebenezer would provide a male heir to the fortune of the childless Haddon-Estaugh couple.

While Elizabeth worked with her family, John preached. He soon received a certificate from the Horsleydown Monthly Meeting attesting to "Satisfaction with his Ministry in & Labour in the Gospel in those parts."[7] The Haddonfield traveling minister did not forget Friends back in New Jersey, penning an epistle to discipline "the unfaithful Professors of Truth" for the Quaker Meetings in Salem and Gloucester counties that was later published by Elizabeth after her husband's death. When not spreading the Inner Light to the unfaithful, Estaugh joined his wife to visit with his ailing in-laws.

Now that his daughter and son-in-law had settled into an extended stay with the Haddon family in London, John Haddon determined to arrange his final business affairs in the New World with them. To this end, Elizabeth's father transferred 150 shares of Pennsylvania Land Company stock to her husband John Estaugh. Haddon and his fellow Pennsylvania Land Company managers then made Estaugh, its "Attorney or Agent" to take charge of Company Treasurer Thomas Story's "landed and personal estate in Pennsylvania." This immediately complicated John Estaugh's life, dragging the Haddonfield traveling minister into a major scandal surrounding Quaker investors from the Pennsylvania Land Company and London Lead Company.[8]

There had been rumors for some time that corrupt members of the boards of directors of the land and lead companies, particularly the former treasurer Dr. Edward Wright, committed major fraud and stole money from both firms. Company financial problems had arisen as part of the complicated investment scandal surrounding the bursting in 1720 of the so-called South Sea Company Bubble, the year before Estaugh's arrival in England. The speculative South Sea enterprise had been formed between 1711 and 1714 to sell stock in a South American trading company that promised great profits for the many investors. The money raised was supposed to finance the never-ending British colonial wars against France and Spain. Mismanagement, over speculation and corruption soon bankrupted the company, losing the investors' money. The collapse of the South Sea Company had a far-reaching impact involving the British government, Bank of England, East India Company and, most importantly for John Haddon and John Estaugh, the London Lead and Pennsylvania Land companies.[9]

Haddon and Estaugh, apparently untainted by any corrupt dealings, stumbled into this tangled web of speculation, bankruptcy, and financial corruption in both the British government and private capital that surrounded the collapse of the South Sea Company. The troubles had started for Haddon in 1719 when the then Pennsylvania Land Company of London Treasurer, Thomas Story, suffered imprisonment in London for refusing to make an affirmation in legal matters because it too closely resembled the shunned oath of allegiance to the Anglican Church and King of England. While in prison, Story gave the Quaker banker James Hoskins over £8,000 of the Company's funds to hold in trust. Instead of depositing the money, Hoskins speculated in the South Sea Company and when the investment bubble "burst," lost everything. Hoskins blamed Story for stealing the money, and though a committee of twelve Quaker elders exonerated Story of any wrong doing, the company's treasurer had to cover this loss. In response Story transferred the deed to 7,200 acres of his Pennsylvania property to trusted Land Company board member and personal friend John Haddon. Haddon, in turn, assigned Estaugh to dispose of Story's property in Pennsylvania. Story's American holdings included 11,000 acres along the Delaware River, a tract near the Mennonite settlement on Pacquea Creek in Chester County (later Lancaster County), a tract of land with mills on the Schuylkill River and land in Bucks County. Story's most important property was a valuable Delaware Riverbank lot and wharf on the Philadelphia city waterfront.[10]

 John Estaugh's personal relationship with Story complicated matters. The Haddonfield minister had known the then Philadelphia Meeting elder and original investor in William Penn's proprietary lands since 1702 and over the years had traveled with Story on missions to comfort Friends. But now it was Haddon family business that directed Estaugh's conduct toward Story. In fact, Story's financial problems and the disposal of his land holdings in America would plunge Estaugh, long after his father-in-law's death in 1724, into years of lawsuits and political machinations both in London and Philadelphia, in a dedicated effort to protect Haddon's legacy. Even following John Estaugh's death eighteen years later in 1742, the Thomas Story affair would continue to plague the widow Elizabeth, as well.

Fortunately John and Elizabeth's real estate transactions with John Haddon concerning West New Jersey lands proved far more pleasant (although equally complicated) than involvement in the Pennsylvania Land Company morass. On March 27, 1722, Elizabeth's father transferred to the Estaughs "freely clearly and absolutely" his "plantation called and known by the name of New Haddonfield in the province of West New Jersey in America." John Haddon made the indenture "in consideration of the endeared love and good will and tender affection which I bear and have toward my dearly beloved children John and Elizabeth Estaugh." This free-will, non-compensation deed included "all the building orchards gardens and all other improvement whatsoever." New Haddonfield comprised about 400 acres that extended from the southerly branch of Cooper's Creek southwest to Lovejoy's former mill pond property and north to the land owned by Joseph Collins. At the same time, Haddon gave the Estaughs a moiety, consisting of a half share of the 112-acre Old Haddonfield tract probably purchased long ago from Matthews and Willis. This property lay near John Kay's gristmill, once occupied by Thomas Kendall and presently by John Haddon's cousin John Gill.

Elizabeth and her traveling companion and closest friend Sarah Dimsdale witnessed this transfer of the Haddon's entire American estate to his daughter and son-in-law.[11]

Elizabeth's father took measures during the 1720-1723 visit, when his children were all together in London, to ensure that the Haddon lineage would continue in America after her parents passed away. None of John and Elizabeth Clarke Haddon's four sons had lived to adulthood, and undoubtedly the elder Haddons had long ago realized that his oldest daughter would never bear children to carry on the family line in America. When she failed to provide a Haddon heir, Elizabeth comforted her father by taking her younger sister Sarah's daughter back to America. But John Haddon wanted a male heir to inherit his vast American estate, so Elizabeth had returned little Sarah to her birthplace and prepared to bring her sister's son Ebenezer back to New Jersey as heir apparent to the considerable Haddon-Estaugh fortune in America. In his last will and testament of July 1723 John Haddon granted Ebenezer future title to the Old Haddonfield property and a substantial endowment of £200 to be delivered when his grandson reached the age of twenty-one.[12]

With their futures arranged by John Haddon, Elizabeth, her husband and young Ebenezer prepared to sail for the Delaware River. Elizabeth's final visit to her London birthplace had been marked by much sadness and personal tragedies. She had served as midwife with her mother at the birth of Sarah and Benjamin Hopkins' twin sons John and Benjamin (II), who both died soon after birth. At the same time, the health of Elizabeth's mother had rapidly declined over the past three years.

The illness of the strong-willed Haddon family matriarch "never kept her [to her] bed much more than usual," but near the end of her life had a nurse to care for her. She also had "swelled" and no longer slept with her husband, the bed only "being Enough for her".[13] Despite her mother's condition, however, Elizabeth decided to return to America. John Estaugh paid £8 to John Annis, master of the LONDON HOPE, in April of 1723 to carry Elizabeth and John Estaugh, six-year-old Ebenezer Hopkins, household goods and business papers from the Haddon family to America. They sailed in the late spring for West New Jersey. Elizabeth would never again return to her birthplace.[14]

Elizabeth's mother died on June 16, 1723 of "dropsy" after a long painful illness. "As she lived so died in quiet," Sarah Hopkins wrote her sister, who had just returned to America; "Resigned to ye will of her great Capt." Sarah explained that: "Sometime before her departure, She called her grandchildren & advised ym [them] to fear ye Lord & be dutyfull to me, . . . & grant that thy Children may be as dutyfull . . . as ye [Sarah] & Sister [Elizabeth] has been to mee.[quoted as written]"[15] Nothing captures the character and personality of her older daughter Elizabeth more poignantly than her younger daughter Sarah's heartfelt description of their mother Elizabeth Clarke Haddon. Everything we know about Elizabeth Haddon Estaugh's undocumented private life and personality echoed her sister's portrayal of their mother. Elizabeth Estaugh, like her mother, emerges from the few sources that we have as a well-educated, quiet, dutiful woman, convinced throughout her life to follow her Inward Light that revealed the Truth as taught by the Word of God in the Bible. Elizabeth Estaugh's own actions and testimony show a woman who dedicated her life (as had her mother) to the Religious Society of Friends, the interests of her husband and her father's vision of a Quaker community in America.

Elizabeth's father drafted his will on July 16, 1723, soon after his daughter had sailed for the last time to America and a few weeks after his wife's interment at Long Lane Quaker Burial Ground in Bermondsey. "My dear Consort being lately departed after near forty seven Years comfortable living together," Haddon wrote, "I do therefore make this my last will and Testament." He left his entire English estate to his younger daughter Sarah Hopkins and her five surviving children: Haddon, Ebenezer, Mary, Sarah and Elizabeth. John Haddon also gave his London house in Southwark and all household goods and plate to his youngest daughter. In addition, Haddon provided substantial endowments for his grandchildren, granted either when they married in Friends Meeting or reached the ages of twenty-one. Haddon presented his grandson and oldest surviving male heir Ebenezer Hopkins, recently sailed to West New Jersey, with "all my plantation [in] America called and known by the name of Old Haddonfield with fifty six acres of Meadow Ground lying near a plantation of John Keys [John Kay], reserved out of the grant of like quantity of fifty six acres granted and given to my son and daughter John and Elizabeth Estaugh, to be for the use of their plantation called New Haddonfield." Haddon explained that he left Sarah and her children more than he willed to her older sister, "in consideration of what I have already done for my daughter Elizabeth Estaugh of West Jersey in America."[16]

Elizabeth Estaugh's father John Haddon died on the "13th day of the 3rd month [May] 1724" at the age of seventy. "He was Resigned to ye will of ye Lord," Sarah Hopkins wrote Elizabeth. She told her sister, that "a while before [he] was taken, [he] heard a Voice Call him by name after he was in bed which I feared was Ominous." Their father "did not seem in much Paine [sic]," Sarah continued, "but died hard was changed very Yeallow [sic]."[17] Horsleydown Friends buried Haddon in the Long Lane Burial Ground next to his wife Elizabeth and close by their old friend Thomas Lurting (who had been buried there in 1713).

John Haddon's daughters faced their future for the first time without their father's guidance in business. Sarah would manage her late father's affairs in London, while Elizabeth and her husband continued their function as his business representatives in America. John Haddon had employed Elizabeth as his agent and attorney in America for more than twenty-five years to deal with matters "whatsoever, as I myself might or could do the same if I was there personally." His complete trust in his daughter's ability to manage his affairs is clear in what he wrote to her in 1720. "My power will natural[l]y Flow to you for when it Shall Please the Lord to take me away you Shall be Remembered by me as If at my Elbow your Services For ye Lord and the Country where you are Placed," Haddon continued.[18]

John and Elizabeth, accompanied by their nephew Ebenezer Hopkins, arrived home in May of 1723 and found that much had changed in their tiny community of Haddonfield, as it had been called by her father in letters to his daughter for more than a decade. The Haddonfield Monthly Meeting house now stood completed. The decision to replace the old Newton meeting with a new place of worship in Haddonfield certainly was made before Elizabeth had left for London in 1720, although it is first mentioned in the meeting minutes on February 13, 1721. "At said Meeting It is Concluded that a Meeting house for Service of the Monthly & Quarterly Meetings is of Absolutely Neceesary [sic] to be Erected the place agreed on is Near John Gills house by the Road."[19]

In the meeting minutes of October 8, 1721 a "Report is Made by the Persons apointed to Gett Subscriptions for the Erecting the new Meeting house that there Subscribed, in order to itt the sum of one hund[red] & one pound & ten shilling and that ye persons are deemed to Gather the Money, . . . and that John Hain[e]s Thomas Sharp & Joseph Cooper Jun. is appointed to agree with a Workman for Building the Same fourty foot Long & Twenty five foot Wide twelve foot Posts , Shingled on ye outside a[nd] Galleries at Each End tenn foot one hoelve [half] of other to accomadate the Womon's Meeting to be Lined back high With Bo[a]rd & Lathed & plaster the other part; and . . . the house, if possible be finished by the Last End of the Seventh Month next.[quoted as written]"[20]

The construction must have proceeded more quickly than expected. Rather than the end of September 1722 ("the Last End of the Seventh Month next"), the first Monthly Meeting in "our new Meeting House in Haddonfield" was held on February 12, 1722.[21]

Old Gloucester County Friends, who had alternated between attending Meeting at the house of Thomas and Alice Shackle and the Newton Meeting house for many years, now held Meeting in the emerging Quaker center of life in Haddonfield. Most Friends shared or transferred memberships from the Newton, Chester and Evesham Monthly Meetings to the Haddonfield Monthly Meeting. John Gill's wife Mary Heritage Gill busily swept and cleaned the tiny wooden meeting hall, receiving eighteen shillings a year for her services.[22]

While the Estaughs were with Elizabeth's family in England, the new Haddonfield Monthly Meeting already had become the central place of business and worship for Quakers residing between the Big Timber, Newton, Cooper's and Pennsauken creeks. The normal joys, such as marriages, continued at the Haddonfield location. Hope Lippincott and Mary Gill's sister Hannah Heritage inquired into the intention of Richard Matlack and Rebecca Haines to marry at the new Meeting house, followed shortly by Agnes Hollingshead and Ruth Atkinson, who were appointed to inquire into the intention of Samuel Nicholson and Sarah Burrough to marry at the Haddonfield Friends Meeting House. The normal difficulties, such as reprimanding or disowning of members, continued as well. An example was the removal, after due deliberation, of Thomas French from his position as an Overseer of the Meeting on March 12, 1722.[23]

Elizabeth's and John's return to Haddonfield in 1723 restored unity among Friends. They presented their certificate of removal from the Friends Yearly Meeting in London and John submitted his own certificate from Horsleydown Monthly Meeting that expressed great "Satisfaction with his Ministry & Labour in the Gospel in those parts."[24] Elizabeth resumed her keeping of the minute book of the Women's Friends Monthly Meeting, a task which she had begun at Newton Friends Meeting in 1706.

Elizabeth Estaugh's presentation of her father's deed transferring more than one acre of land to the Haddonfield Monthly Meeting for the already constructed meeting house and a Friends burial ground further unified the Quaker community. John Haddon had made an indenture on September 2, 1721 that deeded his plot of land to Newton Monthly Meeting elders William Evans, Joseph Cooper, Jr. and John Cooper. Elizabeth had brought a token payment of five shillings from these Newton Township Friends to her father in London to pay for the property. Elizabeth and her best friend Sarah Dimsdale, then in London to settle her late husband Dr. Robert Dimsdale's estate, had witnessed John Haddon's signing of this indenture.[25]

Apparently Elizabeth and Thomas Sharp, a trustee of the Newton Meeting and county surveyor, had already selected the site for the meeting house before she traveled to England in 1720. Her father's grant gave legal title to the land for the Haddonfield Monthly Meeting. It proved the perfect location for the Estaughs, Gills and other Haddonfield village Quaker families to walk to Meeting. Moreover it placed Elizabeth's house close by the busy crossroads that connected her growing Quaker community to Philadelphia, Burlington, Salem and the Atlantic shore. At the same time, her father had transferred a deed of ownership to his "Dear children" for New Haddonfield Plantation, which included the land surrounding the new meeting house. Thus, the Estaughs could decide what Quaker families might purchase property on which to build their shops or houses in the nearby village of Haddonfield.[26]

Soon new Quaker shopkeepers, innkeepers, craftsmen, land owners and visitors from Philadelphia and other parts of the Delaware Valley found their way to settle, work and trade in Haddonfield. Traveling ministers and many Quaker merchants and landowners who came to Meeting or on business stayed at the nearby roomy Haddon-Estaugh plantation house. The Estaughs "had almost a monopoly in the hospitalities given to 'Public Friends' visiting that neighborhood."[27] Meanwhile Friends who hoped to purchase lots along the King's Highway, the Ferry Road (present-day Haddon Avenue), the soon-to-be-opened Tanner Street, or make more ambitious purchases of larger tracts of farm land in the surrounding countryside would need to negotiate for real estate with the Estaughs.

The Estaughs, and their still underage ward Ebenezer Hopkins, now owned outright all the lands that John Haddon had purchased along the Cooper's Creek region over the years. Haddon had advised his daughter and her husband while on their recent visit to London to sell as much of this land as possible to make them financially comfortable for life. John Estaugh planned, as his father-in-law had instructed, to help Elizabeth divide and manage the Haddonfield lands to make them comfortable. But first he confronted a much more difficult real estate assignment.

While in England, John Estaugh had become the sole American agent for the newly reorganized Pennsylvania Land Company. The company had been completely revamped in the wake of the recent financial problems. In March 1722, the Grand Committee of the original Pennsylvania Land Company transferred to the New Pennsylvania Company the huge William Penn purchase of August 1699 that featured nine Philadelphia city lots and two waterfront lots with wharves, one on the Delaware River and the other on the Schuylkill. The transfer included as well the Richard Noble plantation in Bucks County and land to the west toward the Pennsylvania frontier. As usual, the Company wanted their most trusted Friend, John Estaugh, to survey, divide up and sell these properties.[28]

The Company instructed Estaugh to locate copper mines in Burlington County, New Jersey, on land recently purchased from Peter Sonmans. Estaugh soon discovered that the "knavish" land speculator Sonmans had taken Company money, but had never transferred title to the land. Frustrated by Sonmans' fraud, the Land Company next asked its agent John Estaugh to look for copper or iron deposits along the Neshaminy Creek in Bucks County, Pennsylvania, on land that it had purchased from the Richard Noble estate. Unfortunately, Estaugh found that the Company's ownership of the Noble property remained tied up in court.[29]

The search for mining land proved to be an especially difficult and complex real estate job for the now increasingly sickly Estaugh, who chafed at the taxing time away from his travels to spread the Word of the Lord. Once again as with his earlier duty as Haddon's personal agent for the old Pennsylvania Land Company, Estaugh became involved in surveying, recording deeds, collecting rents and other obligations with what were largely undefined wilderness properties. His job included discovery of "unappropriated" lands for development on the Pennsylvania frontier. This time, Estaugh became even more deeply involved in Land Company business. On his recent trip to England, Estaugh had acquired 156 shares of the company and now held far more responsibility as a land company shareholder, real estate agent and attorney in conducting the firm's extensive American business.

John Estaugh's management of Thomas Story's 7,200 acres of Pennsylvania property turned over to John Haddon and other Land Company Trustees in 1723, and then transferred to Estaugh to cover the loss of £8000, proved particularly troublesome. The trustees of the Pennsylvania Land Committee, now managed by London Lead Company governor John Freame, wrote to Estaugh that: "Since thou left England, we Received a letter from Henry Hodge . . . giving an Account of gaining the Trial of the Person claiming the 1100 acres of and purchased of Thomas Story with costs of Suit." Freame had taken over the company's management badly shaken by the apparently corrupt direction of previous directors, particularly that of one-time company treasurer, Dr. Edward Wright. Freame and the trustees wanted Estaugh to help clean up the financial mess surrounding their real estate firm that accompanied the South Sea Company scandal. They instructed their American agent Estaugh, well-known for his honesty, to take care of the Story matter, rebuild the company's fortune in America and "Likewise that Land Advances and many earnest to purchase" pay in paper currency valued "within ten pounds percent as valuable as gold." Estaugh was to send all correspondence and moneys to Benjamin Kirton at the Pennsylvania Coffee House, Birchin Street, London.[30]

Estaugh worked diligently between 1724 and 1727 to meet his Pennsylvania Land Company obligations, and at the same time, to assist his wife Elizabeth in organizing their Haddonfield properties. Each transaction further expanded the Haddonfield Quaker community. Elizabeth and John easily leased 125 acres to their neighbors and members of Meeting Joseph Collins and his wife Catherine. They sold lots to neighbor Timothy Matlack and other West Jersey and Philadelphia Friends. Most importantly, they used their distribution of Haddon's land to ensure that the title to their estate would go to kin when they died. Elizabeth's father had constantly reminded his daughter to make legal arrangements that enabled her to pass down property to family.[31] Consequently John and Elizabeth Estaugh cleverly conveyed in trust all of Haddon's land grants to their cousin Gill and still underage nephew Ebenezer "to defeat the limitations under the will of John Haddon." They first sold Haddon's nephew Gill a part of the land that he already occupied. Cousin Gill would then lease all the property that included the land on the south side of the north branch of Cooper's Creek that he held rent-free from John Haddon as repayment for his labors. This re-conveyance meant that if the Estaughs died early, the property would always remain in the family.[32]

The itinerant minister John Estaugh seemed comfortable for the first time in staying home in Haddonfield. He assisted Elizabeth and members of the new Haddonfield Monthly Meeting to start building a Quaker community surrounding the new Meeting House. But once again, the voice of his Inner Light became too strong. At this moment, John Estaugh received yet another calling to travel to Britain in service of the Truth. Moreover, he needed to go to London "to settle some [business] affairs there."[33] So on October 9, 1725 Newton and Haddonfield Monthly meetings elders Joseph Cooper and Thomas Sharp issued a certificate of removal from the Haddonfield Monthly

Meeting for Estaugh to travel to England and Ireland. Estaugh transferred his letter of attorney issued to him earlier by the Grand Committee for the Pennsylvania Land Company to his kinsman John Gill and close friend Henry Hodge, a Philadelphia merchant whose daughter had married the Estaugh's family attorney William Rawle. As Estaugh's "true and lawful substitutes,"[34] Gill and Hodge took possession of all city lots, town lots, liberty lots and other lands lying in the Province of Pennsylvania for the Pennsylvania Land Company. With this authority they might collect debts, fines, forfeitures and rents; and lease and sell land for Estaugh. At the same moment Estaugh transferred his power of attorney to his wife Elizabeth so that she held all legal authority to deal with their Haddonfield plantation and real estate business. Thus leaving American business affairs in the hands of a trusted friend and family, Elizabeth's husband set sail once again for Britain, where he would soon appear in a personal audience before King George I of England.[35]

CHAPTER 8 NOTES.

[1] Monthly Meeting Newton, July 11, 1720 to Monthly Meeting at "Horsladown" in City of London, copy, in box 2, Lyons Project Papers, HSHL.

[2] Elizabeth Estaugh's "Testimony," in John Estaugh, *Call to the Unfaithful*, iii, xiii.

[3] Certificate of Removal, 1720, in box 2, Lyons Project Papers, HSHL.

[4] John and Elizabeth Haddon to Dear Children, September 5, 1717. HEHP, folder 182.

[5] Receipted order from John Annis to John Estaugh, 1720. HEHP, folder 161.

[6] Lease and indenture, for one year, John Estaugh and wife to John and Susanna Clarke, 1725. HEHP, folder 108.

[7] Haddonfield Monthly Meeting Minutes, June 10, 1723.

[8] Certificates for 150 shares in the Pennsylvania Land Company purchased by John Estaugh, 1726. HEHP, folder 148; Epistle from John Estaugh to the Quarterly Meeting of Friends for Newton and Salem in New Jersey, September 20, 1722. HEHP, folder 194; also, see Estaugh, *Call to the Unfaithful*.

[9] Ackrill and Hannah, *Barclays,* 11–13.

[10] Patents and deeds of lands granted by Thomas Story to John Haddon, record at Philadelphia of 7200 acres in Pennsylvania, undated. HEHP, folder 77; recorded in Philadelphia Deed Books H-19–42, F-4: 265–68 and F-5: 97–105; *Determination of the Case of Mr. Thomas Story and Mr. James Hoskins, Relating to an Affair of the Pennsylvania Company, &c.* (London, July 31, 1723); Rebecca Nicholson Taylor, "Thomas Story's Pennsylvania Estates," *Bulletin of Friends' Historical Association*, vol. 19, no. 2 (Autumn 1930): 92–97.

[11] New Haddonfield, Indenture, to John Estaugh and Elizabeth Estaugh, March 27, 1722, MS. file 2001-004-00, and copies of Haddon's deeds from Sharps Book of Deeds B, New Jersey Division of Archives, Trenton, in box 1, Lyons Project Papers, HSHL.

[12] John Haddon's Will.

[13] Sarah Hopkins to Dear Sister (Elizabeth Estaugh) September 19, 1742. HEHP, folder 184. On the document there is a notation that the date of 1742 is incorrect and that the correct date is 1724. However, recent research confirms that the 1742 date, as written on the letter, is accurate.

[14] Receipted bill to Mrs. Estaugh on board the LONDON HOPE, John Annis, Captain, with sundry goods, for Pennsylvania, Also waterside charges, 1723. HEHP, folder 162.

[15] Sarah Hopkins to Dear Sister (Elizabeth Estaugh) September 19, 1742. HEHP, folder 184.

[16] John Haddon's will.

[17] Sarah Hopkins to Dear Sister (Elizabeth Estaugh) September 19, 1742.

HEHP, folder 184. Other Friends buried in the Long Lane Quaker Burial Ground, close to John and Elizabeth Haddon, included: Jacob Hagen (died 1758), the Haddon and Estaugh family lawyer in London, and a Bermondsey merchant, Land Company stockholder; and, Peter Collinson, London haberdasher, merchant, and world renowned botanist, who probably brought the trees and plants for Elizabeth Haddon Estaugh's garden in Haddonfield.

[18]John and Elizabeth Haddon to Dear Children, January 4, 1720. HEHP, folder 183.

[19]Minutes of the Haddonfield Monthly Meeting, February 13, 1721, on microform in the Quaker collection, Haverford College Library.

[20]Ibid. October 8, 1721.

[21]Ibid. February 12, 1722.

[22]Copy, of the Minutes of the Haddonfield Monthly Meeting of Friends, 1721–1723, in box 1, Lyons Project Papers, HSHL; the original minutes for this early period are on microform at the Haverford Friends Library, Haverford, Pennsylvania, and copies of some later minutes are held in the Frank H. Stewart Room, Special Collections, Campbell Library at Rowan University, Glassboro, New Jersey.

[23]Haddonfield Monthly Meeting Minutes, 1722.

[24]Ibid, June 10, 1723.

[25]Indenture John Haddon to William Evans, Joseph Cooper, Jr., and John Cooper, September 2, 1721, entered by T. Sharp, December 10, 1723, Book B, or Sharp's Book, p. 43, copy, in box 1, Lyons Project Papers, HSHL.

[26]Thomas Sharp's survey of the Haddonfield Friends Meeting House site, in Clement, *First Emigrant Settlers*, 33.

[27]Visitors to the Estaugh plantation house during this period included English traveling ministers and wealthy Philadelphia merchants, including Thomas Wilson (friend of Peter Collinson), William Ellis, Isaac Norris, John Fothergill, Edmund Peckover, James Pemberton, Nicholas Waln, and members of the Drinker, Rawle, Cadwallader families among many others, see Rhoads, "Haddon Hall."

[28]See "John Estaugh's Dealing with the Pennsylvania Land Company of London," 1714–1735. HEHP, folders 83–97.

[29]Transfer of property in New Jersey for one hundred pounds, Peter Sonmans of St. Martins-in-the-Fields to John Haddon, 1723. HEHP, folder 76; Letter from the Pennsylvania Land Company to John Estaugh, in regard to the possibility of finding copper mines on the land of P. Sonmans, London, October 28, 1724. HEHP, folder 89; for Noble plantation complications, see documents 189–192, all in HEHP; also, see Rebecca Nicholson Taylor, "The Business Papers of John and Elizabeth Estaugh," *Bulletin of Friends' Historical Association*, vol. 20, no. 1 (1931), 16–17.

[30]Letters from the Pennsylvania Land Company in London to John Estaugh, 1724–1727. HEHP, folders 91, 93 and 95; Grand Committee Instructions to Estaugh, June 10, 1724. HEHP, folder 90; John Bell, signed for the Trustees to Loving Friend John Estaugh, April 7, 1727. HEHP, folder 148. The Pennsylvania Coffee House of London served as the center of business for Delaware Valley visitors, including Benjamin Franklin.

[31] John and Elizabeth Haddon to Dear Children, February 27, 1717. HEHP, folder 182.
[32] Release to John Gill, to defeat the limitations under the will of John Haddon, 1726. HEHP, folder 167.
[33] John Estaugh transfer Power of Attorney to Henry Hodge and John Gill, 1725. HEHP, folder 86.
[34] Ibid.
[35] Power of Attorney from John Estaugh to Elizabeth Estaugh, witnessed by Sarah Dimsdale, Thomas Sharpe, and John Kay, 1725 folder 133), HEHP; also copies, in box 1, Lyons Project Papers, HSHL.

CHAPTER 9.
To See Good Order Among Friends, 1727–1742.

> He [John Estaugh] was zealous for preserving good Order in the
> Church; and for maintaining Love and Unity, that Badge of true
> Discipleship . . . he freely bestowed much Labour and Time therein,
> for the Good of the Neighbourhood where he dwelt; and especially
> on the Poor, for whom he was much concerned.
> —Friends of the Monthly Meeting of Haddonfield [1]

John Estaugh's trip to England in 1726 turned out to be far more than the usual business and missionary journey to preach the Truth among the unfaithful. When Elizabeth's husband submitted his certificate of removal to the London Meeting, its renowned Meeting for Sufferings asked him to sign a copy of a law from the Pennsylvania Assembly that had arrived earlier, unsigned. This was "An Act Prescribing the Forms of Declaration of Fidelity, Abjuration and Affirmation, instead of the Forms [Oaths of Loyalty to Crown and Church of England] Heretofore Required in Such Cases." The act enabled Quakers to hold public office, serve as directors of corporations, testify in civil court cases and allow affirmation to be used instead of swearing oaths of allegiance in all legal matters.

The affirmation became one of the most important symbols of religious liberty for Quakers. Religious non-conformists, particularly those convinced by the Religious Society of Friends, had struggled for years in Britain against the requirement of swearing oaths of loyalty to the Crown and the Church of England as a pre-requisite for conducting public business or holding any public or private corporate office. Such swearing of an oath in God's name violated, so Quakers believed, their religious and biblical principles. The Crown and Parliament saw the refusal to take oaths as seditious, even treasonous, anti-government activity and a reason to confiscate property, crush organized religious dissent and imprison and sometimes execute Friends.

Gradually, Quaker leaders adopted the concept of an affirmation as an acceptable substitute for the oath. The British government, under the Affirmation Act of 1696, allowed affirmations rather than oaths in most cases, although British authorities often ignored the law and demanded oaths to participate in legal matters. John Haddon and other Quaker members of the London Lead Company and the Pennsylvania Land Company of London held no positions until at least 1704 on the boards of directors by affirmation. Nevertheless, Quakers saw the affirmation concept as a major victory in their struggle for individual rights and religious freedom. Each year, Friends in England presented a "Humble and Thankful acknowledgement of People called Quakers From Yearly Meeting in London." But in 1715, the established Church of England and anti-Quaker factions in Parliament applied pressure to prevent continued application of the law. British lawmakers refused to pass a renewal. Then, in1722, Parliament endorsed a new affirmation act. Three years later, the Pennsylvania Affirmation Act of 1725 further expanded the British law allowing affirmations instead of oaths for all public and private legal conduct in colonial courts. The Council of Trade and Plantation raised no objections, and the Pennsylvania law received acceptance. So the London Committee of Sufferings wanted Estaugh, just arrived in the city from his Haddonfield home in America, to sign a copy of the Pennsylvania law and present its thankful acknowledgment to King George I. On May 19, 1726, Estaugh; London merchant Joseph Wyeth, a Quaker essayist and close friend of the late William Penn; and Joshua Gee, a Quaker merchant and political activist, received an audience with the monarch. At this meeting, the Quaker emissaries expressed Pennsylvania's undying loyalty and the thanks of all Quakers for the King's act of religious toleration.[2]

After his audience with the King, Estaugh preached for a time in Ireland, returning in late 1726 to his home in Haddonfield, New Jersey. Though undoubtedly tired and apparently suffering more than usual from headaches and breathing difficulties, the now frail preacher, always supported by his faithful wife Elizabeth, continued his leadership of the Friends community in West New Jersey. In fact his recurring illness, Haddonfield Friends insisted, actually gave him a larger role in caring for the poor and sick among Friends. John employed his reputed "Skill in Chymistry and Physick." "A Man of great Humility and Compassion, sympathizing with the Afflicted in Body or Mind;" Haddonfield Friends testified, and "being sometimes enabled, as with healing Oil," Estaugh would often "comfort the Sorrowful, the heavy-hearted and sincere, Seeking of Christ Jesus."[3]

Despite his poor health, John assisted Elizabeth in developing the growing Quaker community in Haddonfield. He "bestowed much labor and time For the good of the People of the Neighborhood Where he dwelt," Elizabeth affirmed.[4] The Quaker couple sold a village lot, shop, shed and a wharf on Cooper's Creek to the blacksmith John Burrough for his business. They conveyed, in fee simple, a choice eighty-seven acre tract of land that extended from Cooper's Creek on the west side of Haddonfield's main street (the old King's Highway) to the new Friends Meeting house to John Gill.[5] Elizabeth's cousin already held the entire Haddon property under a complicated lease-trusteeship arrangement to protect the transfer of the John Haddon estate to the Estaughs and their nephew Ebenezer Hopkins. Gill served not only as a trusted partner in land development, but along with his wife Mary Heritage Gill, accompanied Elizabeth, John and Ebenezer to Meeting. They often attended important marriage ceremonies together. On April 2, 1727, Cousin Gill and the Estaughs witnessed the marriage of Ephraim Tomlinson to Sarah Corbut. The following month, the Gills sat with the Estaughs at the most significant marriage ceremony held up to this point in their lives, at the new Haddonfield Monthly Meeting house. On May 18, 1727, Mary Estaugh, daughter of John's brother James Estaugh, married Joseph Kaighin (Kaighn).

The union of these two influential Quaker families in 1727 brought the Estaughs' intimates and kin to the Haddonfield Meeting House, many from families who had first witnessed the Haddon-Estaugh marriage twenty-five years before. Those who witnessed the Joseph Kaighin-Mary Estaugh ceremony that day in May 1727 included Elizabeth's best friend Sarah Collins Dimsdale, close Women's Meeting friends Sarah Ellis, Judath Sharp, Lydia Cooper, Sarah Griscom, Mary Gill and Elizabeth Wills. Haddonfield Monthly Meeting elders John Kay,

Thomas Sharp, Timothy Matlack, Joseph Cooper, Jr., Ephraim Tomlinson and John Lord also signed the marriage certificate for Mary Estaugh and Joseph Kaighin.[6]

Joseph Kaighin's brother John was a particularly important witness. John Kaighin, who never married, became Elizabeth Estaugh's closest male confidant. He often joined Gill and Philadelphia lawyers William and Francis Rawle to manage the legal aspects of her plantation business when her missionary husband left on his frequent travels to spread the Truth and conduct business overseas. John Kaighin had studied "the Arts & Mysteries of Chymistry [sic] & Astral Sciences whereby to make a more perfect Discovery of the Hidden Causes of the more Occult & uncommon Disease," with Germantown, Pennsylvania practitioner of herbal medicine Dr. Christopher Witt.[7] Witt issued Kaighin a medical diploma in 1738, reputedly the first in America according to Pennsylvania historian S. W. Pennypacker.[8] Kaighin would become Elizabeth Estaugh's personal physician and, shortly before her death, Elizabeth gave to "her Kindsman John Kaighin, as a free Gift . . . all the Books in his poss[ess]ion, two Iron morters, one limbeck, still bottles of all Sorts, with the Clinical Glass, or anything else in his actual poss[ess]ion."[9]

The Estaugh-Kaighin ceremony came at one of the busiest times in the daily plantation life of John and Elizabeth Estaugh. Nonetheless, John decided one more time to leave Elizabeth alone in Haddonfield and sail for England, from which he had only just returned. Though John expected to preach in the London and Horsleydown Religious Society of Friends Meetings, his primary mission was to discuss secular affairs with his wife's sister, Sarah Haddon Hopkins, now managing the English portion of the late John Haddon's estate. Apparently, Elizabeth could not accompany John to visit her sister because of a recurring bout with what may have been the yellow fever that killed so many eighteenth century Philadelphians. Besides, she had to oversee her busy farm and real estate business. John Estaugh received a certificate to travel in 1730 from John Kay and John Mickle, overseers of the Haddonfield Monthly Friends Meeting. The Haddonfield minister presented this certificate of removal from his Meeting to the London Meeting in August. In its record of Estaugh's arrival, the London Yearly Meeting mentioned by name, probably for the first time, the Haddonfield Monthly Meeting.

Estaugh crossed the Thames River and visited the Horsleydown Monthly Meeting where he met his sister-in-law Sarah Haddon Hopkins. Sarah was now administering not only her late father's estate but that of her husband Benjamin, who had just died. Sarah focused particularly on her late-father's London Lead and Pennsylvania Land companies' transactions. She worked with a new set of company managers, Sarah told her visiting brother in-law. "Most of them, men well Qualified for trade," Elizabeth's sister advised John Estaugh, "some of them you know." She inquired of her sister and brother-in-law if they might invest with her in a "large share" of Lead Company stock. John proved "not inclined to buy" into this highly speculative venture, however, because company stock had been badly devalued by the South Sea scandal.[10]

Estaugh showed a greater interest in obtaining the indenture for a daughter of Sarah's close Southwark friend, Mary Cross Healey. The elder Healey had served as midwife, along with Elizabeth Estaugh's late mother, for many of the women who belonged to the Southwark Quaker Meeting. So, the Healey family willingly indentured their daughter Mary to be a servant for John and Elizabeth Estaugh in America, probably to help Elizabeth raise her sister's son Ebenezer, who was now twelve-years old.[11]

While conducting these business arrangements in the Horsleydown Meeting community with his sister-in-law, Estaugh met fellow Delaware Valley Quaker, John Dillwyn. A Philadelphia Common councilman and wealthy merchant, Dillwyn had returned to visit his Southwark birthplace that he had left long ago to accompany William Penn to America. Now in 1730, Dillwyn was in England to conduct business at the Pennsylvania Coffee House in London, contact the sons of his late-friend, Dr. Robert Dimsdale, and worship at his former Horsleydown Monthly Meeting in Southwark. Here, Dillwyn renewed unity with his American neighbor John Estaugh. It was not clear whether Estaugh and Dillwyn were business partners but, at one time or other both represented Dimsdale family interests and shared major business relations with James Logan back in Philadelphia. Estaugh had received power of attorney earlier from John and William Dimsdale to settle their father Robert's estate in Burlington County, West New Jersey. Dr. Robert Dimsdale, of course, was the late husband of Elizabeth's best friend Sarah Dimsdale. Years later, Dillwyn became the executor for the widow Dimsdale's estate in America. Thus, Estaugh and Dimsdale had many business and family connections in common.[12]

In November 1730, John Estaugh joined Dillwyn and indentured servant Mary Healey on board a ship sailing to the Delaware Valley. Mary undoubtedly arrived in Haddonfield at a critical moment to help Elizabeth Estaugh. Elizabeth had been ill since summer with a fever. At the same time, after his return from London, her husband's health also worsened. Local remedies and herbal medicines that filled the Estaughs' house failed to stop his periodic violent headaches. Adding to John and Elizabeth's physical sufferings, the Estaughs began to lose their oldest personal, religious and business friends with increasing frequency. Perhaps most distressing for John and Elizabeth, on October 19, 1729, Thomas Sharp passed away. Sharp's relationship with Elizabeth and John Estaugh had defined their early years in West New Jersey. Thomas had served Elizabeth as surveyor and religious guide since her first arrival in America. Between 1702 and 1728, he had assisted her husband John Estaugh, a fellow overseer of the Newton Monthly Meeting, by surveying property, recording deeds and most importantly assuring good order in Meeting.

Sharp was an original settler of the Irish Tenth, first constable, justice and town clerk of Newton Township. Most important for the Estaughs, as the leading elder and an original founder of the Newton and Haddonfield Monthly Meetings, Sharp had often joined with Elizabeth and John to promote love and unity in their West New Jersey Quaker community. Just before his death, however, Sharp expressed a growing discomfort with the local Meeting. He penned a poem (possibly read in Meeting) that lamented the widespread "wavering" in acceptance of the Truth among the unfaithful children and grandchildren of the original families that founded the old Newton Meeting and had recently removed to the newer Haddonfield Monthly Meeting. The Lord's kindness once shined upon the Newton Monthly Meeting, Sharp wrote: "But now poor Newton is decayed; The youth not zealous, I am afraid."[13]

Elizabeth and John Estaugh determined not to let the children of the original Quaker families who had established the Newton Monthly Meeting (and now sat with them in worship at the Haddonfield Meeting) to lose their faith in the Truth. Nor would they allow the Haddonfield Monthly Meeting to decay as Friend Thomas Sharp believed had happened with Newton. To provide unity to their Quaker community, John and Elizabeth continued their service to the Friends Meeting. John "was zealous for preserving good Order in the Church; and for maintaining Love and Unity, that Badge of true Discipleship."[14] The Haddonfield Monthly Meeting appointed John Estaugh to represent it at the Salem Quarterly Meeting. Meanwhile, Elizabeth recorded the minutes of the women's meeting and sat with John as overseers of the separate (but equal) men's and women's meetings. They certified clearances for marriage and then witnessed these blessed unions of second-generation Newton Township Friends to family members from the Haddonfield and other nearby West New Jersey Friends Meetings. This not only expanded the Haddonfield Quaker community, but by overseeing the intermarriage of local families, Elizabeth kept the children of the original settlers tied to the emerging center of the West New Jersey Quaker community in Haddonfield.[15]

Elizabeth and John also witnessed marriages during the 1730s that connected Salem and Woodbury Quaker families more closely to Friends in the Haddonfield, Evesham and Chester meetings. The decade saw an increased number of marriages between prominent West New Jersey Friends. In March, John and Elizabeth Estaugh witnessed the marriage of Josiah Parker to Mary Ladd at the Woodbury Meeting House. Three months later they attended a marriage ceremony at the Haddonfield Meeting House for Elizabeth Tomlinson of Evesham, Burlington County, and Bartholomew Wyatt(e) of Salem County. Wyatt(e) was the son of a wealthy Salem, New Jersey, plantation owner and, not incidentally, one of the leading Quaker slave owners in West New Jersey. The following year the Estaughs witnessed the joining of Anthony Sharp and Mary Dimswick (or Dimack) at the Chester Meeting. In 1733, John and Elizabeth signed the certificate of marriage for Sarah Stephens and Thomas Edgerton.[16]

Then the Estaughs, accompanied for the first time by their fifteen-year-old nephew Ebenezer Hopkins, witnessed the marriage of Haddonfield newcomer Thomas Redman of Philadelphia to their cousin John Gill's daughter Hannah. Next, the Estaughs and young Hopkins attended the marriage testimony in 1737 of Mary Harrison to Thomas Thorne at the Haddonfield Monthly Meeting. These were Ebenezer's first public testimonies, certifying his growing importance in the Quaker community. They forecast as well his own upcoming marriage in 1737 to Sarah Lord of Woodbury. This Ebenezer Hopkins-Sarah Lord marriage in April promised to be the most important nuptial ever witnessed by John and Elizabeth Estaugh (and for the history of their Haddonfield Quaker community).

Aunt Elizabeth had groomed her nephew and ward Ebenezer for just such a day from the beginning of his arrival in 1723 at the Estaugh plantation. Elizabeth, who had become the increasingly dominant Quaker female leader of her community, had carefully nurtured her sister's boy for years. Elizabeth raised Ebenezer to marry into a prominent Quaker family in America, preparing him to inherit the Haddon-Estaugh lands and carry on the Haddon-Estaugh line in America. Consequently she had roomed "Ebby" with her dear friend Dr. John Craig. The only physician-teacher in Haddonfield at the time, Dr. Craig ran a boarding school in a building rented from Elizabeth Estaugh and that was within a short walking distance to her plantation house. John Estaugh paid Craig £12 a year for tuition, room and board. Dr. Craig tutored young Ebenezer in mathematics, reading and science.[17] The Haddonfield teacher left the religious education to the Estaughs and the Haddonfield Monthly Meeting. Craig's

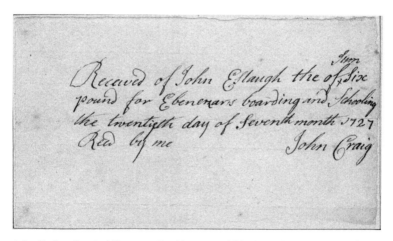

John Craig educated Ebenezer Hopkins, son of Elizabeth Estaugh's sister Sarah Hopkins, in Haddonfield. Ebenezer boarded with Craig while attending school.
Collection 1001, Quaker Collection, Haverford College, Haverford, PA.

tutelage was most successful as Ebenezer became an astute businessman, county tax collector and most acceptable Friend. He would help his aunt Elizabeth, after her husband John's death in 1742, to continue the development of the town of Haddonfield. More significantly, as the son of Elizabeth's sister Sarah Haddon Hopkins, Ebenezer (and his children) would be able to carry the Haddon-Estaugh-Hopkins family legacy on to future generations.

Ebenezer started to fulfill the Haddon and Hopkins' family expectations of having an heir to their fortune in America when he married Sarah Lord of the Woodbury Friends Meeting. The marriage of Ebenezer and Sarah united the most influential and prosperous Quaker communities in old Gloucester County. The Lord (and the Wood) families had founded the Woodbury Creek settlement and Meeting, and Joshua Lord's marriage to Sarah Wood in 1689 was the first recorded ceremony by the Woodbury Friends. These families dominated the Quaker community in the lower part of Old Gloucester County. Sarah's relations who witnessed her marriage to Ebenezer were from the most prominent settlers residing near the Timber Creek and included members of the Wood, Wilkins, Mickle, Gibson, Whitall and Ward families. These Quaker land-owning families had shaped the society and economy of the lower part of Old Gloucester County. Meanwhile Hopkins' kin from the Haddonfield Monthly Meeting who attended the marriage came from the Estaugh, Gill, Kaighn and Cooper families, all leaders in Meeting and prominent landowners in the upper part of the county above the Timber Creek.[18]

This marriage between two powerful and prosperous West New Jersey Quaker clans promised to increase the influence and unity of the Haddonfield Quaker community. Ebenezer and Sarah accompanied their most immediate kin, the Estaughs, Kaighns and Gills, to Meeting and signed certificates of marriage that witnessed their growing unity with a new generation of Haddonfield Friends. After each marriage in Meeting, John and Elizabeth would further design their community by selling or renting property near the Haddonfield Monthly Meeting house to newlyweds, thus forging the new generation's unity with the expanding Quaker community of Haddonfield.

The Estaughs had long envisaged the creation of a vibrant Quaker community through a selective sale of John Haddon's lands that promoted unity and good order among West New Jersey Friends. Elizabeth and John had started the expansion of their Haddonfield community soon after they returned from England in 1723 with full and free title to all of John Haddon's properties. During the next decade they leased, sold and resold these properties between Pennsauken, Cooper's and Newton creeks to the Kay, Gill, Matlack, Clement and Kaighin families to begin the process of expansion. These families quickly profited by dividing up their new properties, and selling or leasing to family and other newly-married Friends from the Haddonfield Monthly Meeting. This brought members of the Whitall, Haines, Ellis, Morgan, Taylor, Andrews and French families, among others, into the inner circle of the wider Haddonfield Quaker community of West New Jersey and Philadelphia.[19]

The marriages of Haddonfield Friends to Quakers from nearby communities, particularly Philadelphia, also increased the growth of business in the Quaker community. Thus John Kay's daughter Sarah married Philadelphia shipwright and carpenter James Norris. The Philadelphia craftsman moved to Haddonfield where his wife opened a dry goods store in 1733 that was worked with the help of several slaves of African descent. By 1739, Sarah Norris also operated a tavern on the southwest corner of Haddonfield's main street (King's Highway) and the road that later became Potter Street.

Meantime, Thomas Perry Webb purchased a large lot nearby from John Kay and ran a blacksmith shop and tavern (corner of King's Highway East and Ellis Street, today). Perry Webb repaired farm tools, plows, and manufactured nails, hardware and iron kitchenware for the increasingly busy Quaker farming and craft-shop village of Haddonfield. The Clement and Howell families operated tanneries during the decade on a dirt path that later became Tanner Street. Thomas Redman moved to Haddonfield from Philadelphia in 1735, bought property from Elizabeth Estaugh and opened an apothecary shop (drug store). Redman married Elizabeth's kin Hannah Gill at the Haddonfield Monthly Meeting in February of 1737, thus linking the Redman family to the Gill, Estaugh, Haddon, and Hopkins families. The Redmans soon became part of Elizabeth's inner circle at Friends meetings and in the real estate business.

Elizabeth's husband seemed reinvigorated by all the local real estate activity and the wonderful marriage of his ward Ebenezer Hopkins into one of West New Jersey's most significant Quaker families. Her acceptable companion, as Elizabeth called husband John, again managed business affairs with his wife. He purchased pumps, livestock and farm equipment for the plantation.

He hired Ralph Leigh for £14 a year to help run the farm. He employed Richard Buckele (Buckle) to cut drainage ditches through the farm's meadows, put up fences and perform other heavy work on the Estaughs' property.[20] John collected quit rents, surveyed land and registered deeds.[21] The Haddonfield yeoman farmer and traveling minister expanded the Haddon-Estaugh property. He acquired 980 acres of untitled land "below the Falls of the Delaware" from the West Jersey Council of Proprietors.

John Estaugh bought the 200-acre John Eastlack plantation and leased it in 1737 to Ebenezer Hopkins and his nineteen-year old bride Sarah Lord Hopkins. Ebenezer and Sarah lived on the property for ten years, finally purchasing it after John's death from Aunt Elizabeth in 1747 for £300 lawful money of New Jersey. Here Ebenezer's wife Sarah gave birth in February 1738 to their first child John Estaugh Hopkins. The following year they had a healthy daughter Elizabeth Estaugh Hopkins.[22] It is noteworthy that Ebenezer and Sarah named their first two children in honor of their beloved great uncle and great aunt rather than for Ebenezer's natural parents back in England, Benjamin and Sarah Haddon Hopkins.

This was a blessed time for Elizabeth and John Estaugh. The wealthy devout couple had become the most respected elder members of the Haddonfield Meeting. Their plantation prospered, land sales and rentals boomed; and their nephew Ebenezer's lovely family was growing. Quaker craftsmen, tanners, blacksmiths and storekeepers purchased lots in the village, rented from the Estaughs or built houses and opened shops and inns. Yet difficulties accompanied this great time of joy. Never comfortable with affairs of business, John Estaugh faced some of the usual challenges associated with the management of a large plantation. An example of these challenges was his relationship with hired-hand Richard Buckele, who leased properties from the Estaughs, Ebenezer Hopkins, Abigail Cooper and Sarah Dimsdale. Apparently Buckele decided to use these properties for his own profit, refused to pay his rent or settle other debts. His entrepreneurial machinations forced Estaugh to employ Isaac Albertson to enter Buckele's house and seize his goods and chattels for back rent.[23]

Other difficulties would have arisen from the normal, ongoing business of the Haddonfield Monthly Meeting, which included the disciplining of members. One example was the disowning of Samuel Dennis, the husband of one of Elizabeth's friends Ruth Tindall, for "drinking and false speaking."[24]

More seriously, the respected Haddonfield elder John Estaugh faced criticism from the Quaker preacher Benjamin Lay. In a biographical article on John Estaugh, published in 1857, the author noted that John Estaugh "was one of those [at] whom Benjamin Lay shot his shafts, but the cause we cannot positively tell. It may have arisen from his rebuking the uncharitable spirit, which manifested itself in that zealous, but often misdirected man."[25] Quite probably John Estaugh's ownership of slaves was Lay's target. Lay was a physically deformed and brilliant character who dedicated his life to social reform, particularly care for the disadvantaged in the community.[26] Most Quakers considered Lay, at best, to be "eccentric" and he was disowned by the Philadelphia Yearly Meeting. Lay endorsed the growing movement against the African slave trade among Delaware Valley

Quakers, writing a path-breaking anti-slavery tract: *All Slave-Keepers that keep the Innocent in Bondage, Apostates* (printed by Benjamin Franklin in 1737). Although historians debate how much direct influence Lay had on his contemporaries, it seems that, despite his eccentricities, "there is evidence to suggest Lay's message was getting through and that slaveholding was becoming increasingly less acceptable in Quaker circles" and was part of an "increasingly sophisticated discourse of anti-slavery that was being articulated in private homes as well as meeting houses, and which had become a mainstream Quaker concern by the start of the 1740's."[27]

It is not known exactly how many slaves were owned by John and Elizabeth Estaugh, or when or how they were acquired. In 1742, John and Elizabeth Estaugh owned two slaves of African descent; whether they owned any others, and if so, in what time period, is not known.

Only four references in the historical record yield any information on the Estaugh slaves. The only original document relating to the Estaugh slaves which survives is a document from John Estaugh to his nephew Ebenezer Hopkins dated October 12, 1742, just prior to his departure for a missionary trip to Tortola. In this document, John Estaugh states: "Whereas I am now going a viage [a voyage] to sea, and being desirous that my dear and well beloved Wife may in my absence as much as can be Eased of all combrances, do there fore assigne and make over all my Negros to Ebenezer Hopkins untill my return, and to serve him in all such imployment as he shall from time to time have acashon to make use of them or either of them, and if they or either of them shall refuse to obey his just commands, then to take and use all proper wayes and meanes as may oblige them or either of them to amor [honor] steady observance of his commands and in ye doing where of this shall be his justifications as witness my hand this 12th day of ye 8th mo [October]1742—John Estaugh.[quoted as written]"[28]

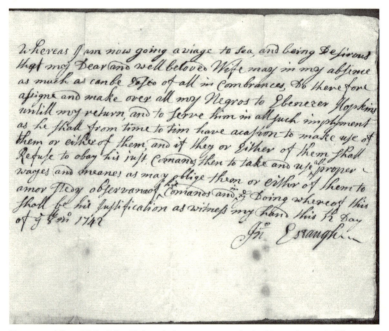

Document in which John Estaugh turns over control of two slaves to Ebenezer Hopkins while Estaugh is on a missionary trip, 1742. *Wittwer Collection, Historical Society of Haddonfield*

In her article on slaves in Haddonfield, Carrie Nicholson Hartel discusses a freed slave named Primus "who once belonged to the Estaughs but as no slaves are mentioned in her will probably he had been freed." However, in the "Inventory of Goods and Chattels of Elizabeth Estaugh", which was compiled and appraised at Elizabeth's death in 1762, the very last listing is "an old Negroe man almost past labour [too old to work]."[29] No monetary value is placed upon him.

When Hartel wrote her article she indicated that she had access to a document dated 1768 titled "An account of the stuff for Primus his house for which he is indebted to John [Estaugh] Hopkins."[30] Undoubtedly, Primus was the "old Negroe man" noted in Elizabeth Estaugh's inventory. Most likely, John Estaugh Hopkins, Elizabeth's primary heir, freed Primus and the Hopkins family continued to assist him and provide for his needs until his death.

The final document relating to Estaugh slaves appeared in the *Pennsylvania Gazette* on May 5, 1773. It too is about Primus, who last name is finally revealed. "Haddonfield April 26, 1773. The day before Yesterday about five'o clock in the afternoon a Fire broke out in a Shed, adjoining the House of Primus Marsh, an ancient Negroe, who formerly belonged to John Estaugh and is now upwards of 90 years of Age."[31]

Unrecorded in the historical record are John and Elizabeth's attitudes toward slavery. However, it is certain they were well aware of the slowly evolving Quaker attitudes and findings on slavery throughout the eighteenth century. Although not yet primarily focused on the abolition of slavery, the Quakers' attitude was profoundly shifting by the late 1730's. The Philadelphia Yearly meeting minutes in 1739, 1741 and 1742 cautioned Friends about "importing of Negroes, and against buying them after they are imported" rather than on abolition of slavery.[32]

John Estaugh was present at the Salem Quarterly Meeting, held in Haddonfield on June 17, 1737. Following the directive of the last Yearly Meeting, the Quarterly meeting "recommends to each Monthly Meeting . . . make an answer to our Next Quarterly Meeting" on the issue "relating to Negros."[33] On September 15 1738, it was reported at the Quarterly Meeting that the Monthly Meetings are "mostly clear of buying Negros."[34]

The issue of abolition became more prominent in Quaker thought throughout the 1740s and 1750s; more and more the "keeping" of slaves, not just the importing or buying of slaves, was part of the Quaker discipline. By 1743, noted Quaker minister John Woolman was beginning to express his concern about slavery. His concerns and ministries against slavery would gradually continue to increase, culminating in his 1754 publication, *Some Considerations on the Keeping of Negroes*. Woolman's attitudes undoubtedly would have been known to Elizabeth Haddon Estaugh. Woolman's sister Elizabeth, a prominent seamstress, rented a house from Elizabeth Estaugh in Haddonfield. Elizabeth Woolman often sewed for her neighbor and close friend Elizabeth Estaugh. (John Woolman also sewed for Elizabeth.) When Elizabeth Woolman lay dying, Estaugh comforted her on her deathbed.

Slaveholding was commonplace throughout the American colonies, including West Jersey, in the seventeenth century and many Quaker families in Old Gloucester and neighboring Salem and Gloucester counties owned slaves and indentured servants to work their large farms. One West Jersey Quaker even owned two Native American slaves. John and Elizabeth Estaugh owned fewer slaves than many of their immediate neighbors. Samuel Cole, William Evans and William, Joseph and Daniel Cooper, among other nearby plantation owners, held large numbers of African slaves. John Hugg of Gloucester town held nine slaves of African descent. The Cooper family, intimate with the Estaughs, owned more than a dozen slaves. Daniel Cooper's will in 1715 mentioned, "three male and one female negro slaves," who were valued at £140.[35] Between the years 1751 and 1762, a later Daniel Cooper, along with his cousin, Benjamin, permitted Philadelphia merchants to hold slave auctions at their respective ferries.

The greatest burden that John Estaugh faced during the 1730s was his never-ending obligations as the sole American agent for the new Pennsylvania Land Company of London. The Company instructed Estaugh in 1732 to comment on its plan to divide up and sell all its real estate holdings and properties in America. This included more than 7,000 acres of southeastern Pennsylvania land (also claimed by Maryland) and a dozen Philadelphia city lots formerly owned by Thomas Story. Estaugh, who was both a Pennsylvania Land Company agent and proprietor, replied that he might manage the division of all their properties, but this task would require a large work force of surveyors.

John Estaugh estimated that three or four managers would be needed to accompany each group of surveyors in order to accurately record the boundaries of each uncharted tract of wilderness land. Estaugh insisted that such "Surveying is a worke yt [that] cannot safely be done in ye heat of summer, without Danger to ye workemen, both as to Surveying & also of Snakes, therefore spring and fall is ye times wherein its to be done.[quoted as written]"[36] Estaugh and the Land Company hired noted Philadelphia attorney William Rawle (II) to help sort out all the deeds and legal papers sent by the Company. The over-worked and tired Estaugh wanted Rawle to substitute for him as manager of the surveying teams, as well, especially for winter service along the Brandywine Creek.[37] "But, If I cannot be Excused from acting in ye Affair," Estaugh wrote the Company, "I shall insist on, not only ye continuance of my Sallary untill ye work be finish, but yt [that] my expences be also born, for it will be a troublesome peace of work.[quoted as written]"[38]

As troubles mounted for her husband, Elizabeth began to suffer more health problems as well. A nagging sickness tempered Elizabeth's momentary happiness engendered by the marriage of her nephew Ebenezer to Sarah Lord and the birth of the Hopkins's first children. The Estaugh's attorney William Rawle observed that Elizabeth had been sick for some time. Rawle wrote Elizabeth's husband that: "I hope thy Spouse has recovered her health."[39] During her lingering illness, Elizabeth learned that Benjamin Hopkins, her sister's husband and father of her ward Ebenezer, had died in London. A short time later Elizabeth's oldest and dearest companion, Sarah Collins Dimsdale, died. According to family tradition Elizabeth sat by her bedside for hours praying and comforting her closest friend. Meanwhile Elizabeth's husband began to suffer more severe headaches. Elizabeth claimed that "he was troubled with an Infirmity in his Head, which rendered him unfit for the Service."[40] Nonetheless John began to talk about leaving his increasingly comfortable home to go on a mission to Friends in the West Indies.

The call to preach again to the unfaithful began for John Estaugh in 1737 when renowned Quaker traveling preacher John Fothergill visited the Haddon-Estaugh plantation house. The assertive minister Fothergill announced plans for a religious mission to comfort Friends in Barbados. His clearance to travel in the service of the Lord stirred John Estaugh to yet again visit Friends in the Caribbean islands. But it was the news that arrived in Philadelphia from the West Indies in December 1741 that finally convinced a frail sixty-six-year-old John Estaugh to undertake one more mission to the Caribbean. He learned that Thomas Chalkley, a Quaker traveling minister, wealthy Philadelphia merchant ship owner and lifelong Haddon-Estaugh family intimate had died while on a mission to comfort Friends and conduct trade on the tiny British West Indies island of Tortola. The Estaughs had known Chalkley and his family for nearly fifty years, since his days as a member with Elizabeth Haddon's family of the Horsleydown Monthly Meeting. After Chalkley removed to Philadelphia and Elizabeth Haddon and John Estaugh to West New Jersey, Chalkley often attended Meeting with the Estaughs across the river. Moreover, for years Estaugh and Chalkley carried on a vigorous West Indies trade together with James Logan and other Philadelphia Quaker merchants.

Spiritual soul searching and "conversation" with Friends moved Estaugh to continue his dear departed lifetime companion Chakley's mission in the British West Indies despite his increasingly comfortable Haddonfield existence. At the same time, the Philadelphia and London Meetings urged Estaugh to replace the deceased Chalkley on Tortola. These supplications convinced the tired Haddonfield minister to make the journey to the tiny British West Indian island of Tortola. It was not a good time for John to travel to the Caribbean, however. Not only did John suffer from poor health, but he would have to sail on dangerous seas once again. Another great war for empire had broken out in 1739, allying Spain and France against Britain in the American phase of military and naval action known as the War of Jenkins's Ear (1739–1743). By 1742 this war had spread to Europe becoming the War of the Austrian Succession (1740–1748). The fighting in America that mostly disturbed the southern colonies and Pennsylvania's frontiers made little immediate impact on the long-settled and most tranquil Haddonfield community, but as Elizabeth's sister Sarah wrote from England, "talk of war" hurt their Pennsylvania Land Company sales and the price of lead.[41] Worse this world-wide warfare threatened British travel and trade with the Americas across the Atlantic and in the Caribbean. For a decidedly unhealthy John Estaugh, sailing into hostile waters to the island of Tortola meant that he would embark on a particularly life-threatening mission.

John Estaugh brushed aside all such concerns. Though he had yielded to the worldly comforts of his pleasant estate, John had never abandoned his willingness to sacrifice everything—house, land, marriage and life—to his calling to spread the Word of God among the unfaithful. In September 1742, Estaugh and Philadelphia minister Thomas Cadwallader received clearance from the Philadelphia Yearly Meeting to travel to Tortola. The following month, although noting that "it hath pleased Almighty God to restore me a state of Good health," nonetheless, on October 5, 1742, Estaugh wrote his final will and testament, "calling to mind the uncertainty of Life ye Great inconveniences that often times Happen to the Family related to the Person that desires the Quiet of his relations after his decease." Consequently he bequeathed "all the rest and remainder Part of my Estate both real and Personall Goods and Chattels whatsoever . . . unto my dear and well beloved Wife Elizabeth Estaugh, daughter of John Haddon late of Saint Georges Southwark in Great Britain deceased."[42]

Elizabeth's husband knew that he was not in good health, but seemed driven to console troubled Friends in the humid, fever-ridden island of Tortola. At least this time the seas proved friendly enough. No enemy warships or privateers intercepted the missionaries' ship, as they had on his 1704 mission to Barbados. Estaugh and Cadwallader arrived safely in November 1742 at the home of John Pickering, the Quaker Governor of Tortola. The two Delaware Valley ministers began at once to comfort Tortola Friends at Pickering's Meeting. Estaugh and Cadwallader prepared to travel through nearly impassable sugar cane fields, thick underbrush and sail across wide expanses of water to reach other Meetings scattered about the islands. However Cadwallader had fallen ill on the voyage and collapsed when he reached Governor Pickering's house. The Philadelphia traveling minister Cadwallader died eighteen days after arriving in Tortola.

John Estaugh attended Cadwallader's burial in the pouring rain and then traveled alone to attend Meeting on these remote islands. Throughout John's journey to assist distant Friends, it rained. When the Haddonfield traveling minister arrived finally at the houses of Quakers, he found that a deadly fever plagued many. Nevertheless, Estaugh not only visited these unhealthy meetings on Tortola but sailed in particularly rough seas to a meeting on the more distant Jost Van Dyke Island. Ultimately Estaugh collapsed and was bedridden in great pain and suffering. Even on the last day of his life, though, John Estaugh insisted on preaching to a small gathering from his deathbed in the "House of William Thomas." Estaugh died on December 6, 1742, and the Tortola Quakers buried him next to Philadelphia ministers Thomas Chalkley and Thomas Cadwallader at the Fat Hog Bay burial ground near Governor Pickering's plain wooden plantation house in Road Town.[43]

The Tortola ministry killed Estaugh as it had the two Philadelphia Quaker preachers Chalkley and Cadwallader. Governor Pickering attested that they had died in the service of the Lord and for the comfort of Friends. When

ANCIENT BURIAL GROUND OF FRIENDS, TORTOLA.   Drawn on the spot by George Truman.
1. Graves of Thomas Chalkley, John Estaugh, John Cadwallader and Mary Hunt.
2. Foundation of Meeting-house.   3. Farm of Long Look.

Print of George Truman's original drawing depicting the Quaker burial ground at Tortola containing the interments of Thomas Chalkley, John Estaugh, John Cadwallader, and Mary Hunt. *Courtesy of Friends Historical Library of Swarthmore College.*

the Haddonfield Monthly Meeting received news of Estaugh's death, it announced that he had died answering his Inner Light, the voice of God, to spread the Truth. When Elizabeth heard the news a few weeks after her husband's death, she testified that she was content to have given up John most willingly, as she had since their marriage in 1702, to his lifelong calling to sermonize the Word of the Lord. Sadly his death occurred just six days after their 40th marriage anniversary. "Oh! What shall I say of him, but that he was a Man endowed with many good Gifts, which rendered him very agreeable to his Friends, and much more to me, his Wife."[45]

Despite this comforting testimony, John's passing devastated Elizabeth. In her meticulously detailed record book for the Haddonfield Women's Monthly Meeting, she left a blank page after learning of the death of her beloved husband. More significantly, for nearly ten years after his decease, Elizabeth did not witness Quaker marriages at her beloved Haddonfield Monthly Meeting house. During this interval Elizabeth inquired into just one clearance for marriage and that for her close kin and then-widow Mary Gill to John Thorne. The widow Sarah Hopkins tried to comfort her "Sorely tried & afflicted (though) not forsaken Sister," Elizabeth Estaugh. "May ye god of peace Accompany us while hear [sic] & where our troublesome life Shall end Receive us into ye Kingdom of Eternall [sic] Rest where our Dr. friends & worthy parents are Doubt not enter'd."[46]

Ultimately Elizabeth emerged from her private suffering. Perhaps to obtain inner peace, Elizabeth now dedicated the rest of her life to continue the building the Quaker community of Haddonfield, a task that she had begun forty years before when she sailed to America on her father John Haddon's instructions. After her father's death, Elizabeth had continued the prominent London Quaker blacksmith's mission over the next two decades with the prayers and support of her dear companion John Estaugh. Now with her husband's passing, Elizabeth was once again left alone to continue her great task of building a Quaker community on her Haddon family's lands. This time, however, she could call upon and receive constant assistance from her many male and female Friends, who shared unity with her in the Haddonfield Monthly Meeting.

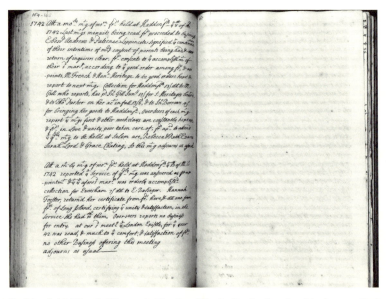

Haddonfield Friends Women's Meeting Minute Book showing blank page that Elizabeth Estaugh left as a tribute to her husband John Estaugh after learning of his death in 1742. *Collection 1250 P3.5, Quaker Collection, Haverford College, Haverford PA.*

CHAPTER 9 NOTES.

[1] Estaugh, *Call to the Unfaithful*, xiii.
[2] J. William Frost, "The Affirmation Controversy and Religious Liberty," in Richard S. Dunn and Mary Maples Dunn, *The World of William Penn* (Philadelphia: University of Pennsylvania Press, 1986), 303–35.
[3] Estaugh, *Call to the Unfaithful*, xiv–xv.
[4] Ibid. xv.
[5] Release to John Gill, 1726. HEHP, folder 167.
[6] Joseph Kaighin [Kaighn]-Mary Estaugh certificate of marriage, May 18, 1727, in Camden County Historical Society Library, Camden, NJ; copy, in box 1, Lyons Project Papers, HSHL.
[7] Kaighin's medical diploma.
[8] Edward W. Hocker, *A Doctor of Colonial Germantown* (Philadelphia, Germantown Historical Society, 1948).
[9] Elizabeth's gifts to Kaighin, October 23, 1760. HSHL, file 1914–005-208.
[10] S. Hopkins to Dear Bro & Sister [John and Elizabeth Estaugh] September 17, 1734. HEHP, folder 184.
[11] Southwark Records.
[12] Note regarding land in dispute between Francis Collings [sic] and Robert Dimsdale, 1722, HEHP,folder 103; Power of Attorney from John and William Dimsdale (Chirurgions) to John Estaugh, 1722, HEHP.
[13] Thomas Sharp's Poem, in Clement, *First Emigrant Settlers*, 31.
[14] Estaugh, *Call to the Unfaithful*, xiv.
[15] Minute Book 1, Part B, Haddonfield Women's Monthly Meeting in Frank H. Stewart Room, Special Collections, Campbell Library at Rowan University, Glassboro, New Jersey.folder 134.
[16] Marriage Certificate, Thomas E[d]gerton and Sarah Stephens, signed by John and Elizabeth Estaugh, 1733. HEHP, folder 208.
[17] Receipts, signed by John Craig, for board and schooling of Ebenezer Hopkins, paid by John Estaugh, 1727–1728. HEHP, folder 169.
[18] Marriage Certificate, Ebenezer Hopkins and Sarah Lord, 1737. HEHP, folder 209.
[19] For a list of these marriages from 1730–1739, see Clement, *First Emigrant Settlers*, 395–410.
[20] Agreement of Richard Buckele with John Estaugh for cutting a trench through the meadow, 1735. HEHP, folder 118.
[21] Receipts by Ralph Leigh in connection with the business of John Estaugh, 1735 and 1737. HEHP, folder 142.
[22] Clement, *First Emigrant Settlers*, 374.
[23] Authorization by John Estaugh to Isaac Albertson and his assistants to

enter the house of Richard Buckele, and distrain [sic] his goods and chattels for rent, 1742. HEHP, folder 121; for the entire Buckele affair, see documents 117–122, in HEHP

[24]Haddonfield Monthly Meeting Minutes, September 14, 1730.

[25]John Estaugh "was one of those against whom Benjamin Lay shot his shafts," *The Friend: A Religious and Literary Journal* (Philadelphia: Robb, Pile & McElroy, 1857) 30: 124.

[26]For description of Lay, see Albert Cook Myers, ed., *Hannah Logan's Courtship: A True Narrative* (Philadelphia: Ferris & Leach, 1904), 8.

[27]Brycchan Carey, *From Peace to Freedom: Quaker Rhetoric and the Birth of American Antislavery, 1657–1761.* (New Haven, Yale University Press, 2012), 174.

[28]John Estaugh Instructions to Ebenezer Hopkins, 12th day of yet 8th mo 1742, file 1991-001-0115, Wittwer Collection, HSHL.

[29]Copy of Inventory of Elizabeth Estaugh. HSHL, file 1913-001-0642.

[30]Carrie Elizabeth Nicholson Hartel, "Notes on Slaves in Haddonfield and Vicinity," file 12-08 in Hartel Collection, HSHL.

[31]New Jersey Archives, XXIII, 501.

[32]Minutes of the Haddonfield Quarterly Meeting, June 17, 1737, on microform in the Quaker collection, Haverford College Library.

[33]Carey, *From Peace to Freedom.*

[34]Haddonfield Quarterly Meeting Minutes. September 15, 1738.

[35]New Jersey Archives, 1st series, XXIII, 107.

[36]Jno Estaugh letter to Pennsylvania Land Company, July 29, 1733, copy, in box 1, Lyons Project Papers, HSHL.

[37]Letter from the Pennsylvania Land Company, London. Approves of the appointment of William Rawle, July 8, 1735, folder 97; Letter of Attorney, John Estaugh makes William Rawle his true attorney, 1736, HEHP, folder 135; for William Rawle-John Estaugh relationship, 1732–38, see documents 163–165, all in HEHP.

[38]Jno Estaugh letter to Pennsylvania Land Company, July 29, 1733, copy, in box 1, Lyons Project Papers, HSHL.

[39]William Rawle to John Estaugh, January 6, 1733. HEHP, folder 164.

[40]Estaugh, *Call to the Unfaithful,* v.

[41]S. Hopkins to Dearest Broe. & Sister, London, September 17, 1734, and, S. H. [Sarah Hopkins] to Dearest Sister [Elizabeth Estaugh], March 17, 1744. HEHP, folder 184.

[42]John Estaugh Will, October 5, 1742, New Jersey State Archives Lib. 4, p. 357-B, copy, in box 1, Lyons Project Papers, HSHL.

[43]Generations of researchers, including Betty and Stuart Lyons, visited the Tortola site trying unsuccessfully to locate the Friends burial ground with its unmarked graves, long ago lost in thick undergrowth.

[44]John Jackson, "Worthy Friends of the Nineteenth Century III in *Friends' Intelligencer*, Seventh Month 4, 1903, vol. LX, no. 27, (Philadelphia: Friends Intelligencer Association), 419.

[45]Estaugh, *Call to the Unfaithful,* vi.

[46]S. H. [Sarah Hopkins] to Dearest Sister [Elizabeth Estaugh], March 17, 1744. HEHP, folder 184.

CHAPTER 10.
Maintaining Love and Unity, 1743–1762.

I have a secret Satisfaction in that I was enabled to give him up unto the Service into which he was called. This is but just a Hint for those who may be under the like Exercise and Tryal [sic], that they may not hold back, but submit, and freely give up their All leaving the Consequence to the wife disposing Hand, who knows for what Cause it is.

—Elizabeth Haddon Estaugh[1]

Shortly after John Estaugh's death on the tiny Caribbean island of Tortola, Elizabeth Estaugh contracted with Philadelphia printer Benjamin Franklin to publish her husband's essay: *A Call to the Unfaithful Professors of Truth*. Elizabeth had carefully hand written the tract, possibly as her husband dictated it to her a few months before he left for Tortola. Now, Elizabeth paid the sizeable sum of £46.18.9 Pennsylvania money to Franklin's type-setter John Bringhurst to print and bind two-hundred copies.[2] She planned to distribute them to all the members of the Haddonfield Monthly Meeting. The widow Estaugh dispatched close friend Joseph Cooper and her nephew Ebenezer Hopkins to Philadelphia to pay in two installments for publication of the sacred volume. This was arguably the most important act of her life, more important to Elizabeth than her father's

A CALL TO THE Unfaithful Professors OF TRUTH.

WRITTEN BY

JOHN ESTAUGH

In his Life-time; and now Published for General Service.

TO WHICH IS ADDED

Divers **EPISTLES**

Of the same AUTHOR.

PHILADELPHIA:
Printed by B. FRANKLIN.
M,DCC,XLIV.

Title Page of John Estaugh's *A Call to the Unfaithful Professors of Truth*, which Elizabeth Estaugh organized and had published in 1744, after John Estaugh's death. *Rhoads Collection, Historical Society of Haddonfield*

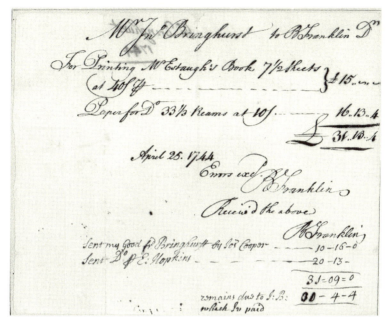

Receipt from Benjamin Franklin for printing "the Widow Estaugh's book," 1744. Collection 1001, Quaker Collection, Haverford College, Haverford, PA.

assignment to her as his American real estate agent forty years earlier or the marriage ceremony with John Estaugh. Elizabeth told her Haddonfield Friends Meeting on February 9, 1743: "I cannot be altogether Silent" any longer and must reveal at last the "Truth" about her forty-year relationship with John Estaugh. "For sure, few, if any Man ever left a sweeter Savor [sic], both at home and abroad, than he has done."[3]

In her "Testimony to the Memory of her beloved Husband," Elizabeth Estaugh revealed, perhaps for the first time in a public record, her personal feelings and character. Her testimony emerges as one of the few sources with which to document how Elizabeth evaluated her own life. Elizabeth wrote many personal letters over the years to her parents in England, but none have ever been located. She also recorded numerous routine minutes for the Newton and then Haddonfield Friends Women's Meetings. She left a handful of personal business papers, as well. Few of these formal reports or records provided insight into the "real" Elizabeth. Therefore, this affirmation of affection for John Estaugh remains one of the rare sources with which we can try to understand Elizabeth Haddon Estaugh.

In her testimony, Elizabeth showed an intensely personal, passionate and total commitment to her Inner Light and to the Word of God as professed in the Bible. At the same time, she revealed a clear understanding of the need to participate "at home" in the worldly affairs of community. Elizabeth embodied the birth-right Quaker who recognized no dividing line between religious (the Meeting House) and the secular (Counting House). As this biography has demonstrated, Elizabeth served not only God in everyday worship and at the Friends Meeting, but the secular needs of building her own farm and helping male and female members of her rural West New Jersey Quaker community to establish their own places.[4]

Elizabeth explained in her mid-eighteenth century epistle what it meant to be a follower both in England and the New World of the long-suffering Religious Society of Friends, now known as Quakers. Using her late-husband John Estaugh as a model, Elizabeth explained how during the tumultuous period of religious and civil crises that convulsed late-seventeenth century England, many young people struggled to find a true religion, trying as her future husband had during his early years to receive comfort from the Baptists and other reformed English Protestant sects. In the end, the teachings of George Fox, founder of the Religious Society of Friends, and the tutelage of "worthy Minister of the Gospel Francis Stamper of London" awakened John (and many other young "seekers of the Truth") to the Society of Friends. A blessed few such as Estaugh received the "Gift" to spread the word of the Lord through traveling ministries. Elizabeth explained in her testimony to the Haddonfield Monthly Meeting that her husband constantly "grew in his Gift," preaching in England, Scotland, Ireland, the West Indies and throughout British North America. Finally, John decided to settle and marry in West New Jersey. Elizabeth explained in her testimony after her husband's death, that for forty years "he was a Sweet Companion . . . at Haddonfield in the County of Gloucester, and Western Division of the Province of New-Jersey."[5]

Elizabeth admitted that at first John "traveled pretty much" in his ministry, "but in the latter Part he was troubled with an Infirmity in his Head, which rendered him unfit for the Service." It was then that Estaugh devoted more time to help his wifely companion build a prosperous plantation and a Quaker community in the village of Haddonfield. Elizabeth remembered that John was so blessed in Haddonfield, being "very easy at home; where, thro' Mercy, we lived very comfortably." Yet even after he had reached such comfort, Elizabeth sighed, he gave up everything "to travel in the Service of Truth," for one last time, "enabled by the great Hand that drew him forth, to perform that Service to the great Satisfaction of Friends."

Yet Elizabeth troubled that, though John had "freely given up their all," he had left "the Consequence to the wife disposing Hand, who knows for what Cause." She implied that John had improved their wealth so that he would be free to travel when called by the Lord to spread the Truth. Elizabeth explained that he did this work, since no Quaker minister was free to fulfill God's mission of preaching to "the great Satisfaction of Friends" everywhere unless they had a firm economic base from which to launch their missions. In the end, Elizabeth wondered "who knows for what Cause it is" that she surrendered her husband to the Lord, concluding, that it was "the Cause yet hid."[6]

Gradually, Elizabeth came to believe that John had left her for the higher purpose of completing their lifetime work of building a Quaker community upon her father's lands in order "to comfort the sorrowful, the heavy-hearted and sincere, seeking of Christ Jesus." Now that John was gone, she received strength from so many intimate Haddonfield Friends to continue this work. Those closest to Elizabeth included her kin through marriage: Ebenezer Hopkins, John Gill, Joseph and John Kaighn, Thomas Redman, Timothy Matlack, Joseph Cooper, John Hollinshead, Samuel Lippincott and Joshua Lord. These elders and overseers of the Haddonfield Monthly Meeting revealed to widow Estaugh that they must continue her late husband's work together and further strengthen the Quaker community, particularly the Haddonfield Monthly Meeting. They testified that: "He was zealous for preserving good Order in the Church; and for maintaining Love and Unity, that Badge of true Discipleship."[7]

After her husband's passing, Elizabeth continued to work with the Quaker community in Haddonfield and the surrounding Chester, Woodbury, Evesham and more distant Burlington and Salem Meetings. To this end, Elizabeth "constantly kept up" her report of Meeting "in a general way in love & unity." She had retired as an Overseer of the Poor, but continued recording reports on care for the poor. She meticulously listed donations to support the Evesham and Chester meetings and each payment to Joseph Thackara for looking after the old Newton Meeting House. The long-time clerk of the Haddonfield Women's Meeting Elizabeth Estaugh reported on all women members who were selected to attend the Quarterly and Yearly Meetings in Salem and Burlington. At the same time, she recorded dissatisfaction with the actions of any female member of the Meeting, particularly "for early familiarity with her husband" before she inquired as to clearness to marry. For instance, Susann Sloan had to present a paper condemning "her outgoing," while Rebeckah Crispin brought a paper admitting to "her unchaste freedom [that] has brought shame & trouble on herself & Friends." Usually the Women's Meeting gave the condemnation of its women members to the Men's Meeting for review and public reading. Occasionally the women, probably at the behest of the widow Estaugh, took care of the case and kept it within their own meeting.[8]

Elizabeth continued her service as clerk of the Women Friends of the Monthly Meeting of Haddonfield. However, she avoided the witnessing of important Quaker marriages for many years after her husband's death. Such conduct seemed contrary to Elizabeth's mission in life since these marriages lay at the center of her vision of building a Quaker community around the Haddonfield Friends Meeting. Inquiry into a couple's search for clearance to marry in Meeting was most important to Elizabeth. It provided the best method with which to arrange for the union of the most "satisfactory" and "serviceable" Quaker families, particularly those related to the original settlers. Nonetheless, Elizabeth failed to witness even the most acceptable arrangements. Perhaps she remained so grief stricken by the loss of her husband that she became something of a recluse in her great plantation house where she focused on maintaining her farm for the benefit of the Hopkins family.

More likely, Elizabeth now deferred to other trusted women Friends of the Monthly Meetings to inquire into clearness to marry. Most of these women came from the older families that first settled Old Gloucester County. Moreover these "acceptable" female Friends were related directly through marriages held in Meeting to the Gill and Hopkins clans, and thus to the Estaugh and Haddon families. Most of these newly married Quaker women became during her later years Elizabeth's dearest and constant companions. These included Elizabeth Lippincott for the Evesham Meeting, Mary Heritage Gill and Sarah Lord Hopkins for the Haddonfield Monthly Meeting and Phoebe Burrough for the Chester Meeting. All led inquiries into a couple's clearance to marry in the Friends Meeting House in Haddonfield. Though not witnessing the marriages, Elizabeth Estaugh carefully recorded each inquiry for clearness to marry and subsequent marriage in her record book for the Haddonfield Women's Meeting.

Elizabeth finally agreed eight years after the death of her husband to sit on a committee that inquired into the clearness to marry for one of her closest kin. Thus Elizabeth joined Sarah Hopkins in 1750 on the committee that inquired into the intention of John Thorne to marry Mary Gill, the widow of Elizabeth's cousin John Gill who had died a few months earlier. The Thorne family had deep roots in the original Quaker community and had intermarried with nearly every other significant Haddonfield family. Consequently, Elizabeth and Sarah found the marriage acceptable and cleared Mary Gill to marry John Thorne. Such intermarriage of leading Quaker families provided the security for the estates and landholdings of women members, particularly for widows, by uniting them with unmarried or widowed Quaker landowners or shopkeepers. Thus the widow Gill married a wealthy Gloucester landowner John Thorne, who now moved to Haddonfield and managed his new wife's estate.

After witnessing the marriage of her cousin's widow, Elizabeth withdrew once more to her plantation house and failed to witness the union of members of other prominent Quaker families in her neighborhood. She recorded the conjoining through marriage of acceptable Friends, however. These included the marriages of Archibald Mickle to Mary Burrough, Thomas Hinchman and Letitia Mickle, Jacob Ellis and Cassandra Albertson and Benjamin Matlack to Susanna Hewitt. These newlywed couples settled in the center of the growing village of Haddonfield or on farms in the surrounding countryside between the Pennsauken, Cooper's and Newton creeks. Letitia Mickle, for instance, resided in "A Commodious brick house" on an acre-and-a-half lot with a good shop and barn and "near 100 fruit trees."[9]

For many years prior to John's death, Elizabeth and other prosperous landowning Friends had started to shape their community through the division and sale of land. They built houses for sale or rent on lots on both sides of the King's Highway, Tanner Street and Ferry Road (Haddon Avenue). The Estaughs had already constructed four rental properties during the previous decade along these Haddonfield roadways. Such transactions placed acceptable newlyweds, those married in Meeting, in houses close by the Haddonfield Monthly Meeting house and within a short walking distance up a tree-lined lane to the nearby Haddon-Estaugh plantation house. Already, Samuel Mickle, Sarah Norris, Thomas Perry Webb, John Kay, Isaac Smith and Thomas Redman owned shops, stables, inns and/or houses in the center of town. Elizabeth diligently recorded all transactions, probably from her desk in the sitting room and library of her house, preserving her father's vision of a Quaker community in West New Jersey and continuing the work that she had initiated with her husband years before his death in Tortola.

Now after John's death, Elizabeth determined to further develop this Quaker community. She directed business from her plantation house office and through her agents Ebenezer Hopkins, John Gill, William Rawlins, John Kaighin and others. Their work led to Jacob Clement opening a tannery on a lot purchased from Timothy Matlack, who had originally acquired it from the Estaughs. This land adjoined that of Sarah Kay Norris, proprietor of a shop and tavern on that spot. In 1747 Jacob Clement married Hannah Alberston, one of Elizabeth's closest neighbors and friends in the Women's Meeting. Rebecca Collins Clement, widow of Jacob's brother Samuel, maintained her small frame house on the lane to the Haddonfield Friends Meeting House. Joseph Collins had deeded the property that he had purchased earlier from the Estaughs to his daughter Rebecca as a wedding gift. Her house stood a few steps away from her kin Jacob Clement. Next door Samuel Clement, Jr., who married into the Evans family from the neighboring Evesham Meeting, maintained his surveyor's office on another lot purchased in 1740 from the Estaughs. The Clement family, originally from Long Island, intermarried with others from that community who had moved with them long ago to West New Jersey. This Long Island Quaker connection included the Hinchman and Harrison families. John Hinchman married the widow Elizabeth Norris Smith and in 1747 moved to Haddonfield's main street near the Cooper's Creek. This marriage united the couple with the Hugg, Wood and Cole; Matlack, Kay and Evans families among many other Friends in the Haddonfield Monthly Meeting deemed most acceptable by Elizabeth Estaugh.

That same year, Elizabeth's cousin John Gill built a brick house on the King's Highway in the center of the growing Quaker community of Haddonfield. Gill sold this fine residence to his son John, Jr. after the elder Gill moved in 1748 to a large farmhouse a few miles away. The Gills helped Elizabeth sell land adjoining their property along the main street running between Cooper's Creek and the Ferry Road to Pyne Poynt (Camden). The following year, Elizabeth sold a lot to Robert Stephens. Stephens was related to Elizabeth through his sister Mary's marriage to John Kaighin, Sr. (Kaighn), whose son Joseph had married Mary Estaugh. This property bordered on the lots containing the Haddonfield Friends burying ground and the properties of Timothy Matlack and Joseph Kaighn. In December 1745, Elizabeth closed a deal with the saddler William Griscom for sale of her lot "by the bounds of the Burying ground . . . to a stone at the most Northerly Corner of the Burying ground Thence North-esterly . . . to a Stake in the Line of Timothy Matlack[']s Land." Griscom paid Estaugh £10 for the prime property upon which he opened a saddle shop.[10]

In the two decades after her husband's passing, Elizabeth pushed the sales and rentals of her real estate with increasing intensity. Elizabeth also leased a parcel of land near her house to William Sharp for clearing and selling timber. In 1746 she sold land to Peter Andrews, along what would become the corner of the King's Highway and Tanner Street. Isaac Andrews already maintained a tannery on Tanner Street, purchased in 1735 from the Estaughs. Andrews' daughters soon married into the Sharp and Brown families with all marriages witnessed at the Haddonfield Friends Meeting House. Elizabeth maintained an intimate relationship with the Andrews family, leaving money in her will to them. Nearby, Elizabeth leased an adjoining lot to her dear friend and personal physician Dr. John Kaighin. Here, Kaighin built his residence and doctor's office.[11]

Real estate development and construction of shops attracted newcomers to the growing town of Haddonfield. Local land owners aggressively advertised their properties for sale in the *Pennsylvania Gazette*. Inevitably some buyers were not birthright Quakers. Others were not acceptable members of the Religious Society of Friends Meeting or had married out of Meeting. However the Quaker community welcomed a few non-Quakers if they brought wealth to Haddonfield. Such was the case with Mathias Aspden, Hugh Creighton and Robert

Friend Price, the latter arguably the most prominent owner of Haddonfield properties during Elizabeth's lifetime. Innkeeper Creighton married the Quaker widow Mary French out of meeting in 1759, and they built a brick house on the King's Highway, opposite the present-day Indian King Tavern, and within the Haddonfield village boundary. In 1750 Robert Friend Price bought the tavern owned by the late Margery Perry Webb, who had just died. To secure his place in the village and enhance his property, Price eventually married Mary Thorne, the daughter of well-connected Friends Thomas and Mary Harrison Thorne. Although, the ceremony took place out of Meeting, Price established vital connections for his business with Haddonfield's Quaker community, including with the Estaugh-Hopkins family. This latter connection arose from the marriage, witnessed by Elizabeth Estaugh Hopkins at the Haddonfield Friend's Meeting House, of widow Mary Heritage Gill to Mary Thorne's brother John Thorne.

Robert Friend Price demonstrated how the use of marriage might gain an outsider full acceptance by the Quaker community of Haddonfield. He maximized such relationships despite the fact that he was not of Meeting and had married outside of Meeting. His marriage to Thorne and later to Leze Collins Hugg connected Price to the Hinchman, Burrough, Haines, Roberts, Heritage, Kaighn, Hugg, Collins, Mickle and other leading Quaker families. His Haddonfield tavern became a center for political and economic discourse that included Quaker and non-Quaker Gloucester County residents. After his first wife's death, Price immediately married Leze Hugg, daughter of the late John Collins and the widow of Samuel Hugg. Hugg had been Gloucester town's most prominent store keeper and political leader. Price and fellow Haddonfield resident John Hinchman eventually became involved with the growing protest movement against British imperial polices and would become leaders of the Committees of Correspondence. While Hinchman remained a Loyalist, Price would become a militant patriot against Britain in the Revolutionary War.

As more newcomers, not yet accepted in Meeting, began to settle in the area, Elizabeth became active once again in witnessing marriages between Friends at the Haddonfield Monthly Meeting. She witnessed the 1758 marriage of Sarah Andrews, her immediate neighbor, to newcomer John Miller. The following year, Elizabeth witnessed the marriages of Sarah Sloan to John Branson, Sarah Albertson to Sam Webster and after Webster's death Sarah's marriage to Constantine Lord. Elizabeth's last recorded witnessing occurred in August of 1761 when she went to Meeting to sign the certificate of marriage of Elnathan Zane to Bathsheba Heartly. There was no evidence that she attended months later what must have been a very important affair for her: the marriage of her closest relative in America, her grandnephew John Estaugh Hopkins to Sarah Mickle at the Upper Greenwich Monthly Meeting in Cumberland County, New Jersey. Elizabeth, at age 81 and in failing health, could have sailed down the Delaware or traveled more than thirty miles over badly rutted roads to reach this meeting in her "chaise" four-wheeled carriage that had been recently repaired for a broken axle and "hup Round Kittle."[12] So she failed to make this trip.

Still, Elizabeth maintained love, unity and good order in her own Haddonfield Monthly Meeting. At the same time, she continued to develop her special town in memory of her beloved father. Ebenezer Hopkins's family gave her constant comfort. Ebenezer had become a prominent figure in local politics, serving between 1749 and 1754 as the Gloucester County tax collector. Meanwhile, Ebenezer and Sarah's family continued to grow, providing the childless Elizabeth with the surrogate grandchildren, that she was never able to nurture in her own household. Haddon Hopkins, the Hopkins' third child, was born in 1743, and two years later, Ebenezer (II) was born. A large family soon followed with Sarah born in 1748, Mary in 1750 and Ann in 1757. Everyone who stopped at Elizabeth Estaugh's plantation during her later years noted the neighborly atmosphere that surrounded her household. Widely traveled Quaker missionary Mary Pace Weston visited Elizabeth's mansion in 1750 with William Logan, Peter and Isaac Andrews and the noted Burlington minister and businessman Peter Fearon where they met Ebenezer and Sarah Hopkins and their young family. The visitors noted how the Hopkins's "Pretty children" created a warm and friendly surrounding.[13] Elizabeth made certain that the Hopkins were comfortable in their own place, as well, while continuing to enhance her own estate. She sold them two-hundred acres of prime land, known as the Hopkins Plantation, where they had lived since their 1737 marriage. Elizabeth charged her nephew's son £300 for the property.[14]

Elizabeth was outliving all the earlier generations and her immediate family. Her "Very serviceable Friend" Elizabeth Evans died in 1748, followed the next year by kinsman Joseph Kaighn. Cousin John Gill died in 1749 on a business trip to England. Although Gill's son John Jr. continued to manage some of Elizabeth's real estate affairs, the elder Gill's death marked the beginning of the passing of her oldest and closest kin. In 1754 Hannah Cooper passed away and in 1757 her dearest nephew Ebenezer Hopkins died unexpectedly of smallpox at the age of thirty-eight. Ebenezer died intestate and Elizabeth and her lawyer Francis Rawle had to settle his affairs for his wife Sarah Lord and his mother Sarah Haddon Hopkins, Elizabeth's sister back in England.[15] Coincidentally, Elizabeth learned that her sister Sarah had also died in the London borough of Southwark at the age of seventy-two. Friends buried Sarah Hopkins near Elizabeth's parents in the Long Lane burial ground. After this sad news, Elizabeth gave her great nephew John Estaugh Hopkins, the eldest son of her late nephew Ebenezer Hopkins, her most sacred possession, the *Treacle Bible*.

Even now, though, the widow Estaugh was not ready to withdraw from worldly affairs. She continued to sell lots and build houses for her closest remaining friends, family and members in Meeting. Elizabeth sold choice land on the King's Highway to the blacksmith Edward Gibbs, son of a prominent Quaker family that had first settled in Salem in 1675 and was now married to Mary Burrough, the daughter of Estaugh's close friend John Burrough. She deeded the cordwainer Thomas Cummings a lot next to the Gibbs property. The widow Estaugh and John Estaugh Hopkins also developed other properties along the main roads of the growing Haddonfield town. She employed Daniel Smith to build rental properties with shops on the first floor and residences on the upper story. Elizabeth Estaugh paid Smith "one Hundred Pounds Lawful money of New Jersey to be paid at four separate times, i.e. £15 at beginning, and £15 at nailing, £15 at enclosing Said Tenement, and the remaining part when finished."[16]

The long-lingering Pennsylvania Land Company management left to her in John Estaugh's will also kept Elizabeth busy in her large, comfortable house. Francis Rawle, Elizabeth's Philadelphia attorney, warned her that the London-based company had found errors in her late husband's accounting of Pennsylvania land sales. Rawle delivered a lengthy dispatch to her in early 1759 from company executive Thomas Hyam that detailed Elizabeth's obligations to settle her husband's debt to the company. Hyam warned that this must be accomplished before the English Parliament arranged for a breakup of the company and sale of all land for cash dividends. Hyam wrote from London that he was "so perplexed" by the "very deficient" accounts of Pennsylvania Land Company business that "Friend Elizabeth" had sent him. He lashed out at her deceased family and attorneys John Estaugh, William Rawle and Ebenezer Hopkins for their "Indolence Inactivity or Negligence" in keeping good records. Worse, Hyam blamed them for not returning money owed the Company from the sale of timber land, rent from tenants and the distribution of surveyed land in America. The Land Company attorney claimed that "because of thy Husband & Nephews remissness during the Time of their agency, the Company's Estate is not now worth, by many Thousand pounds Sterling, what it would now yield, If all the concerned in the management of it had done their duty." Hyam even blamed Elizabeth's long-departed father John Haddon for not returning the deed to Richard Noble's plantation that he had held in trust for the Company. Elizabeth expected her attorney Francis Rawle to take care of these matters, but Rawle accidentally shot himself while hunting and died suddenly. In the end, Elizabeth Estaugh never settled the Pennsylvania Land Company account. Her nephew's widow Sarah Lord Hopkins completed legal arrangements only after Elizabeth's death.[17]

Though still active in the local real estate business in 1759, Elizabeth had begun to slow down. She stopped going to Meeting sometime in late 1760 or early 1761. A visitor to the Estaugh's plantation house, Ann Cooper Whitall from nearby Red Bank, reported that Elizabeth appeared to be in some pain. Indeed, Elizabeth wrote Philadelphia Quaker merchant John Smith, husband of her dear friend Hannah Logan, that I "am so afflicted with my head, that deeply affects and unqualifies me for much writing." She closed her letter to Smith in late 1761 with a poignant: "Farewell Saith Eliza. Estaugh."[18]

On November 30, 1761 Elizabeth decided, at last, to write her will. She insisted that she was still in fair health. "I, Elizabeth Estaugh, of Haddonfield," she began, "being at this time (through mercy) in a good state of health of body, and of sound disposing mind—praised be the Lord . . . do make and ordain this my last Will and Testament." In her will, Elizabeth left the Haddon-Estaugh legacy to relatives and closest friends who were "being of the People called Quakers." She granted the widow Hopkins the use of the Upper House and lot in Haddonfield purchased from the executors of Samuel Mickle. "I also farther give unto my kinswoman Sarah Hopkins aforesaid," Elizabeth continued, "the liberty and use of which House, either that wherein I now dwell or that wherein she now dwells [the Hopkins plantation]." In actuality Elizabeth was directing her grandnephew, John Estaugh Hopkins to allow his mother Sarah Hopkins to have first choice as to where she would live, even though he became the legal owner of both properties upon Elizabeth's death.[19]

Elizabeth carefully provided for other Hopkins family members as well. She bequeathed Sarah's oldest son John Estaugh Hopkins all her plantation called New Haddonfield. She gave him all her tools, furniture, cherished clock and horse-drawn "chariot." In addition, Elizabeth granted the twenty-four-year old future head of the Hopkins' family a 1/8th share of the Proprietary lands "which my dear father Jno. Haddon purchased of Richard Matthews." Elizabeth also instructed her late nephew's son to provide "corn sufficient" for his mother and his younger siblings. The widow Estaugh bequeathed to twenty-three-year old kinswoman Elizabeth Estaugh Hopkins a substantial endowment of £500 "proclamation money" upon her marriage. She granted her nineteen-year old kinsman Haddon Hopkins (later read out of Meeting), her house and lot adjacent to Isaac Andrews and her farm called "Little Stebbing," comprising 157 acres along the Ferry Road (Haddon Avenue) several miles to the west of Elizabeth's plantation house. The elder Elizabeth also devised to seventeen-year old Ebenezer Hopkins half of the Proprietary land granted long ago to her father John Haddon by Thomas Willis. Elizabeth bequeathed her house and lot then occupied by her dear friend the widow Elizabeth Craig to young Ebenezer. Elizabeth Estaugh next awarded property and monies to twelve-year old Mary, ten-year old Sarah and four-year old Ann Hopkins, still living with their mother. This bequest would be held in trust until these underage children reached the age of eighteen or married. Mary would receive £300 and the house and lot on the corner of what is now Tanner and Clement streets, then occupied by the widow Elizabeth Collins Cooper. Elizabeth gave Ann Hopkins her house and lot in town presently occupied by the widow Rachel Lippincott, and £300 "current money of the Province" of New Jersey.[20]

Hoping to assure the continuation of good order in the Haddonfield Quaker community that she had helped to build for sixty years in her father's name, Elizabeth warned that "if any of them [the Haddon-Estaugh-Hopkins relations] run out in marriage contrary to the rules of our Society, that in such case the part and sums or sum prefixed to that name or names shall be void, and equally divided to each other of the children or survivor of them, who do not marry contrary to the rules aforesaid." At the same time, Elizabeth's last will and testament took care of some of her closest Quaker friends and family. She granted her husband John's niece Mary Estaugh Kaighn Stephens the house and lot next to Elizabeth Craig's rented house, a cash endowment of £50 and a beautiful gold chain. Mary had earned Elizabeth's complete acceptance through marriage in the Haddonfield Monthly Meeting to Joseph Kaighn, a most serviceable Friend. Elizabeth gave her late cousin John Gill's son a one-sixteenth part of all her meadows joining his late-father's proprietary lands. She allotted £100 to his mother Mary Gill Thorne. Elizabeth was a bit less generous with her sister-in-law Hannah Estaugh, widow of James. She allowed Hannah's three young children Joseph, David and Grace Estaugh only a £50 endowment. The smaller grant most likely reflected her late husband's sometimes cool relationship with his brother, and certainly Elizabeth's apparent concern that James Estaugh had never really achieved an acceptable unity with Meeting.[21]

Elizabeth provided some money to help care for widowed women friends Rachel Lippincott, Mary Sharp, Abigail Cooper Fisher and Elizabeth Craig. She supplied funds as well to neighbors Thomas Redman and Isaac Andrews to finance the continued development of the center of Haddonfield. Elizabeth also bequeathed £10 to Abigail Spicer's husband Daniel Stanton, perhaps in memory of young Elizabeth Haddon's first days in Old Gloucester County, when the widow Spicer and her daughter Abigail accepted her into the West New Jersey Quaker community. As Elizabeth wrote a friend in 1761, the names of these Newton Monthly Meeting Friends "are pretty much forgotten being but few left who can remember them but by the names."[22]

Elizabeth Haddon Estaugh died on May 30, 1762 and was buried on the first day of June in the Haddonfield Friends Burial Ground, just down the lane from her residence of nearly fifty years. The "Testimony from Haddonfield Monthly Meeting in New Jersey concerning Elizabeth Estaugh" reported that her last illness confined Elizabeth for three months in great bodily pain "but favored with much calmness of mind and sweetness of spirit." The Meeting remembered her as "a serviceable member, having been clerk to the Women's Meeting near fifty years, greatly to satisfaction." The Meeting revealed its version of her legacy: "[Elizabeth Haddon Estaugh] was a sincerer sympathizer with the afflicted, of a benevolent disposition, and in distributing to the poor, was desirous to do it in a way most profitable and durable to them, and if possible, not to let the 'Right hand know what the left did;' and tho' in a state of affluence to this world's wealth, was an example of plainness and moderation; zealously concern'd for maintaining good order in the church in attending meetings at home, where her service seemed principally to be, and from her awful sitting, we have good cause to believe she was an humble waiter therein, which administered edification to the solid behavior. Her heart and house was open to her friends, whom to entertain, seemed one of her greatest pleasures; was prudently cheerful, and well knowing the value of friendship, was careful not to wound it herself, nor encourage others in whispering and publishing their failings or supposed weaknesses." Her life, "sanctified by the Spirit of Christ," served as a "matter of encouragement to survivors, to press after the mark of the high calling in Christ Jesus."[23]

Perhaps in her final moments Elizabeth took comfort in knowing that Elizabeth Estaugh Hopkins had announced her intention to marry John Mickle. Simultaneously, John Estaugh Hopkins sought clearance to marry Sarah Mickle. Elizabeth undoubtedly hoped that they and other members of the Haddon-Hopkins family would carry on the Quaker legacy and to continue to maintain good order in the Haddonfield Friends Meeting. Elizabeth provided that the Hopkins family would benefit only if they married in and maintained unity with the Haddonfield Monthly Meeting. It seemed that she had achieved her purpose as Ebenezer and Sarah Lord Hopkins' children married into some of the best Quaker families: the Mickles, Stokes, Albertsons and Cressons. The second generation of Hopkins also followed good order, achieving unity through marriage to the Clement, Hugg and Morgan families. The third generation featured acceptable marriages to the Redman, Barton, Hugg and Nicholson families. However, there were signs that the Estaugh-Haddon-Hopkins legacy might not live on in Haddonfield, New Jersey, forever. Several Hopkins family members moved out of the area. Meanwhile, Ann Hopkins, daughter of Ebenezer Hopkins, Jr., married Mark Brown in 1793 "contrary to the good order amongst us." When visited by a committee from the Haddonfield Meeting to inquire into her condition, she failed to give satisfaction. Apparently, Ann Hopkins Brown was eventually disowned.[24]

Gradually Hopkins family and collateral kin focused less on maintaining good order in Meeting and building a Quaker community than in memorializing their distant-relative Elizabeth Haddon as Haddonfield's founder. Few remembered that Elizabeth, herself, and all of her contemporaries always called her Elizabeth Estaugh during her life in America. Moreover, future accounts presented Elizabeth Haddon as a Christian woman reformer more than as a dedicated birthright member of the Religious Society of Friends who spent her entire life building a Quaker community in Haddonfield, New Jersey. More significantly for future generations, by the end of the eighteenth century only the name "Elizabeth Haddon" was remembered as the "founder" of Haddonfield, a town that very gradually changed into a more religiously diverse village of well-kept houses, profitable little shops and nearby successful farms. In the final analysis, over the years, each new generation gradually imagined "Elizabeth Haddon" as a "larger-than-life" female hero, whose persona was adopted by many of the American women's reform movements. Perhaps such deification of Elizabeth was inevitable, for her distant kinsman John Clement wrote at the end of the nineteenth century: "It is unfortunate that she did not, near the close of her life, prepare or dictate her autobiography, so that the incidents of her eventful career could have been preserved, as she would not then have left the most interesting and romantic parts of her life to vague and uncertain tradition."[25]

CHAPTER 10 NOTES.

[1]"Elizabeth Estaugh's Testimony," in Estaugh, *Call to the Unfaithful*, xii.
[2]Receipt to Jno. Bringhurst to B. Franklin, April 24, 1744. HEHP, folder 227.
[3]"Elizabeth Estaugh's Testimony," in Estaugh, *Call to the Unfaithful*, iii–xii.
[4]See Tolles, *Meeting House and Counting House*, viii.
[5]"Elizabeth Estaugh's Testimony," in Estaugh, *Call to the Unfaithful*, ii–vi.
[6]Ibid, iii–xii.
[7]Ibid, xvi.
[8] Leaders of the Women Friends of the Monthly Meeting of Haddonfield that helped Elizabeth Estaugh maintain love and unity included: Ester Eldredge, Hannah French, Ann Stokes, Mary and Kathleen Tomlinson, Mary Sharp, Mary Wilkins, Ann Cooper, Elizabeth Lord, Amy Gill, Naomi Ballinger, and Mary Lippincott, see "Minutes of the Women Friends of the Monthly Meeting of Haddonfield, 1749–1750", copy, in box 1, Lyons Project Papers, HSHL; original Minutes of the Women Friends Monthly Meeting, on microfilm at the Haverford Quaker Collection, and copies of later minutes in Frank H. Stewart Room, Special Collections, Campbell Library at Rowan University, Glassboro, New Jersey.
[9]*Pennsylvania Gazette,* September 22, 1748.
[10]Indenture between Elizabeth Estaugh and William Griscom, saddler, December 2, 1745, file 14-00-5091, Rhoads Collection, HSHL; copy in box 1, Lyons Project , HSHL.
[11]Elizabeth Estaugh lease to William Sharp. HEHP, folder 185. Map of Andrews and Kaighn properties along Tanner Street, drawn by Jacob L. Rowand in 1842 and copied by Carrie Nicholson Hartel in 1947.
[12]Receipt, signed by Isaac Smith, payment received from Elizabeth Estaugh for 'Mending Axells [sic], 1743. HEHP, folder 156. Many historians insisted later that no-one owned a four-wheeled vehicle in West Jersey until the American Revolutionary War era, however, Elizabeth Estaugh did, see Mickle, *Reminiscences,* 57.
[13]A Burlington traveling minister and longtime business associate in the Barbados trade with John Estaugh, Peter Fearon, a Burlington traveling minister, had just come back from Tortola where he had hoped to find John Estaugh's grave, see John Estaugh's account of sales by Peter Fearon, in Barbadoes, and financial statement. HEHP, folder 110. Mary Pace Weston Diary, entry February 10, 1752, Devonshire House Library of Friends, copy in Biographical File, box 3, Lyons Project Papers, HSHL.
[14]Deed of Sale, Elizabeth Estaugh to Ebenezer Hopkins, two hundred acres of land, 1747. HEHP, folder 173.

[15] Report made by Francis Rawle for Sarah Hopkins, executor of Ebenezer Hopkins, 1757, HEHP, folder 175; Receipt signed by Francis Rawle for £46, received from Sarah Hopkins, 1757, HEHP, folder 159.

[16] Elizabeth Estaugh indenture to Thomas Cummings, September 1, 1761, item 1913-00-0331, Founder's Collection; Elizabeth Estaugh to Edward Gibbs, December 24, 1761, item 1977-134-0001, Rhoads-Estaugh-Gibbs Collection; Smith contract with Estaugh, 11 August 1757, file 14-00-7056, box 1, Lyons Project Papers, all in HSHL.

[17] Letters to and from Elizabeth Estaugh, 1757–1761. HEHP, folders 186–189.

[18] E. Estaugh to John Smith, Sept 18, 1761, *New Jersey Historical Society Proceedings,* VII: 104.

[19] Will. Copy of Elizabeth Estaugh's Will, made by Samuel Allinson, Surrogate. Registered in the Prothonotary Office in Burlington, April 23rd, 1762, HEHP, folder 207; Elizabeth Estaugh's Will, November 30, 1761, copy of original handwritten will from Lib. 4, p. 357-B, New Jersey State Archives, and typed copy of complete Inventory of Estaugh's estate, in box 1, Lyons Project Papers, HSHL.

[20] Elizabeth Haddon's Will.

[21] Ibid. "Little Stebbing" was located near present-day Crystal Lake in Haddon Township, see Farr, *Place Names,* 45–46.

[22] E. Estaugh to John Smith, 104.

[23] "Testimony from the Monthly Meeting of Haddonfield in New Jersey Concerning Elizabeth Estaugh," undated. HEHP, document 218.

[24] Haddonfield Monthly Meeting Minutes, June 10, 1793.

[25] Clement, *First Emigrant Settlers,* 124; see Ryan, *Imaginary Friends.*

CONCLUSIONS.

While both [Quaker] men and women struggled against and came to affirm the relational in their lives, women had a different vantage point because as women they had been socialized to see the importance of living in relationship to various others and to use this to shape their lives.
—Carol Stoneburner[1]

Betty and Stuart Lyons had concluded after nearly forty years of research that Elizabeth Haddon was the most "unusual woman" for her time. "Perhaps one marvels most when learning of her daring solo undertaking to the New World and her subsequent trips back to England under hazardous conditions, challenged by motives at which we can only guess," the Lyons argued. The amateur Haddonfield historians explained that Elizabeth faced great hardships when she crossed the dangerous ocean in a small wooden sailing ship to settle in America and then three times to visit her family in England. But her traveling experiences were not unusual. Hundreds of strong, deeply religious and independent-minded Quaker women crossed the Atlantic throughout the late seventeenth and early eighteenth centuries. Many journeyed alone, not only across the ocean but as traveling ministers struggling into the wilderness of the British North American colonies and the island jungles of the Caribbean to spread the Word of the Lord. Most suffered incredible hardship: some were imprisoned; others banished and a few like Mary Dyer and the Boston Martyrs were executed for preaching the Truth in Puritan-dominated Massachusetts.[2]

Elizabeth Estaugh never became a traveling minister, leaving that mission to her husband and the men and women from her own neighborhood who "had a good gift in the ministry." Like many other strong women throughout the Quaker settlements in West New Jersey, the City of Philadelphia and surrounding southeastern Pennsylvania and Delaware communities, Elizabeth stayed home to manage her plantation and regularly attend Meeting. She spent most of her life in her Haddonfield neighborhood, and except for the trips home to England to visit family and discuss business affairs with her father, Elizabeth almost never traveled beyond old Gloucester County or crossed the Delaware River to the great Quaker community of Philadelphia. Moreover, contrary to traditional accounts, she was never alone in the wilderness, but received the constant support from her very first days in America in all her religious and business transactions by many Friends, both male and female. These close Friends, mostly from the more prosperous land-owning neighbors and members of the nearby Quaker Meetings played a most important and central part in the founding of the Quaker community of Haddonfield that was named after Elizabeth's father John Haddon.

Though a well-educated, strong-willed and courageous woman, Elizabeth Estaugh willingly merged her own identity, first with her service to the Lord in Meeting, then to her father's vision of building a Quaker community on his property in America, and lastly to support her husband John Estaugh's ministry. Even though Elizabeth Haddon Estaugh's real life was not as colorful as her legend, her story is vital in helping us to understand the equality that Quaker women enjoyed and the role they played in colonial America. She exemplified the ideal first presented by founder of the women's meeting Margaret Fell Fox that Quaker women who did not travel to spread the Truth must use their homes to provide public space for Friends to seek spiritual comfort together and to conduct worldly business.

Elizabeth's long life provides further evidence of how American Quakers merged their religious testimony in the Meeting Houses with the secular business activities of their "Counting Houses" designed to gain the most profit from any transaction. Her life also reveals that she, like other Quakers of her era, gained economically through the labor of slaves and indentured servants. Her biography illuminates, as well, the Quakers community's humanistic commitment to education, study of agriculture, helping the poor and development of medicine to treat the ill and infirm.

Elizabeth's life also demonstrated how gradually her community advanced the interest of Quakers over other Christian sects as she sought to create a society built mainly for the faithful followers of the Truth. Any of her kin who married out of meeting would be summarily disowned and deprived of any inheritance. Before her death, however, Elizabeth sold property to and probably accepted many newcomers not of Meeting who settled and prospered in her beloved Quaker village of Haddonfield.[3]

For all these reasons, in the end Elizabeth Haddon Estaugh stands out as one of the more significant woman in the early history of American settlement, and particularly that of New Jersey, Pennsylvania and the Delaware Valley. She used every family, religious and business connection to (help) develop a vibrant Quaker community in Haddonfield, New Jersey. Although her father, mother and husband were great influences on her, Elizabeth Haddon Estaugh, after their deaths, continued to work both openly and behind the scene, depending on the circumstances, to protect her kin and Quaker neighbors. In particular, she provided comfort in Meeting and creating places of residence and employment for women, especially women and widows not protected by the law in a still male-dominated culture. In the process, she became one of the independently wealthiest women in colonial America. Executors Isaac Andrews and Samuel Clement Jr., assessed her goods and chattel, alone, at over £7,800 (a multi-millionaire by today's standards), and extensive land holdings in New Jersey and Pennsylvania most likely doubled the value of her estate. Moreover, the extent of her English mining stock at her death may never be known.[4]

How much Elizabeth Estaugh helped those women around her cannot be determined with certainty. Nor can we evaluate without full documentation her actual role in building and forming the Quaker community of Haddonfield. Letters that she wrote monthly to her father, sister and others in England have never been found. Many dedicated researchers tried: from John Clement and Samuel Nicholson Rhoads in the nineteenth century to Rebecca Nicholson Taylor and most intensely by Betty and Stuart Lyons with their never-ending "Search for Elizabeth" in the twentieth century. But no one discovered Elizabeth's long lost letters. So we have to construct her life from a few remnants of her own writings and from what others remembered about her character. Whether that image was the real Elizabeth Haddon Estaugh, or not, may never be known. Her voice in history, as this study has demonstrated, remains muted. Her faded portrait in history, nevertheless, reveals the silhouette of one incredibly strong woman who imprinted the Haddon name indelibly on the town of Haddonfield and on the history of colonial New Jersey and America.

CONCLUSIONS NOTES.

[1]"Drawing a Profile of American Female Public Friends as Shapers of Human Space," in Stoneburner, *Influence of Quaker Women*, 9.

[2]Lyons, "The Search for Elizabeth," HSHL; also, see Larson, *Daughters of Light* and Richard L. Greaves, ed., *Triumph Over Silence: Women in Protestant History* (Westport, CT: Greenwood Press, 1985).

[3]See Tolles, *Meeting House and Counting House;* Wulf, *Not All Wives*, and Stoneburner, *Influence of Quaker Women*.

[4]See Margaret Hope Bacon, *Mothers of Feminism: the Story of Quaker Women in America,* 1st ed. (San Francisco: Harper & Row, 1986).

BIBLIOGRAPHY.

This bibliography contains published and unpublished sources that deal primarily with Elizabeth Haddon Estaugh, her family, friends and relatives. It includes studies of the development of the Religious Society of Friends in America and Britain, particularly the influence of Quaker women. It also lists books that deal with the settlement and development of Haddonfield and the Quaker communities in West New Jersey, Pennsylvania, and the British West Indies.

For individual letters from primary sources, and evidence from secondary books, articles and studies, see each set of chapter endnotes.

Manuscript Collections

Campbell Library at Rowan University, Glassboro, New Jersey
    Minutes of the Haddonfield Women's Meeting (Elizabeth Haddon Estaugh),
    Frank H. Stewart Room, Special Collections

Friends Historical Library of Swarthmore College, Swarthmore, Pennsylvania
    Records of the Haddonfield Monthly Meeting of the Religious Society of Friends, 1658–2002

Friends Library, London, England
    Book of the Monthly and Two Weeks Meeting of the People Called Quakers at "Horsleydown," 1666–1696.

London Yearly Meeting Advices.

Southwark Monthly Meeting List of Members.

Gloucester County Historical Society

    Diary of Anne Cooper Whitall

Haverford College Library, Haverford College, Haverford, Pennsylvania

    Haddon-Estaugh-Hopkins Papers, 1676–1841, Collection no. 1001, Special Collections

        Deeds and Indentures Relating to John Haddon's Purchases of Land in the Neighborhood of the Present Haddonfield, New Jersey

        John Estaugh's Dealings with the Pennsylvania Land Company of London

        Miscellaneous Business Papers of John Estaugh

        Letters of Attorney and Power of Attorney

        Receipts

        Receipted Bills for Ocean Voyages

        William Rawle

        Papers Relating to Family Affairs and Settlments John Haddon-Elizabeth Estaugh and the Hopkins Family

        Family Letters

        Elizabeth Estaugh's Business Correspondence and Papers

        Wills

        Marriage Certificates

        Miscellaneous Papers

Historical Society of Haddonfield, Haddonfield, New Jersey

    Carrie Nicholson Hartel Papers and Articles

    Lyons Project Papers and Notes

    Drafts for Elizabeth Haddon Estaugh biography

    Samuel N. Rhoads Collection, Papers and Articles

    Wittwer-Hopkins Collection

Historical Society of Pennsylvania, Philadelphia, Pennsylvania
  Carpenter Family Papers
  Contributions to the Biography of Elizabeth Estaugh
  John Clement Collection, 1616–1884
  Newton Township town meeting minute book, 1724–1822
  James Logan Papers, 1670–1749
  Logan-Fisher-Fox Family Papers, 1703–1940
  Series 1: James Logan, 1703–1718
  Rawle Family Papers, 1682–1921

Library of the North of England, Institute of Mining Engineers, Newcastle-on-Tyne
  Fair Minute Books of the Court of Assistants of the London Lead Company, 1692–1899
  General Court Minutes: The Society of Royal Mines Copper and the Ryton Company, 1695–1704

New Jersey Division of Archives and Records Management, Trenton, New Jersey
  Records of the Council of Proprietors of the Western Division of New Jersey,
  Received on Deposit by the New Jersey State Archives
  Sharp's Survey Book
  Leed's Survey Book

Published Primary Sources

Armstrong, Edward, ed. and notes by Deborah Logan. *Correspondence between William Penn and James Logan and others, 1700–1750.* 2 vols. Philadelphia: J. B. Lippincott for the Historical Society of Pennsylvania, 1870–1872.

Besse, Joseph. *A Collection of the Sufferings of the People Called Quakers for the Testimony of a Good Conscience from the Time of their being first distinguished by that Name in the Year 1650 to the Time of the Act commonly called the Act of Toleration granted to Protestant Dissenters in the first Year of the reign of King William the Third and Queen Mary in the year 1689. London: George Yard on Lombard Street, 1753.

Budd, Thomas. *Good Order Established in Pennsilvania* [sic] & *New-Jersey in America, Being a true Account of the Country; with its Produce and Commodities there made.* Philadelphia: William Bradford, 1685, reprinted Ann Arbor: University Microfilms, 1966.

Chalkley, Thomas. *A Collection of the Works of that antient, faithful servant of Jesus Christ, Thomas Chalkley.* London: printed and sold by Luke Hinde, 1751.

Dunn, Richard S., and Mary Maples Dunn, eds. *The Papers of William Penn.* 5 vols. Philadelphia: University of Pennsylvania Press, 1982–85.

Estaugh, John. *A call to the unfaithful professors of truth / written by John Estaugh in his life-time; and now published for general service. To which are added divers epistles of the same author.* Dublin: Printed by Isaac Jackson, 1745 and London: printed and sold by T. Sowle Raylton and L. Hinde, 1745.

Graunt, John, Citizen of London. *Natural and Political OBSERVATIONS Mentioned in a following INDEX, and made upon the Bills of Mortality.* London: printed by Tho: Roycroft, for John Martin, James Allestry, and Tho: Dicas, at the Sign of the Bell in St. Paul's Church-yard, 1662; reprinted New York: Arno Press, 1975.

Myers, Albert Cook. *Hannah Logan's Courtship: A True Narrative.* Philadelphia: Ferris & Leach, 1904.

_____. *Narratives of Early Pennsylvania, West New Jersey and Delaware,* New York: Charles Scribner's Sons, 1912.

_____. *Quaker Arrivals at Philadelphia, 1682–1750: Being a List of Certificates of Removal Received at Philadelphia Monthly Meeting of Friends.* Baltimore: Genealogical Book Company, reprint 1957.
New Jersey Archives: First Series. *Documents Relating to the Colonial, Revolutionary and post-Revolutionary History of the State of New Jersey.* 34 vols. Newark, Paterson, etc., N.J., 1880–1949.

Nickalls, John L., editor. *The Journal of George Fox.* Cambridge University Press, 1952.

Reed, H. Clay, and George Julius Miller, editors. *The Burlington Court Book: A Record of Quaker Jurisprudence in West New Jersey, 1680–1709*

Richardson, John. *An Account of the life of that Ancient Servant of Jesus Christ, John Richardson.* Philadelphia: Friends' Book Store, 1880.

Stewart, Frank, ed. *Notes on Old Gloucester County, New Jersey.* Vol. I. Camden, N.J.: New Jersey Society of Pennsylvania, 1917.

_____. *The Organization and Minutes of the Gloucester County Court; also Gloucester County Ear Mark Book, 1686–1728.* Woodbury, New Jersey: Gloucester County Historical Society, 1930.

Story, Thomas. *A Journal of the Life of Thomas Story.* Newcastle upon Tyne, Printed by I. Thompson, 1747.

Weiss, Harry B. and Grace M. Weiss. *The Early Promotional Literature of New Jersey.* Trenton: New Jersey Agricultural Society, 1964.

Stories, Essays, and Articles about Elizabeth Haddon Estaugh

Child, Lydia Maria. "The Youthful Emigrant: A True Story of the Early Settlement of New Jersey." *Fact and Fiction: A Collection of Stories.* New York: C. S. Francis & Co., 1846.

Clarke, Walter Irving. "Found—Elizabeth Haddon's Bible." *New Era Magazine*, v. 25, November, 1920: 760–67.

Clement, J. and Lydia H. Sigourney, eds. "Elizabeth Estaugh." *Noble Deeds of American Women: Biographical Sketches of Some of the More Prominent.* Buffalo: Geo. H. Derby and Co. (1851): 284–96.

Clement, John. "Elizabeth Estaugh." *Sketches of the First Emigrant Settlers in Newton Township, Old Gloucester County, West New Jersey.* Camden, NJ: Sinnickson Chew, (1877): 109–25.

_____. "Elizabeth Estaugh and some of her Contemporaries." *Proceedings of the New Jersey Historical Society,* 3rd. ser. (1912–1913) vol. 7:103–105.

Cooper, Howard M. "Newton Meeting: A Retrospect." *Friends' Intelligencer and Journal,* 56 Philadelphia, (1899): 707–8.

Hartel, Carrie E. Nicholson. *Estaugh Plantation—Wood Farm.* Haddonfield, NJ: Haddonfield Historical Society, 1947.

Haydock, Edna L. "Elizabeth and the Indians," in *This Is Haddonfield.* Historical Society of Haddonfield, (1963): 262.

Heston, Alfred M. "Courtship of Elizabeth Haddon." *Jersey Waggon Jaunts.* 2 vols. Atlantic County Historical Society, (1926) I: 229–39.

Hopkins, Anna Garrison. *Sketches relating to colonial Haddonfield.* Haddonfield, N.J.: printed for the [Hopkins] family, 1954.

Longfellow, Henry Wadsworth. "The Theologian's Tale: Elizabeth," in *Tales of A Wayside Inn.* Boston and New York: Houghton Mifflin, 1913 edition of 1873 work.

Lyons, Elizabeth A. "Elizabeth Haddon," in *Past and Promise: Lives of New Jersey Women, the Women's Project of New Jersey Inc.* Metuchen, NJ: Scarecrow Press, hardcover, 1990; Syracuse: Syracuse University Press, paperback, 1997: 21–22.

_____. "Haddon, Elizabeth," in *Encyclopedia of New Jersey.* Maxine N. Lurie and Marc Mappen, eds. New Brunswick, NJ: Rutgers University Press, 2004.

Lyons, George, and Elizabeth A. Lyons. *"The Search for Elizabeth."* Haddonfield, New Jersey: The Historical Society of Haddonfield: unpublished manuscripts, n.d.

McDonald, Gerald D. "Elizabeth Haddon Estaugh," in *Notable American Women: A Biographical Dictionary, Volumes 1–3: 1607–1950.* Edward T. James, Janet Wilson, James and Paul Boyer, eds. Cambridge: Belknap Press of Harvard University Press, (1971) I: 584–85.

Nicholson, R. [Rebecca]. *Contributions to the Biography of Elizabeth Estaugh / compiled in part from original MSS, in possession of the editor.* Philadelphia: Dewey & Eakins, 1894.

Rhoads, Samuel N. "Haddon Hall of Haddonfield." *Bulletin of Friends' Historical Society of Philadelphia*, (vol. 1906–1910): III: 58–67.

Sheldon, Edward Austin. "Elizabeth and John Estaugh." *The Fifth Reader*. Charles Scribner's Sons, 1875.

Sturge, Hannah J. *Fragmentary Memorials of John and Elizabeth Estaugh*. Gloucester, NJ: printed by J. Bellows, 1881.

Taylor, Rebecca Nicholson. "The Business Papers of John and Elizabeth Estaugh." *Bulletin of Friends' Historical Association* (1931): 13–18.

_____. "Original Papers Belonging to Elizabeth Estaugh in Possession of Rebecca N. Taylor." *Bulletin of Friends' Historical Association*. Philadelphia, 1930.

Willits, Harriet O. Redman. "Incidents in the Life of Elizabeth Haddon," in *Two Hundredth Anniversary of the Settlement of Haddonfield, New Jersey: Celebrated October eighteenth, nineteen hundred and thirteen*. Haddonfield, NJ: 1913.

Works Project Administration. "Elizabeth Haddon." *Stories of New Jersey Prepared for Use in Public Schools by the New Jersey Writers' Project, Bulletin No. 1*. Newark, N.J.: Works Project Administration, 1940–41.

Histories of Haddonfield and West New Jersey

Boyer, Charles S. *Early Forges & Furnaces in New Jersey*. Philadelphia: University of Pennsylvania Press, 1931.

_____. *Rambles Through Old Highways and Byways of West Jersey*. Camden, NJ: Camden County Historical Society, 1967.

Clement, John. *Sketches of the First Emigrant Settlers Newton Township, Old Gloucester County, West New Jersey*. Camden, NJ: Sinnickson Chew, 1877.

Cooper, Howard M., and Emily Cooper Johnson. *Historical Sketch of Camden, Including Papers on the Cooper and Kaighn Families.* Camden, NJ: Haddon Craftsmen, Inc., 1931.

Dorwart, Jeffery M. *Camden County, New Jersey: The Making of a Metropolitan Community, 1626–2000.* New Brunswick, NJ: Rutgers University Press, 2001.

Farr, William R. *Place Names in and About Haddonfield.* Haddonfield, NJ: Historical Society of Haddonfield, 1979.

_____. *Waterways of Camden County: A Historical Gazetteer.* Camden, NJ: Camden County Historical Society, 2002.

Godfrey, E. L. B. *History of the Medical Profession of Camden County, N. J.* Philadelphia: F. A. Davis Co., 1896.

Haddonfield Publication Committee. *The Two Hundredth Anniversary of the Settlement of Haddonfield, New Jersey.* Philadelphia: Franklin Printing Company, 1913.

Hartel, Carrie Elizabeth Nicholson. *"History of Haddonfield: Colonial Period."* Unpublished manuscript, Historical Society of Haddonfield Library, 1948.

Heston, Alfred M. *South Jersey: A History, 1664–1924.* 5 vols. New York: Lewis Historical Publishing Company, 1924.

Historical Society of Haddonfield. *This Is Haddonfield.* Haddonfield, NJ: The Historical Society of Haddonfield, 1963.

Mickle, Isaac. *Reminiscences of Old Gloucester County or Incidents in the History of Gloucester, Atlantic and Camden, New Jersey.* Philadelphia: Townsend Ward, 1845, reprint Woodbury, NJ: Gloucester County Historical Society, 1968.

Monshaw, Harriet Gotchel. *Elizabeth French Gill, 1794–1854: First Mistress of Greenfield Hall.* Haddonfield, NJ: The Historical Society of Haddonfield, 1998.

Pennypacker, James Lane. *The Story of an Old Road.* Camden, NJ: Camden County Historical Society, 1921.

Pomfret, John E. *The Province of West New Jersey, 1609–1702: A*

History of the Origins of an American Colony. Princeton: Princeton University Press, 1956.

Prowell, George R. *The History of Camden County, New Jersey*. Philadelphia: L. J. Richards, 1886, reprinted by the Camden County Historical Society and Camden County Cultural and Heritage Commission, 1974.

Raible, Dennis G. *Down a Country Lane*. Camden, NJ: Camden County Historical Society, 1999.

Raible, Dennis G. *Haddon Township's Hopkins Plantation: The First Three Hundred Years*. Philadelphia: St. Joseph's Press, 1990.

Rauschenberger, Douglas B. *Haddonfield History: a Bibliography and Index to Sources in the Haddonfield Public Library*. Haddonfield, NJ: Haddonfield Public Library, 1977.

Rauschenberger, Douglas B., and Katherine Mansfield Tassini. *Lost Haddonfield*. Haddonfield, NJ: The Historical Society of Haddonfield, 1989.

Snyder, John P. *The Story of New Jersey's Civil Boundaries, 1606–1968*. Trenton, NJ: Bureau of Geology and Topography, 1969.

Tassini, Katherine Mansfield, and Douglas B. Rauschenberger with the Historical Society of Haddonfield. *Haddonfield*. Charleston, SC: Arcadia Publications, 2008.

Histories about the Quakers

Ackrill, Margaret, and Leslie Hannah. *Barclays: The Business of Banking 1690–1996*. Cambridge: Cambridge University Press, 2001.

Bacon, Margaret Hope. *Mothers of Feminism: the Story of Quaker Women in America*. San Francisco: Harper & Row, 1986.

Barbour, Hugh, and J. William Frost. *The Quakers*. New York and Westport, CT: Greenwood Press, 1988.

Carey, Brycchan. *From Peace to Freedom: Quaker Rhetoric and the Birth of American Antislavery, 1657–1761*. New Haven, CT: Yale

University Press, 2012.

Deyle, Steven. "By farr the most profitable trade': Slave trading in British colonial North America." *Slavery & Abolition: A Journal of Slave and Post-Slave Studies,* volume 10, Issue 2 (1989): 107–25.

Dunn, Richard S. and Mary Maples Dunn, eds. *The World of William Penn.* Philadelphia: University of Pennsylvania Press, 1986.

Evans, William. *A Brief Statement of the Rise and Progress of the Testimony of the Religious Society of Friends, Against Slavery and the Slave Trade.* Philadelphia: Joseph and William Kite, 1843.

Gragg, Larry. *The Quaker Community on Barbados: Challenging the Culture of the Planter Class.* Columbia: University of Missouri Press, 2009.

Greaves, Richard L., ed. *Triumph Over Silence: Women in Protestant History.* Westport, CT: Greenwood Press, 1985.

Ingle, H. Larry. *First among Friends: George Fox and Creation of Quakerism.* New York: Oxford University Press, 1994.

Jennings, Judith. *Gender, Religion, and Radicalism in the long Eighteenth Century: the 'Ingenious Quaker' and her Connections.* Aldershot, England: Ashgate Publishing, 2006.

Jones, Rufus M. *The Quakers in the American Colonies.* London: Macmillan, 1923.

Larson, Rebecca. *Daughters of Light: Quakers Women Preaching and Prophesying in the Colonies and Abroad, 1700–1775.* New York: Alfred A. Knopf, 1999.

Levenduski, Cristine. *Peculiar Power: A Quaker Woman Preacher in Eighteenth-Century America.* Washington and London: Smithsonian Institution Press, 1996.

Levy, Barry. *Quakers and the American Family: British Settlement in the Delaware Valley.* New York: Oxford University Press, 1988.

Moore, John M., ed. *Friends in the Delaware Valley: Philadelphia*

Yearly Meeting, 1681–1981. Haverford, PA: Friends Historical Association, 1981.

Raistrick, Arthur. *Quakers in Science and Industry*. New York: Augustus M. Kelley, 1968.

Ryan, James Emmett. *Imaginary Friends: Representing Quakers in American Culture, 1650–1950*. Madison: University of Wisconsin Press, 2009.

Stoneburner, Carol and John, eds. *The Influence of Quaker Women on American History: Biographical Studies*. Lewiston, N.Y.: Edwin Mellen Press, 1986.

Tolles, Frederick B. *Meeting House and Counting House: The Quaker Merchants of Colonial Philadelphia, 1682–1763*. Published for the Institute of Early American History and Culture at Williamsburg, Virginia. Chapel Hill: University of North Carolina Press, 1948.

Wax. Darold E. "Quaker Merchants and the Slave Trade in Colonial Pennsylvania." *The Pennsylvania Magazine of History and Biography*, v. 86, no. 2 (April 1963), 143–59.

Wulf, Karin A. *Not All Wives: Women of Colonial Philadelphia*. Ithaca, NY: Cornell University Press, 2000.

Websites
(all accessed 23 August 2013)

Bulletin of the Friends' Historical Society of Philadelphia
http://www.archive.org/details/bulletinoffriend190910frie

Elizabeth Haddon – Wikipedia, the Free Encyclopedia
http://en.wikipedia.org/wiki/Elizabeth_Haddon

English Short Title Catalogue-Full View of Records-Standard format.
http://estc.bl.uk

Finding Aid for the Haddon-Estaugh-Hopkins Papers, Haverford College Library http://www.haverford.edu/library/spcial/aids/haddonestaughhopkins/hadeshop.xml

Hopkins Family
Art Hopkins has created the definitive Hopkins family history and genealogy, using extensive primary research materials. The homepage of his website is:
http://home.comcast.net/~adhopkins

Haddonfield Monthly Meeting Marriages
http://home.comcast.net/~adhopkins/hadmar.rtf

Haddonfield Monthly Meeting Hopkins References
http://home.comcast.net/~adhopkins/hadhopkins.htm

Records of Haddonfield Monthly Meeting: A Finding Aid
http://trilogy.brynmawr.edu/speccoll/mm/haddomm.xml

Records from Southwark Monthly Meeting in Surrey, England.
http://home.comcast.net/~adhopkins/swkgrecs.htm

Settlement pattern for Delaware River
http://jerseyman-historynowandthen.blogspot.com/2010/10/best-laid-schemes-o-mice-men-gang-aft.html

Sufferings of the People Called Quakers
http://home.comcast.net/~adhopkins/suffer.htm

West Jersey History Project – Early Settlements
http://www.westjerseyhistory.org/articles

INDEX.

Throughout the text there are countless references to Elizabeth Haddon Estaugh, John Estaugh and Haddonfield. Accordingly, the entries under Elizabeth Haddon Estaugh, John Estaugh and Haddonfield give only broad subject headings rather than a page by page listing. The number of references to Quakers, Friends and the Religious Society of Friends also are too numerous to make a page by page listing useful. Individual Friends Meetings are included in the index.

A

Adams, Deborah, 85
Adams, Elizabeth, 82, 83, 95
Adams, John, 78, 95, 105, 113
Adams Family, 33, 183
Affirmations, 143, 144, 158, 186, 205, 206
African Descent, Slaves of, *see* Slaves
Albertson, Cassandra, 243
Albertson, Hannah, 244
Albertson, Isaac, 220
Albertson, William, 88
Albertson Family, 33
Allen, Judah, 94
Allen Family, 33
Andrews, Isaac, 246, 249, 253, 255, 264
Andrews, Peter, 246
Andrews, Sarah, 248
Andrews Family, 217, 246
Anglicans, *see* Church of England
Anglo-Dutch War, 79
Anne Arundel County (MD), 3
Annis, John, 121, 160, 172, 189
Antigua, 130, 173, 174
ARUNDEL (ship), 104
Arundel, Lady Anne, 3
Aspden, Mathias, 246

B

Ballinger, Henry, 113
Ballinger, Naomi, 259, *n. 30*
Ballinger, Thomas, 139
Baltimore, Lord, 3, 128
Baptists, 102, 239
Barclay, Robert, 136, 137, 157
Barclay Family, 33
Barclay Farm, 109, 131
Bartram, John, 161
Bate, Jeremiah, 88
Bates, Joseph, 165

Berkeley, Lord John, 50, 51
Bermondsey, 19, 21, 35, 37, 36, 41, 42, 71, 81, 190
BETTY (ship), 183
Birthright Quakers, 35, 38, 246, 257
Big Timber Creek, *see* Timber Creek
Bitters, 12, 159
Blackburn, Anne, 32
Blanchard, Jane, *see* Breintnall, Jane Blanchard
Borton Family, 33
Breach, Ann, 63
Breach, John, 62, 63, 68, *n.2*, 71
Breach, Simon, 63, 65, 68, *n. 2*, 91, 93, 94, 155
Breach Family, 59, 63, 71
Breintnall, David, 80, 115
Breintnall, Elizabeth, 80
Breintnall, Jane Blanchard, 115, 135
Bringhurst, John, 235
Bristol (England), 2, 108, 144, 182, 183
BRISTOL TRADER (ship), 72, 122
British West Indies, *see* West Indies
Buckele, Richard, 219, 220
Bucks County (PA) 56, 71, 107, 147, 167, 186, 196
Budd, Thomas, 48, 49, 73
Burlington (NJ), 11, 48, 54, 58, 76, 80, 87, 95, 114, 116, 118, 119, 122, 135, 148, 160, 194, 249
Burlington Assembly, 113, 132
Burlington County (NJ), 54, 57, 76, 77, 95, 117, 119, 129, 131, 154, 166, 196, 211, 214
Burlington County Court, 59, 61, 77, 95, 119
Burlington Friends Meeting, 78, 79, 116, 127, 139, 153, 181, 241
Burlington-Salem Road, 86, 87, 119, 131. *See also* King's Highway
Burlington Yearly Meeting, 78, 81, 82, 113, 130, 172, 241
Bull and Mouth Inn, 39, 55, 143
Bull and Mouth Monthly Meeting, 142

Burrough, John, 88, 208, 250
Burrough, Mary, *see* Gibbs, Mary Burrough
Burrough, Mary, *see* Mickle, Mary Burrough
Burrough, Phoebe, 242
Burrough, Samuel, 166, 193
Burrough, Sarah, 193
Burrough Family, 33, 247
Bye, John, 71
Bye, Margaret, 71
Bye, Thomas, 71
Bye Family, 33, 71,
Byllynge (Billings), Edward, 51, 52, 59, 62, 118, 166

C

Cadwallader, Thomas, 228, 229, 230
Cadwallader Family, 202, *n. 27*
Calendar, Quaker (Julian), 125, *n. 15*
Callowhill, Hannah, *see* Penn, Hannah Callowhill
Calvert, Cecil, 3
Camden (NJ), 19, 78, 120, 129, 245
Camden County (NJ), 21, 27, 54
Camden County Historical Society, 18
Carpenter, Elizabeth, 36
Carpenter, Samuel, 111-115, 118, 122, 128, 130, 134
Carpenter, Hannah, 80, 135
Carteret, Lady Elizabeth, 3
Carteret, Philip, 3
Carteret, Sir George, 4
Chalkley, Martha, 120, 135
Chalkley, Mary, 129
Chalkley, Thomas, 21, 41 43, 82, 105, 106, 108, 115, 120, 129, 131, 174, 227, 230
Chalkley Family, 33
Champion, Esther, *see* Palmer, Esther Champion
Cherry Hill (NJ), 68n18, 78, 109, 121, 131
Chester Creek, 134

Chester County (PA), 107, 169, 186
Chester Friends Meeting (Moorestown, NJ), 78, 82, 95, 105, 174, 193, 213,214, 241, 242
Chester (Moorestown, NJ), 78, 83, 113, 128
Child, Lydia Maria, v, vii, 1, 7, 9, 16, 17, 26, n. 19, 70, 71, 152, n. 24, 259, 264
Church of England, 27, 30, 31, 41, 50, 51, 79, 101, 109, 143, 186, 205, 206
Claridge, Richard, 158
Clarke, Elizabeth, see Haddon, Elizabeth Clarke
Clarke, John, 32, 34, 36, 37, 41, 106, 184
Clarke, Mary, see Lurting, Mary Clarke
Clarke, Suzanna, 184
Clement, Jacob, 245
Clement, John, 10-12, 68, n. 21, 86
Clement, Rebecca Collins, 244
Clement, Samuel, Jr., 245, 264
Clement Collection, 91
Clement Family, 33, 217, 218, 245, 256
Clement Street, 254
Charles I, 27, 29, 51, 157
Charles II, 29, 30, 40, 41, 49, 50, 58, 79
Cogshall Friends Meeting, 103
Cole, Samuel, 96, 166, 224
Cole Family, 33
Coles Landing, 18, 88
Coles Mill Road, 18, 88, 92
Collins, Benjamin, 154
Collins, Elizabeth, see Cooper, Elizabeth Collins
Collins, Elizabeth, see Southwick, Elizabeth Collins
Collins, Francis, 11, 22, 41, 48, 57, 63-64, 68, n. 15, 77, 79, 83, 86, 87, 96, 119, 131, 139, 153, 154
Collins, Joseph, 87, 154, 166, 187, 198, 244, 247
Collins, Leze Hugg, see Price, Leze Collins Hugg

Collins, Rebecca see Clement, Rebecca Collins
Collins, Sarah, see Dimsdale, Sarah Collins
Collins Family, 33, 73, 119, 19, 247
Collinson, Peter, 40, 161, 169, 202, n. 17
Concessions and Agreements (West New Jersey), 52-55, 57, 73, 77, 86, 118, 119
Conestoga Creek, 169
Conestoga Village, 104
Conventicle Acts, 30, 32
Cooper, Abigail, 220, 255
Cooper, Ann, see Whitall, Ann Cooper
Cooper, Daniel, 254, 255
Cooper, Elizabeth, see Mickle, Elizabeth Cooper
Cooper, Elizabeth, see Wood, Elizabeth Cooper
Cooper, Elizabeth Collins, 254
Cooper, Hannah, see Mickle, Hannah Cooper
Cooper, John, 194
Cooper, Joseph, 64, 120, 138, 165, 166, 192, 198, 224, 235, 240
Cooper, Joseph, Jr., 194, 209
Cooper, Lydia, 208
Cooper, Mary, 32
Cooper, Sarah, see Richardson, Sarah Cooper
Cooper, Thomas, 56, 143-145
Cooper, William, 78, 81, 88, 120, 121, 129
Cooper Family, 32, 32, 73, 120, 121, 139, 183, 216
Cooper's Creek; Estaughs on, 3, 6, 62-3, 85-86, 88-93, 115, 116, 136-138, 187, 195, 198, 208, 217; ferries, 120; Friends on, 64, 78, 81, 82, 83, 87-88, 112, 119, 211, 122, 245; land transactions, 59, 60-61, 62, 166, 217, 243, 245; settlement on, 3, 6, 60-61, 64, 75-77

Cooper's Point, 133
Corbut, Sarah, *see* Tomlinson, Sarah Corbut
Coxe, Daniel, 160, 166, 178, *n. 13*
Craig, Elizabeth, 253-255
Craig, John, 215
Creighton, Hugh, 246, 247
Creighton, Mary French, 247
Cropwell Creek, 76, 88, 100, *n. 19*, 166. *See also* Pennsauken Creek
Cross, Mary, *see* Healey, Mary Cross
Cromwell, Oliver, 27-30, 51, 79
Cumberland County (England), 132
Cumberland County (NJ), 248

D

Dare, Virginia, 4
Davies, Samuel, 145
Delaware Bay, 48, 50, 54, 81, 122, 130, 138, 173
Delaware Indians, *see* Native Americans
Delaware River, vii, xii, xiv, 128, 166, 168, 262; drowning, 121; Dutch and Swedes on, 3, 75; early settlement, 1, 2, 6, 11, 48-50, 54; ferries, 133; Native Americans on, 72; Penn estate, 87, 104; privateers on, 127; ships, 72, 108, 122; slaves, 225; trading posts, 75
Delaware, 75, 128, 262
Delaware Valley; vii, 2, 21, 23, 37; Dutch and Swedes in, 3, 75; Estaughs in, 87, 95, 105, 110, 111, 115, 116, 139, 153, 161, 211, 264; Penn in, 118, 128; Quaker families in, 32, 48, 79, 133, 142, 195, 211, 229, 264; settlement of, 49, 51, 56, 57, 70, 79, 83, 96; slave trade in, 220
Deptford (England), 42
Deptford Friends Meeting (England), 39, 42, 43, 64
Deptford (NJ), 7, 181
Dillwyn, John, 211

Dillwyn Family, 33
Dimsdale, Robert, 119, 140, 154, 183, 211
Dimsdale, Sarah Collins, 83, 140, 154, 172, 183, 185, 194, 208, 211, 220, 226
Dimsdale Family, 211
DOLMAHOY (ship), 1, 2
Disownment, 109, 193, 220, 257, 263
Drinker Family, 202, *n. 27*
Driscoll, Alfred E., 18
Durborow, Elizabeth, 135

E

Earmarks, 79, 83, 163
Eastlack, John, 219
Edridge, John, 52
Eldridge, Ester, 259, *n. 8*
Ellis, Jacob, 243
Ellis, Sarah, 121, 208
Ellis, Simeon, 88, 121
Ellis, William, 166, 202, *n. 27*
Ellis Family, 121, 217
Ellis Street, 218
Ellisburg (Cherry Hill, NJ), 121
Elizabeth I, 4
Elizabethtown (Elizabeth, NJ), 3
Ellwood, Thomas, 158
Elsinboro (NJ), 112
English Civil War, 27-29, 50, 51, 79
Estaugh, David, 254
Estaugh, Elizabeth Haddon; arrival in West New Jersey (1701), 1, 70-86; birth of (1680), 37; building of New Haddonfield plantation house (1713), 153-165; death of, (1762), 255-258; death of husband John Estaugh (1742), 230-232; development of Haddonfield, 207-208, 217-219, 243-249; family in England, 28-44; early life in West New Jersey, 127-149; first house in West New Jersey 89-94; legends of, 1-24; marriage to John Estaugh (1702), 101-124; trip to

England (1708-1712), 140- 149 ; trip to England (1715-1716), 172; trip to England (1720-1723), 182-189, 193-194; will of, 252-255
Estaugh, Grace, 254
Estaugh, Hannah, 254
Estaugh, James, 114, 132, 133, 135, 138, 169, 208, 254
Estaugh, John; birth of (1676), 101; death of (1742), 230-232; early life 101-103; legends of 7-9; marriage to Elizabeth Haddon (1702), 101-124; meets Elizabeth Haddon, 43-44; missionary trips, 103-107, 173-175, 226-231; smallpox, 107, 108
Estaugh, Joseph, 254
Estaugh, Mary, *see* Stephens, Mary Estaugh Kaighn
Estaugh, Mary Lawson, 114, 132, 133,. 135
Estaugh Family, 104, 227
Evans Pond, 78
Evans, Elizabeth, 78, 113, 249
Evans, John, 147, 155
Evans, Joshua, 154
Evans, William, 113, 194, 224,
Evans Mill, 122
Evans Family, 73, 96, 113, 139, 183, 193, 213, 142, 242, 245
Evesham (NJ), 113, 214
Evesham Friends Meeting, 78, 182, 193, 213, 241, 242, 245

F

Fairman, Robert, 41
Fairman, Thomas, 81, 120, 168
Falls of the Delaware, 53, 76, 219
Fat Hog Bay, 230
Fell, Margaret, *see* Fox, Margaret Fell
Ferries, 58, 77, 82, 112, 120, 133
Fenwick, John, 51-53, 60, 111
Ferry Road, 94, 155, 161, 195, 244, 245, 251. *See also* Haddon Avenue

Fisher, Abigail Cooper, 255
Floyd, Enoch, 141, 144
Fort Casimir, 77
Fort Nassau, 75
Fort Trinity, 76
Fothergill, John, 133, 202, *n. 27*, 226
Founder's Day (Haddonfield), 3, 18, 19
Fox, George, 30-32, 41, 43, 47, 48, 103, 239
Fox, Margaret Fell, 30, 132, 135, 159, 263
Franklin, Benjamin, 161, 202, *n. 30*, 221, 235-237
Freame, John, 56, 143, 144, 197
French, Hannah, 259, *n. 30*
French, Mary, *see* Creighton, Mary French
French, Thomas, 193
French Family, 183, 217
French West Indies, *see* West Indies
Friends, Religious Society of; early history in England, 26-44; early history in America, 47-65. *See also* Individual Friends Meetings
Friends Historical Society, 17
Freeborn, Susanna, 129

G

Gardiner, Hannah Matthews, 59
Gardiner, Thomas, 53, 59, 60, 68, *n. 18*
Gardiner, Thomas, Jr., 60
George I, 158, 199, 207
Germantown (PA), 209
Gibbs, Edward, 250
Gibbs, Mary Burrough, 250
Gibson, Joseph, 181
Gill, Amy, 259, *n. 30*
Gill, Ann Haddon, 138
Gill, Hannah, *see* Redman, Hannah Gill
Gill, Henry, 31, 41
Gill, John, 23, 31, 138, 165, 174, 187, 192, 193, 198, 199, 208, 209, 214, 240, 243-245, 249, 250

Gill, John Jr., 138, 249, 254
Gill, Mary Heritage, *see* Thorne, Mary Heritage Gill
Gill Family, 32, 138, 194, 216-218, 242
Glorious Revolution, 29
Gloucester (NJ), 75, 248
Gloucester County, vii, xii, xiv, 2, 6, 8, 54, 57, 58, 59, 60, 61, 65, 69, 70, 72, 76, 77, 78, 106, 110, 117, 123, 131, 132, 136, 137, 216, 242, 262; Friends in, 216, 242, 247, 255; poll tax, 83
Gloucester town, *see* Gloucester (NJ)
Graisbery, James, 88
Gould, Thomas, 56, 143, 144
Goulding, Henry, 56
Gouldney, Henry, 178, *n. 26*
Gove, Richard, 115, 134
Gove Family, 33
Grimes, Sibill (Sybill)
Griscom, Sarah, 208
Griscom, William, 246
Grove, John, 36, 129, 134
Grove Street, 88
Guinea, 174, 225. *See also* Slave Trade

H

Haddon, Ann, *see* Gill, Ann Haddon
Haddon, Elizabeth, *see* Estaugh, Elizabeth Haddon
Haddon, Elizabeth (aunt of Elizabeth Haddon Estaugh), 11
Haddon, Elizabeth Clarke (mother of Elizabeth Haddon Estaugh), 11, 32, 34-40, 64, 71, 96, 97, 142, 153, 161, 165, 175, 188, 189
Haddon, John, vii, ix, 2-6, 9, 12, 21, 23, 27-44, 47-49, 54-63, 69-73, 78, 80, 84, 86, 88-95, 102, 106, 111, 120-123, 127, 131, 136-148, 157, 159, 163-167, 170-173, 183-188, 191, 194-195, 197-198, 206, 208, 210, 217, 229, 232, 251, 253, 262
Haddon, Mary, 142
Haddon, Mathew, 138
Haddon, Phillipiah Marriott, 135
Haddon, Roger, 34-35
Haddon, Sarah, *see* Hopkins, Sarah Haddon
Haddon, Simon, 33, 34, 142
Haddon, Thomas, 34, 141
Haddon Avenue, 5, 94, 133, 155, 161, 195, 244, 253. *See also* Ferry Road
Haddon Hall, viii, 126, *n. 21*
Haddon Heights (NJ), 5
Haddon Family, 20, 21, 28, 34, 38, 40-42, 81, 93, 95, 102, 105, 106, 119, 138, 140-142, 154, 161, 175, 183-184, 186, 189, 232
Haddon Township (NJ), 5, 18, 260, *n. 21,*
Haddonfield Historical Society, *see* Historical Society of Haddonfield
Haddonfield (NJ); development of,70, 82, 94, 111, 112, 131, 149, 217-219, 239, 243-248, 250, 255, 257; earliest reference to, 74, 99, *n. 8*; first settler, 11, 86; founding of, 5, 7, 17, 22, 24, 257, 262; naming of, 10, 184; New Haddonfield, 88, 90, 162, 187, 190; Old Haddonfield, 88, 165, 187, 188, 190; seal of Borough, 14; 75th anniversary of Borough incorporation, 18; 200th anniversary (1913), 3,15, 16; 250th anniversary (1963), 19
Haddonfield Friends Cemetery, 4, 15, 245, 255
Haddonfield Friends Meeting, vii, 3, 70, 82, 191, 193, 194, 198, 207, 208, 210, 212-220, 231, 232, 235, 239, 237, 240-245, 244, 251, 254, 255-257
Haddonfield Women's Meeting, 39, 193, 208, 213, 231, 232, 238, 241, 242, 255
Hagen, Jacob, 40, 202, *n. 17*
Hagen Family, 33
Haines, Mary, 121, 182
Haines, Rebecca, *see* Matlack, Rebecca Haines
Haines, Richard, 121

Haines Family, 88, 121, 183, 217, 247
Hancock Family, 33
Hardingstone (England), 28, 31-34, 135
Harker, Grace, 135
Harris, Mary, *see* Matlack, Mary Harris
Harrison, Mary, *see* Thorne, Mary Harrison
Harrison Family, 245
Hartel, Carrie Elizabeth Nicholson, 26, *n. 17*, 85, 86, 222, 223
Hartel, Joseph Nicholson, 85, 86
Haverford College, 21, 85, 165, 202, *n. 22*, 215, 232, 237, 258, *n. 8*
Healey, Mary, 211
Healey, Mary Cross, 210
Healey Family, 211
Heartly, Bathsheba, *see* Zane, Heartly Bathsheba
Herbal Medicine, *see* Medicine, Herbal
Heritage, Hannah, 193
Heritage, Mary, *see* Thorne, Mary Heritage Gill
Heritage Family, 88, 183, 247
Hewitt, Susanna, *see* Matlack, Susanna Hewitt
Higgs, William, 138
Hill, Hannah Lloyd, 135
Hinchman, John, 248
Hinchman, Letitia Mickle, 243
Hinchman, Thomas, 243
Hinchman Family, 245, 247
Historical Society of Haddonfield, ix, xi, xii, xiii, 4, 5, 9, 13, 14, 18-20, 22, 85, 92, 97, 125 *n. 9*, 156, 162, 222, 236
Historical Society of Pennsylvania, 89, 91
Hodge, Henry, 197, 199
Hollingshead Family, 33
Hooten Family, 33
Hopkins, Ann, 141, 253, 254, 257
Hopkins, Benjamin (father), 126, *n. 23, n. 33,136*, 141, 142, 162, 164, 189, 210, 214, 219, 226
Hopkins, Benjamin (I) (son), 175

Hopkins, Ebenezer (father), viii, 9, 16, 23, 38, 94, 184, 189, 191, 195, 208, 215, 218, 219, 220-222, 226, 235, 240, 244, 249, 250, 251
Hopkins, Ebenezer II (son), 253, 257
Hopkins, Elizabeth, 141, 191
Hopkins, Elizabeth Estaugh, 219, 247, 253, 256
Hopkins, Haddon, 141, 191, 249, 253
Hopkins, John, 188
Hopkins, John Estaugh, 15, 219, 223, 248, 250, 252, 253, 256
Hopkins, Mary, 141, 142, 191, 253
Hopkins, Sarah (daughter of Sarah Haddon Hopkins), 141, 172, 183, 191
Hopkins, Sarah (daughter of Sarah Lord Hopkins), 253
Hopkins, Sarah Haddon (sister of Elizabeth Haddon Estaugh, mother of Sarah Hopkins), 9, 126, *n. 23, n. 33*, 136, 141, 142, 154, 164, 184, 189, 190, 191, 209, 210, 215, 219, 250
Hopkins, Sarah Lord (wife of Ebenezer Hopkins), 9, 94, 214, 219, 226, 231, 249, 252, 253, 256, 257
Hopkins, Sarah Mickle (wife of John Estaugh Hopkins), 248, 256
Hopkins Family, 10, 16, 17, 23, 33, 38, 46, *n. 8*, 141, 142, 154, 155, 184, 216, 223, 242, 247, 249, 253; genealogy of Sarah Haddon Hopkins and Benjamin Hopkins, 152, *n. 20*
Hopper, Isaac T., 7
Horsleydown Friends Meeting, 21, 35-41, 43, 55, 64, 70-72, 83, 101, 102, 106, 124, 129, 141, 142, 148, 164, 175, 183, 184, 191, 193, 203, 210, 211, 227
Horsleydown Women's Meeting, 35, 43
Hoskins, James, 186
Howell, Catharine, 82
Howell Family, 218
Hugg, John, 137, 182, 224
Hugg, Leze Collins, *see* Price, Leze Collins Hugg

Hugg, Priscilla, 182
Hugg, Samuel, 247, 248
Hugg Family, 247, 256
Hunterdon County (NJ), 166
Hyam, Thomas, 251
Hyde, Edward, the Lord Cornbury, 117, 127

I

Indentured servants, 49, 52, 59, 63, 65, 76, 79, 91, 121, 163, 211, 224, 263
Indian Fields, 73
Indian King Tavern, 247
Indians, *see* Native Americans
Indulged Meetings, 78, 82
Ireland, 28, 56, 76, 102, 106, 111, 122, 148, 199, 207, 239
Irish Quakers, 49, 76, 79, 169
Irish Tenth, 54, 76, 212

J

Jamaica, 145, 174
James, Duke of York, 29, 50, 58, 74
Johnson, Robert Gibbon, 158, 177, *n. 8*
Jones, John, 111-113, 116, 134, 135
JOSIAH (ship), 106

K

Kaighin, John, *see* Kaighn, John
Kaighn, John, 159, 177, *n. 11*, 182, 209, 240, 244, 246
Kaighn, John, Sr., 245
Kaighn, Joseph, 208, 209, 245, 246, 249
Kaighn, Mary Estaugh, *see* Stephens, Mary Estaugh Kaighn
Kaighn Family, 139, 183, 208, 216, 217, 247
Kay, Elizabeth, 78, 82, 108-110, 121, 122, 135
Kay, Isaac, 154
Kay, John, 64, 78, 82, 122, 131, 132, 173, 187, 190, 208, 210
Kay, John, Jr., 131

Kay, Joseph, 139
Kay, Mary, *see* Wood, Mary Kay
Kay, Sarah Langston, 131
Kay, Sarah, *see* Norris, Sarah Kay
Kay Family, 82, 96, 122, 13, 139, 217, 218, 244, 245
Keith, George, 114
King's Highway, 12, 13, 94, 119, 161, 195, 208, 218, 244-247, 250. *See also* Burlington-Salem Road
Kirton, Benjamin, 197

L

Ladd Family, 33
Lancaster County (PA), 169, 186
Langdale, Josiah, 104
Langston, Sarah, *see* Kay, Sarah Langston
Lawrie, Gawen, 47, 52
Lawson, Mary, *see* Estaugh, Mary Lawson
Lay, Benjamin, 220, 221, 234, *n. 25*, *n. 26*
Leigh, Ralph, 219
Lenape Indians, *see* Native Americans
Lewes (DE), 123
Lippincott, Elizabeth, 242
Lippincott, Hope, 193
Lippincott, Mary, 259, *n. 8*
Lippincott, Rachel, 254, 255
Lippincott, Samuel, 88, 240
Lippincott Family, 33, 183
Lloyd, Grace, 135
Lloyd, Hannah, *see* Hill, Hannah Lloyd
Lloyd, Mary Haddon, 142
Lloyd, Samuel, 88, 142
Lloyd Family, 142, 143
Logan, Hannah, 252
Logan, James, 56, 104, 115, 118, 122, 123, 128, 130, 134, 146-148, 157, 168-170, 173, 174, 21, 227
Logan, William, 249
LONDON HOPE (ship), 189

Long Lane Burial Ground, 40, 161, 175, 190, 191, 202, *n. 17*, 250
Lord, Constantine, 248
Lord, Elizabeth, 259, *n. 8*
Lord, John, 209
Lord, Sarah, *see* Hopkins, Sarah Lord
Lovejoy, William, 59-63, 68, *n. 15*, 83, 86, 187
Lovejoy Smith Shop, 93
Lucas, Nicholas, 47, 52, 58
Lurting, Mary Clarke, 37
Lurting, Naomy, 39
Lurting, Thomas, 37, 39-41, 49, 55, 106, 161, 191
Lyons, Elizabeth Alice, ix-xiv, 1, 19, 20, 21-24, 87, 88, 92, 234, *n. 45*, 261, 264-265
Lyons, George Stuart, ix-xiii, 19, 20, 21-24, 234, *n. 45*, 261, 264-265

M

Marriott, Phillipia, *see* Haddon, Phillipiah Marriott
Marriott Family, 31, 32
Martinco, *see* Martinique
Marsh, Primus, 163, 222, 223
Martinique, 134, 173
MARY HOPE (ship), 160, 172
Maryland, 2, 16, 95, 104, 106, 115, 122, 128, 132, 147, 225
Masters, Sybilla Righton, 80, 83, 116, 117
Masters, Thomas, 80, 116, 117, 126, *n. 25*
Matlack, Benjamin, 243
Matlack, George, 166
Matlack, John, 166
Matlack, Mary Harris, 182
Matlack, Rebecca Haines, 193
Matlack, Richard, 193
Matlack, Susanna Hewitt, 243
Matlack, Timothy, 154, 166, 209, 240, 244

Matlack, William, 154, 166
Matlack Family, 33, 73, 88, 100, *n.19*, 217, 245
Matthews, Hannah, *see* Gardiner, Hannah Matthews
Matthews, Richard, 35, 44, 45, *n. 5*, 53, 55, 56, 58-60, 62, 63, 83, 90, 137, 143, 165, 167, 187, 253
Matthews, Thomas, 56, 59, 60, 62, 137
McConnell, Emlen, 14
Medicine, Herbal, 13, 83, 117, 158, 159, 209, 212
Men's Meeting, 44, *n. 7*, 213, 241
Mennonites, 169, 186
Michel, Francois Luis, 147, 148
Mickle, Archibald, 243
Mickle, Elizabeth Cooper, 140
Mickle, Hannah Cooper, 129
Mickle, John, 129, 210, 256
Mickle, Letitia, *see* Hinchman, Letitia Mickle
Mickle, Mary Burrough, 243
Mickle, Samuel, 140, 244, 252
Mickle, Sarah, *see* Hopkins, Sarah Mickle
Mickle Family, 10, 139, 216, 247, 256
Moorestown, *see* Chester and Chester Friends Meeting
Morris, Anthony, 41, 80, 113, 114, 135
Morris, Elizabeth, 80, 113, 114, 135

N

Native Americans, vii, x, 5, 6, 11-14, 17, 22, 23, 47, 52, 72, 73, 77, 104, 117, 131, 133, 148, 168, 224
Neshaminy Creek, 196
New Castle (DE), 1, 2, 75, 76, 107, 108, 122, 128
New Haddonfield, *see* Haddonfield
New Jersey Mirror and Burlington County Advertiser, 7
New Netherlands, 50
New York (NY), 7, 16, 29, 50

Newcastle-on-Tyne (England), 21
Newton Creek, 58, 59, 60, 64, 76, 77, 88, 119, 121, 193, 217, 243
Newton Friends Meeting, 39, 78, 82, 97, 109, 119, 121, 122, 124, 131, 134, 137-140, 148, 149, 172, 181-183, 192-194, 198, 212, 213, 238, 241, 255
Newton Quarterly Meeting, 121
Newton Women's Meeting, 39, 82, 122, 134, 139, 149, 172
Newton Township, vii, xiv, 6, 68, 10, 11, 61, 87, 89-93, 106, 110, 121, 128, 131, 133, 138, 212
Nicholson, Rebecca, 16
Nicholson, Samuel, 193
Nicholson, Sarah, 16
Noble Plantation, 167, 168, 196
Noble, Richard, 167, 196
Non-Conformists, 206
Norris, Isaac, 114, 117, 118, 122, 130, 143, 145, 146, 168, 174, 202, *n. 27*
Norris, James, 218
Norris, Sarah Kay, 218, 244
North Carolina, 6, 29, 104, 105, 115, 132
Northampton River, 121
Northamptonshire (England), 28, 31-33, 138

O

Old Haddonfield, *see* Haddonfield
Oldman's Creek, 54, 60, 136, 137, 166
Owen, Griffith, 1, 2, 107, 140, 146

P

Pace, Mary, *see* Weston, Mary Pace
Padley, Thomas, 36
Palmer, Esther Champion, 129, 132, 135
Peachee, William, 53
Peckover, Edmund, 202, *n. 27*
Pemberton, James, 202, *n. 7*
Penn, Hannah Callowhill, 1, 118
Penn, Letitia, 1
Penn, William, 1, 56,-58, 81, 118, 128
Pennsbury Manor, 87, 104, 105, 118, 157
Pennsauken Creek, 54, 60, 61, 64, 75, 76, 77, 87, 88, 92, 121, 136, 193, 217, 243. *See also* Cropwell Creek
Pennsylvania Coffee House of London, 211
Pennsylvania Gazette, 223, 246
Pennsylvania Land Company of London, 56, 57, 80, 137, 145, 167, 169, 173, 184-187, 196-199, 206, 225, 228, 251
Pennsylvania, vii, x, xii, xiii, 1, 2, 29, 33, 36, 41, 48, 55-56, 71, 75, 79, 81, 104, 106, 110-112, 115, 117, 118, 123, 128, 134, 145-148, 167-170, 185-186, 196-199, 207, 225, 228, 235, 251, 262, 264
Pennsylvania Affirmation Act, 225
Pennsylvania Assembly, 205
Penstone, Anne Willis, 60-62
Penstone, Stephen, 60, 61
Perquimans (NC) Friends Meeting, 104
Perry Webb, Margery, 247
Perry Webb, Thomas, 218, 244, 247
Peter the Great, 42
Philadelphia (PA), xii, 2, 21, 58, 63, 157, 194; court, 138; Estaughs in, 5, 139-140, 172-175, 182, 187, 218, 251, 262; Friends in, xiv, 2, 6, 7, 11, 21, 43, 60, 71, 78-81, 83, 84, 97, 105, 106-108, 110-119, 123, 129, 131-133, 134, 198, 209, 214, 217, 227-230, 252; government, 128, 148; land transactions, 186, 195; merchants, 130, 134, 143, 145-146, 199, 211, 235-236, Port of, 5, 80; ships in, 122, 172-174; slaves in, 173-174, 220, 223; smallpox, 107
Philadelphia Friends Meeting, 108, 110, 111, 112
Philadelphia Women's Meeting, 116, 135

Philadelphia Yearly Meeting, 78, 99, 81, 110, 112, 114, 116, 129
PHILADELPHIAN (ship), 108, 122
Pickering, John, 229, 230
Pike, Joseph, 157, 158
Plumstead, Clement, 5
Pocahontas, 5
Potter Street, 218
Price, Leze Collins Hugg, 247
Price, Mary Thorne, 247
Price, Robert Friend, 247, 248
Prime Hook (DE), 123
Primus, *see* Marsh, Primus
Privateers, 116, 130, 147, 173, 229
Puckle, Nathaniel, 72, 87, 108, 122, 123, 130, 138
Puritans, 85
Pusey, Caleb, 134
Pyne Poynt, 78, 81, 120, 129, 133, 245

Q

Quaker Lead Company, 55, 144, 145, 147, 185
Quakers, *see* Friends, Religious Society of
Queen Anne, 117, 128, 144
Queen Anne's War, 130, 147

R

Raccoon Creek, 75
Rancocas Creek, 54, 77, 121
Rauschenberger, Douglas B., vi, xi
Rawle, Francis, 209, 250, 251
Rawle, William, 117, 209, 225, 226, 251
Rawle Family, 202, *n. 27*
Rawlins, George, 36
Redman, Hannah Gill, 218
Redman, Harriet O., *see* Harriet Redman Willits
Redman, John Evans, 155-157
Redman, Thomas, 214, 218, 240, 244, 255
Redman Family, 256

Redriff, *see* Rotherhithe
Religious Society of Friends, *see* Friends, Religious Society of
Reeve, Rebecca C. Wood, 155-157
Restoration, The, 27, 29, 49, 143, 158
Rhoads, Evan Lawrie, 92
Rhoads, Samuel Nicholson, 4, 9, 12, 15, 18, 19, 88, 92, 93, 155, 156, 162, 236
Richardson, Francis, 114
Richardson, John, 95, 104, 105
Righton, Sybilla, *see* Masters, Sybilla Righton
Righton, William, 116
Road Town (Tortola), 230
Roberts, John, 166
Roberts Family, 88, 247
Rotherhithe (England), 34, 36, 42-44, 60, 62, 72, 84, 123, 140, 175
Royal Mines Copper and Ryton Company, 55, 143
Royden (Roydon), William, 58, 112

S

Salem County (NJ), 53, 60, 77, 112, 136, 137, 159, 166, 214, 224
Salem Friends Meeting, 78, 113, 114, 184, 213, 241
Salem Quarterly Meeting 6, 172, 213, 223, 241
Salem Yearly Meeting, 158
Salmon, William, 158
Schopp, Paul W., vi, 92
Schuylkill River, 75, 186, 196
Scroggins, Jonah, 154
Searchers, 37, 38, 46, *n. 9*
Servants, *see* Indentured Servants
Sewell, William, 157, 158
Shackamaxon, 78, 81, 120
Shackle, Alice, 78, 82, 83, 109, 110, 192
Shackle, Thomas, 78, 88, 121, 166, 192
Shackle Family, 109, 121, 139
Sharp, Anthony, 146, 214
Sharp, Elizabeth, 194

Sharp, Judath, 208
Sharp, Mary, 255, 259, *n. 8*
Sharp, Thomas, 61, 77-78, 88-93, 96, 137, 138, 146, 163, 165, 166, 192, 194, 198, 209, 212
Sharp, William, 246
Sharp Family, 33
Shippen, Edward, 114, 115
Slave trade, 146, 163, 174, 220, 221, 225
Slaves and Slavery, 42, 76, 112-113, 121, 146, 163, 174, 218, 224, 225
Smallpox, 37, 73, 96, 106, 107, 109, 250
Smith, Daniel, 250
Smith, Elizabeth Norris, 245
Smith, Isaac, 244
Smith, John, 252
Smith, Nicolas, 59
Snakes, 168, 225
Society of Friends, *see* Friends, Religious Society of
Sonmans, Peter, 196
South Sea Company, 185, 186, 197, 210
Southwark (England), 19, 21, 32-36, 40, 41, 64, 95, 106, 108, 122, 124, 141, 142, 148, 161, 183, 184, 190, 211, 229, 250
Southwark (England) Friends Meeting, 211
Southwick, Josiah, 131, 154
Spicer, Abigail, 255
Spicer, Esther, 82, 88, 120, 255
Spicer, Martha, *see* Chalkley, Martha Spicer
Spicer, Samuel, 82, 120
Spicer, Sarah, 120
Spicer's Ferry, 82
Stacy, Hannah, 58
Stacy, Henry, 53, 58, 88, 167
Stacy, Mary, 58, 64
Stacy, Sarah, 58
Stacy Family, 62, 167
Stamper, Francis, 56, 102, 239

Stanbury, Mary, 116, 154
Stanbury, Nathan, 116, 117, 134, 154
Stephens, Mary, 245
Stephens, Mary Estaugh Kaighn, 208, 209, 254
Stephens, Robert, 245
Stephens, Sarah, 214
Stiles, Benjamin, 88
Stoneburner, Carol, 261
Story, Thomas, 41, 56, 105, 106, 115, 117, 122, 128, 129, 133, 140, 143, 168, 185-187, 197, 225
Stoy's Landing, 88
Sturge, Hannah, 16, 26, *n. 19*
Sufferings, The, 31, 41, 48, 138, 205
Susquehanna Land Company, 117
Sutton, Mary, *see* Wood, Mary Sutton
Swarthmore College, 230

T

Tanner Street, 161, 195, 218, 244, 246, 254
Tassini, Katherine Mansfield, v, vi, xi
Taylor, Isaac, 169
Taylor, Rebecca Nicholson, 15, 16, 17, 85, 265
Thackara, Joseph, 241
Thackara, Thomas, 78, 121
Thames River, 5, 19, 34, 36, 42, 47, 55, 111, 122, 141, 210
Thomas, Gabriel, 48, 49, 79, 80, 123
Thomas, William, 230
Thorne, John, 243
Thorne, Mary, *see* Price, Mary Thorne
Thorne, Mary Heritage Gill, 231, 243, 254
Thorne, Thomas, 214, 247
Thorne Family, 243
Tice, Patricia, 22
Timber Creek, 54, 74, 76, 112, 99, *n.* 7, 193
Tindall, Elizabeth, 220
Tindall, Ruth, 220

Tiplady, John, 31
Tolles, Frederick B., xiv
Tomlinson, Elizabeth, *see* Wyatt(e), Elizabeth Tomlinson
Tomlinson, Ephraim, 208, 209
Tomlinson, Kathleen, 258, n. 8
Tortola Island, 22, 221, 227-232, 235, 244, 259, n. 13
Treacle Bible, 157, 250
Trenton (NJ), 23, 53

V

Van Name, Elmer Garfield, 18
Vernon's Coffee House, 55, 84, 144
Virginia, 4, 6, 95, 104-106, 115, 132, 147

W

Waln, Nicholas, 134, 140, 166, 202, n. 27
Warner, Anne, 36
Warner, Edmond, 52
Warner Family, 33
War of Jenkins's Ear, 228
War of the Austrian Succession, 228
War of the Spanish Succession, 127, 130, 147, 168
Ward Family, 33
Warner Family, 33
Wasse, James, 53
Waterford (NJ), 62, 68, n. 16, 78, 82, 96, 128, 131, 137, 166, 181, 182
West Indies, x, xii, 76, 80, 116, 129, 130, 146, 173, 174, 182, 226, 227, 239, 271
West New Jersey; early settlement, 29, 33, 35-37, 41, 49-65, 72-81, 86-87; Estaughs in, vii-xiv, 2-8, 11, 36-37, 39, 43-44, 55-65, 69-70, 72, 77-85, 87, 93-97, 103, 110-124, 121-131, 134-139, 148, 151-152, 155-158, 161, 163, 166-168, 170-172, 174, 182, 187, 189, 211, 121, 216-217, 224, 238-239, 262; Friends in, 43-44, 48, 56, 77-85, 95-97, 104-105, 110-114, 117, 118-124, 129-131, 182-183, 207, 211, 213-214, 227, 244-245, 255; Friends Meetings in, 133, 148-149, 217; government, 52-54, 73, 77, 86, 118-119, 127-128; Haddons and, 48, 55-65, 69, 72, 86, 93, 103, 136-138, 164-165, 170-172, 183, 187, 189, 190-191; Hopkins in, 141, 164, 172, 183, 189, 190, 216-218; land transactions, 49-65, 116-168, 187, 198, 211, 212, 219; merchants and craftsmen, 116; Penn in, 49-55, 118-123; slaves in, 42, 76, 112-113, 121, 163, 174, 224-225
Weston, Mary Pace, 249, 257
Whitall, Ann Cooper, 252, 259, n. 30
Whitall, James, 132, 139
Whitall, Job, 172
Whitall Family, 216, 217
Wilkins, Mary, 259, n. 30
Willis, Ann, *see* Penstone, Ann Willis
Willis, Henry, 134
Willis, John, 60, 61, 92, 137
Willis, Thomas, 44, 60, 62, 85, 86, 137, 165, 188, 253
Willis Family, 60-62
Willits, Harriet O. Redman, 15, 16
Wills, Elizabeth, 208
Wills, Hope, 121
Wills, John, 121
Wills Family, 121
Wilson, Thomas, 202, n. 27
Witt, Christopher, 159, 209
Woman's Christian Temperance Union, 5, 12, 13, 15
Wright Family, 33
Wood, Benjamin, 131
Wood, Elizabeth Cooper, 155
Wood, Hannah, 81-83, 88, 100, n.16
Wood, Isaac, 155
Wood, Joshua, 34, 36
Wood, Mary Kay, 131

Wood, Mary Sutton, 16
Wood, Rebecca C., *see* Reeve, Rebecca C. Wood
Wood Family, 33, 35, 36, 216, 245
Wood Lane, 94
Woodbury (NJ), 9, 132, 213, 214, 126
Woodbury Friends Meeting, 139, 214, 241
Woolman, Elizabeth, 224
Woolman, John, 224
Women's Meetings, 44, *n. 7*, 135, 213, 241
Wright, Edward, 44, 143-146, 148, 185, 197
Wright Family, 33
Wright, Kathryn, 141
Wyatt(e), Bartholomew, 214
Wyatt(e), Elizabeth Tomlinson, 214
Wyeth, Joseph, 207

Y

Yorkshire (England), 32, 33, 54, 104, 133

Z

Zane, Bathsheba Heartly, 248
Zane, Elnathan, 248
Zane, Robert, 88

COLOPHON.

ELIZABETH HADDON ESTAUGH *has been composed in Century Schoolbook, a typeface designed by Morris Fuller Benton in 1924 for the American Type Foundry as a variation of his father's earlier design, Century Oldstyle. Subtitles, captions, and credit lines have been composed in Helvetica Neue condensed, designed in 1983 by D. Stempel AG for Linotype. Book design by Paul W. Schopp of Biblio-Graphics, Palmyra, New Jersey, based principally on a variety of nineteenth-century Quaker journals and texts. Typesetting by Laura Baird of Studio B, Allentown, New Jersey. Thomson-Shore of Dexter, Michigan has printed the book on 60lb. Natures Book Natural recycled paper, which consists of 30% Post Consumer Waste and meets the Forest Stewardship Council standards. Smythe-sewn case binding by printer.*